P9-CAN-456

A Fresh Exposition of the Epistle to the Hebrews

George Allen Turner

the new & living way

BETHANY FELLOWSHIP, INC.
Minneapolis, Minnesota

Copyright © 1975
Bethany Fellowship, Inc.
All rights reserved

Published by Bethany Fellowship, Inc.
6820 Auto Club Road, Minneapolis, Minnesota 55438

Printed in the United States of America

Library of Congress CIP data:
Turner, George Allen.
   The new and living way.

   Bibliography: p.
   1. Bible. N. T. Hebrews—Commentaries. I. Title.
BS 2775.3.T87   227'.87'07   74-23104
ISBN 0-87123-388-6 pbk.

To Lucile
my "helpmeet," constant companion, solace
and support for more than three decades,
this volume is lovingly dedicated

A Study Guide for *The New and Living Way* is available for personal use or for group study. See your book dealer, or write to the publisher for information.
Bethany Fellowship, Inc.
6820 Auto Club Road
Minneapolis, Minnesota 55438

Foreword

Benjamin Disraeli once said that "the best way to become acquainted with a subject is to write a book about it." The second best way, perhaps, is to prepare to teach that subject to others.

My longtime colleague at Asbury Theological Seminary, Dr. George A. Turner, meets both of these qualifications. For years he has taught courses of study in both Testaments. This commentary presents us with his mature insights into basic biblical theology as found in the Hebrew epistle. He is eminently equipped, both by his graduate studies and his professorial labors, to produce such a volume.

The Hebrew epistle is one which has influenced me greatly across my entire Christian life. As a new, late-teen convert to Christ, my first memorized scripture verse was Hebrews 2:1, "Therefore we ought to give the more earnest heed to the things which we have heard, lest at any time we should let them slip." One of the two favorite Bible courses in my early ministerial training was a semester's study of this unique epistle. My senior sermon, preached before the entire faculty and student body, was an exposition of Hebrews 12:14, "Follow peace with all men, and holiness, without which no man shall see the Lord." And during my first year in full-time ministry, spent in interdenominational evangelism, more of my sermon texts were taken from Hebrews than any other book of the Bible. I discovered there a preachable theology which has great evangelistic as well as pastoral potential. And during my own teaching years in the seminary classroom, I have found the Hebrew epistle to be a thrilling challenge, both spiritually and theologically, to my students. A careful study of this New Testament book helps the Christian discover quickly the true genius and uniqueness of his faith.

Taken as a whole, the Epistle to the Hebrews is a rare literary jewel. No one has better pointed up this fact for us than Dr. Adam Clarke. Claimed he:

> So many are the beauties, so great the excellency, so instructive the matter, so pleasing the manner, and so exceedingly interesting the whole, that the work may be read a hundred times over without perceiving anything of sameness, and with new and increased information at each reading. This latter is an excellency which belongs to the whole revelation of God; but to no part of it in such a peculiar and supereminent manner as to the Epistle to the Hebrews.

Dr. Clarke's continued comment further underscores its towering importance for biblical Christianity:

> The Epistle to the Hebrews . . . is by far the most important and useful of all the apostolic writings; all the doctrines of the Gospel are in it embodied, illustrated, and enforced in a manner the most lucid, by references and examples the most striking and illustrious, and by arguments the most cogent and convincing. It is an epitome of the dispensations of God to man, from the foundations of the world to the advent of Christ. It is not only the sum of the *Gospel*, but the sum and completion of the *Law*, on which it is also a most beautiful and luminous comment. *Without* this, the law of Moses had never been fully understood, nor God's design in giving it. *With* this, all is clear and plain, and the ways of God with man rendered consistent and harmonious. . . . All rites, ceremonies, and sacrifices of the Mosaic institution are shown to have had *Christ* for their *object* and *end* . . . (*Clarke's Commentary*, VI, 681).

The timeliness of Dr. Turner's commentary on this epistle can scarcely be exaggerated. In a day of great, even revolutionary, change, this biblical document deals with both the passing and the permanent, with both the temporal and the eternal. In an era of questing for meanings, this epistle takes one beyond ritual to reality, behind the shadows to the substance. In an age of ecumenism and religious syncretism, this epistle points up what cannot be surrendered, and at the same time preserves the finality of Jesus Christ and His great salvation.

In an age of widespread apostasy, both doctrinally and ethically, this New Testament book warns against those who would cast away their confidence in Christ as Savior, and highlights the timelessness of the Christian faith and ethic.

Dr. Turner's work accentuates in a commendable way the great biblical message of "the second rest," Christian perfection rightly understood, and the life of holiness. This commentary will serve well the pulpit minister, the classroom teacher, and the serious lay student of the Scriptures.

I heartily commend both the author and the publisher for mak-available to the Christian world this scholarly volume.

October 1974

Delbert R. Rose, Ph.D.
Professor of Biblical Theology
Asbury Theological Seminary
Wilmore, Kentucky

Preface

> If we hold that the judgment of the Spirit makes itself felt
> through the consciousness of the Christian Society, no Book of the
> Bible is more completely recognized by universal consent as giving
> a divine view of the facts of the Gospel, full of lessons for all
> time, than the Epistle to the Hebrews.—Westcott.

This assessment by Bishop Westcott, one of the foremost expositors of all time, deserves as much consideration today as when it was uttered. In every generation since its appearance Christian consciousness has considered this letter indispensable.

This exposition of Hebrews was prepared with the needs of pastors, Sunday school teachers and adult Bible study groups in view. It is the outgrowth of several years of studying, teaching and preaching from this epistle in a variety of different situations. The final preparation of material for the press extended over a period of two years.

Although an exegesis of the Greek text is not included in this volume, the exposition is based upon a close study of the Greek text and of several versions. The exposition proceeds upon a paragraph-by-paragraph rather than on a verse-by-verse approach, thus seeking the overall thrust and movement of the letter.

In this treatment of the epistle special attention is given to three areas. The analytical outline, more detailed than most, endeavors to trace the author's argument, step by step, displaying the relation of the part to the whole. The attention given to topical studies, after the precedent of an "excursus" of older German scholars and the "detached notes" of certain English commentaries, is in line with the contemporary emphasis on biblical theology. The third feature is in the inclusion of illustrative material for the convenience of the teacher and preacher.

Since this commentary seeks to follow the inductive method it has seemed best to reserve questions of author, date, locale, recipients and purpose until after the epistle itself is examined. Therefore these matters are treated as appendices rather than being presented as an introduction. This procedure is designed to reduce the natural tendency to approach the letter itself with prior assumptions.

The Bible text on which this exposition is based is the American Standard Version of 1901. However, various translations of the Bible have been used in this book, along with some free paraphrasing by the author, in order to get the clearest sense.

Indebtedness is hereby acknowledged to the many students who have interacted with the author and thus have contributed in a large measure to the perspective here presented. Several competent typists helped the project to completion. But in a real sense the project is still incomplete. It is to be hoped that the use of this commentary will lead the reader to feel that he has just begun his own study of the Epistle to the Hebrews.

George Allen Turner
Professor of Biblical Literature
Asbury Theological Seminary
Willmore, Kentucky

Table of Contents

man scholars and the "detached notes" of certain English commentaries, is in line with the contemporary emphasis on biblical theology. The third feature is in the inclusion of illustrative material for the convenience of the teacher and preacher.

Since this commentary seeks to follow the inductive method it has seemed best to reserve questions of author, date, locale, recipients and purpose until after the epistle itself is examined. Therefore these matters are treated as appendices rather than being presented as an introduction. This procedure is designed to reduce the natural tendency to approach the letter itself with prior assumptions.

The Bible text on which this exposition is based is the American Standard Version of 1901. However, various translations of the Bible have been used in this book, along with some free paraphrasing by the author, in order to get the clearest sense.

Indebtedness is hereby acknowledged to the many students who have interacted with the author and thus have contributed in a large measure to the perspective here presented. Several competent typists helped the project to completion. But in a real sense the project is still incomplete. It is to be hoped that the use of this commentary will lead the reader to feel that he has just begun his own study of the Epistle to the Hebrews.

George Allen Turner
Professor of Biblical Literature
Asbury Theological Seminary
Willmore, Kentucky

Abbreviations

BIBLE VERSIONS

ASV—American Standard Version (1901)
ASVm—American Standard Version margin
AV—King James Version
HEM—Herman E. Mueller (the author's translation of Hebrews)
JB—The Jerusalem Bible
JBP—J. B. Phillips, The New Testament in Modern English (1958)
JM—James Moffatt, The New Testament, a New Translation (1930)
LB—The Living Bible
LXX—The Septuagint
NAB—The New American Bible
NASB—New American Standard Bible
NEB—The New English Bible, New Testament (1960)
NIV—The New International Version
RSV—Revised Standard Version

GENERAL REFERENCE WORKS

A.G—W. F. Arndt and F. W. Gingrich, eds., *A Greek-English Lexicon of the New Testament.* Chicago: University of Chicago Press, 1957

GA-S—G. Abbott-Smith, *A Manual Greek Lexicon of the New Testament,* New York: Scribner's, 1922

JHT—J. H. Thayer, *A Greek-English Lexicon of the New Testament,* New York: American Book Co.

Jos. *Ant.*—Flavius Josephus, *Antiquities of the Jews*

Jos. *Wars*—Flavius Josephus, *Wars of the Jews*

L-S—Liddell and Scott, *A Greek-English Lexicon of the New Testament,* New York: American Book Co.

M-G—W. F. Moulton & A. S. Geden, *A Concordance to the Greek Testament*, Edinburgh: T. & T. Clark, 1897

M-M—W. F. Moulton & G. Milligan, *Vocabulary of the Greek New Testament*, Grand Rapids: Eerdmanns, 1949

MRV—Marvin R. Vincent, *Word Studies in the New Testament*. New York: Scribners, 1906

RCT—R. C. Trench, *Synonyms of the New Testament*, London: Macmillan, 1871

TWNT—G. Kittel, ed., *Theologisches Wörterbuch sum Neuen Testamentum*, Stuttgart; 1933

COMMENTARIES

MD—Marcus Dods, "Epistle to the Hebrews," *Expositor's Greek Testament*, Grand Rapids: Eerdmans, n.d.

WB—William Barclay, *The Letter to the Hebrews*, Philadelphia: Westminster, 1957

ABB—A. B. Bruce, *The Epistle to the Hebrews*, Edinburgh: T. & T. Clark, 1908.

FFB—F. F. Bruce, *The Epistle to the Hebrews* (NICNT), Grand Rapids: Eerdmans, 1964

JC—John Calvin, *Epistle to the Hebrews* (tr. by J. Owen), Eerdmans, 1948

FD—Franz Delitzsch, *Commentary on Hebrews* (2 vols), T. & T. Clark, 1883

FWF—F. W. Farrar, *Epistle to the Hebrews* (Cambridge Bible), Cambridge U. Press, 1883

TH—Thomas Hewitt, *Epistle to the Hebrews* (Tyndale Commentaries), Grand Rapids: Eerdmans, 1960

JM—James Moffatt, *Epistle to the Hebrews* (I.C.C.), T. & T. Clark, 1948

OM—Otto Michel, *Der Brief an die Hebraer*, Gottingen: Vanderhoeck & Rupreche, 1949

BFW—B. F. Scott, *The Epistle to the Hebrews*, London: Macmillan, 1889

EFS—E. F. Scott, *The Epistle to the Hebrews*, Edinburgh: T. & T. Clark, 1922

IB—G. A. Buttruck, Edit., *Interpreter's Bible*, Nashville: Abingdon Press, 1955

CS—C. Spicq, *L'Epitre aux Hebreux*, Paris: J. Gabalda, 1952 (2 vols.)

PERIODICALS

BA—*Biblical Archaeologist*
CBQ—*Catholic Biblical Quarterly*
ET—*Expository Times*
JBL—*Journal of Biblical Literature*
NTS—*New Testament Studies*
RB—*Revue Biblique*

SCROLLS

IQS—Manual of Discipline or Rule of the Community (Qumran)
IQH—Hymns
IQM—War of the Children of Light vs. the Children of Darkness

Chap.	Son of God	Son of Man	Moses	Joshua	Aaron	"Press On
	1	**2**	**3**	**4**	**5**	**6**
Paragraphs	1-2 Son superior to prophets 3-4 Son superior to angels in nature 7-14 Superior to angels in ministry	1-4 Take heed Son of Man 5-7 Abased and exalted 8-13 Reason for Son's humiliation 14-18 Consequences of Son's abasement	1-6 Christ superior to Moses 7-12 Danger of unbelief 13-19 Necessity of obedience	1-5 Rest dependent on faith 6-10 Danger of procrastination 11-13 Diligence imperative 14-16 The throne of grace	1-4 Human priests sympathetic 5-10 Christ experienced human infirmity 11-14 Readers immature	1-8 "Unto perfection" 9-12 "Be not sluggish" 13-20 God's immutab promise

Segments	The Person of Christ

Sequence	Exposition Predominates

Exposition / Exhortation	Son's revelation superior	Heed	Son superior in glory	Beware of unbelief	Christ superior to Aaron	Press on unt perfection
	Exposition	/////	Exposition	//////////	Exposition	/////////

Jesus superior	As Prophet / Son	As Apostle	As Priest

"Better"	A better Saviour	A better Leader	A better priesthood 4:14

(Steele)	A better Revelation	A better High Priest

(White, G.T.)	Prophets and angels	Moses and Joshua	Melchizedek and Aaron

	Key Verse 4:14 Key Words	⎫ "better" (15 times); "perfect" (16 times) ⎬ "confession" (3:1; 4:14; 10:23; 11:13; 13:1 ⎭

Jesus, cf.	Prophecy	1:1 Angels 1:4	Adam 2	Moses 3:1	3:7 Joshua	

Hebrews—Outlined

Melchizedek	Covenant	Tabernacle	Sanctification	Pilgrims	Endurance	Perfection
7	8	9	10	11	12	13
3 Melchizedek unique 10 Melchizedek greater than Aaron Levitical priesthood inferior ?-25 Jesus was superior to priesthood ?-28 Jesus unchangeable and accessible	1-5 Jesus' ministry superior Jesus mediates superior covenant 7-9 Old covenant inadequate 10-13 To a new covenant provided	1-10 Old tabernacle man-made 11-14 Better tabernacle 14-22 Better covenant 23-28 Better sacrifices	1-18 A more effective and final sacrifice 14-22 Let us draw near 23-31 Apostasy fearful 32-39 A better possession	1-12 Faith defined or exemplified 13-16 A better country 17-31 Other examples 32-39 Summary, conclusion	1-4 Jesus also 5-17 Design of discipline 18-28 Mt. Sinai, cf. Mt. Zion	1-6 Love, purity, trust 7-16 Without the camp 17 Obedience 18 Prayer 19-21 Benediction 22-24 Salvation

The Work of Christ

Exhortation Predominates

Priesthood of Christ The New Covenant	Importance of enduring afflictions	Two Mts.	Closing exhortations

Exposition

As Minister		As Exemplar	
A better covenant 7:13	A better sacrifice 9:11	A better Example	A better Kingdom

A better ritual and offering	A better life motive 10:14
The tabernacle	The city (11:10, 16 [cf. 10:34]; 12:22; 13:14)

"faith" (31 times); "consider" (3:1; 7:4; 10:23; 12:3; 13:7);
"well-pleasing" 11:5 [cf. 11:4], 6, 7; 12:28; 13:16, 21)

5:1 Aaron	10:19 Patriarchs

17

Outline Analysis of the Argument

THEME: The superiority of the person and work of Jesus Christ, and the importance of continuing in the faith. KEY VERSE: 4:14.

PART ONE: THE SUPERIORITY OF JESUS' PERSON (1-7)

I. The Superiority of Jesus' Person as Son (1:1-2:18)

   A. JESUS IS SUPERIOR TO THE PROPHETS (1:1-3)
     1. In time
       a. Then—"of old time"
       b. Now—"these days" (vv. 1, 2)
     2. In finality (1:1, 2)
       a. Then—by diversity (prophets)
       b. Now—completely (a Son)
     3. In person
     4. In creative work
     5. In relationship to God (1:2, 3)
     6. In His service (1:3)

   B. JESUS IS SUPERIOR TO THE ANGELS BY NATURE (1:4-2:18)
     1. In name (1:4-7)
       a. Called a Son (Ps. 2:7; II Sam. 7:14)
       b. Angels commanded to worship the Son (Ps. 97:7)
       c. Angels created to be servants (Ps. 104:4)
     2. In character (1:8, 9)
       a. Stability
       b. Righteousness
       c. Joyousness
     3. In permanence (1:10-12)
     4. In honor (1:13, 14)

C. A SUPERIOR REVELATION DEMANDS AN EAGER RESPONSE (2:1-4)
   1. The danger of drifting away is imminent (2:1)
   2. This better revelation must be heeded (2:2-4)

D. JESUS IS SUPERIOR TO THE ANGELS IN DOMINION (2:5-18)
   1. Angels not given dominion (2:5)
   2. Adam (man) failed to dominate the world (2:6-8)
   3. Jesus (Son of man) alone given this dominion (2:9)
   4. The rationale of the Cross (2:9-18)
      a. The means was appropriate to the end (v. 10)
      b. Jesus' incarnation made salvation available (vv. 11-15)
      c. Jesus' death makes salvation adequate (vv. 15, 16)
   5. Jesus' oneness with humanity qualifies Him as High Priest (2:17, 18)

II. The Superiority of Jesus' Person as Apostle (3:1-4:16)

A. JESUS IS SUPERIOR TO MOSES (3:1-6)
   1. He is fully equal to Moses (3:1, 2)
   2. His glory exceeds that of Moses (3:3-5)
   3. He has the higher claim on our allegiance (3:6)

B. JESUS IS SUPERIOR TO JOSHUA (3:7-4:11)
   1. In the accessibility of His rest (cf. 4:3)
      a. Accessibility contingent on obedience (vv. 7-19)
         (1) It was so in Joshua's day
         (2) It is also in our day (vv. 12-14)
         (3) An object lesson for us (vv. 15-19)
      b. Access to rest now to those who heed (4:1-3)
         (1) It is possible to come short of this rest (v. 1)
         (2) The Word must be believed as well as heard (v. 2)
         (3) Rest conditioned on obedience (v. 3)
   2. Christ's rest Superior (4:4-10)
      a. The rest involves a cessation of self-effort (vv. 4, 5, 10)
         (1) God "rested" on the Sabbath after creation ceased (v. 4)
         (2) Believers also may now have rest
      b. This rest more real (vv. 6-10)
   3. The importance of entering God's rest (4:11-13)
   4. Christ now leads believers into this better rest (4:14-16)

III. The Superiority of Jesus' Person as Our High Priest (5:1-7:28)

   A. JESUS IS EQUAL TO THE AARONIC PRIESTHOOD (5:1-6:20a)

      1. Qualifications of a good high priest (5:1-4)

         a. He stands officially between God and man (v. 1)

         b. He is capable of human sympathy (vv. 2, 3)

         c. He is divinely appointed (vv. 4-6)

      2. Christ meets these qualifications (5:5-10)

         a. He was appointed by God (vv. 5, 6)

         b. He was sympathetic (vv. 7, 8)

         c. He was perfected by these disciplines (vv. 8, 9)

      3. Spiritual condition of the readers hinders instruction (5:11-14)

      4. Maturity is imperative (6:1-3)

         a. "Let us advance" (v. 1)

         b. First principles should be "left behind" (vv. 1-3)

      5. Failure to "press on" has tragic consequences (6:4-8)

         a. Repentance impossible for apostates (vv. 4-6)

         b. In grace as in nature, barrenness brings a curse (vv. 7, 8)

      6. The writer's confidence in his readers (6:9-12)

      7. Hope has a sure foundation (6:13-20)

         a. God's promise to Abraham immutable (vv. 13-15)

         b. The validity of God's oath (vv. 16-18)

         c. God's promise the basis for our hope (vv. 18b-20)

   B. JESUS IS SUPERIOR TO THE AARONIC PRIESTHOOD (6:20b-7:28)

      1. Jesus is of Melshizedek's order (5:6, 10; 6:20; 7:14-17)

      2. Melchizedek unique (7:1-3)

      3. Melchizedek's order superior to that of Aaron (7:4-25)

         a. In status (vv. 4-10)

            (1) Reception of tithes from Abraham (and Levi) implies superiority

            (2) Blessing Abraham implies superiority

         b. In permanence (vv. 11-25)

            (1) Levi temporary; Melchizedek permanent (vv. 11-14)

            (2) A hereditary priesthood compared with a personal and eternal one (vv. 15-19)

            (3) Law or oath (vv. 20-22)

            (4) The continuity of the messianic priesthood (vv. 23-25)

            (5) The adequacy and finality of Christ (vv. 26-28)

PART TWO: THE SUPERIORITY OF JESUS' MINISTRY (8-13)

I. The Superiority of Jesus' Ministry as Ministering a More Effective Covenant (8:1-10:18)

   A. A BETTER SANCTUARY (8:1-5)
     1. The chief point (8:1, 2)
     2. Comparison with the earthly sanctuary (8:3-5)

   B. A BETTER COVENANT (8:6-13)
     1. Inauguration of the new implies the inadequacy of the old (8:6-9, 13)
     2. The characteristics of the new covenant (8:10-12)

   C. A BETTER SACRIFICE (9:1-10:18)
     1. The inadequacy of the old system (9:1-10)
       a. The tabernacle plan (vv. 1-5)
       b. The tabernacle ministry (vv. 6-10)
     2. The effectiveness of the new system (9:11-22)
       a. A better place and sacrifice (vv. 11-14)
       b. The provisions of the new covenant (vv. 15-22)
         (1) It provides an "eternal inheritance" (vv. 15-21)
         (2) It provides forgiveness of sins (vv. 15, 22)
     3. Summary: a better remedy for sin was necessary and is available (9:23-28)
     4. Christ's one offering alone makes the believer "perfect" (10:1-18)
       a. The limitations of the Law are obvious (vv. 1-4)
       b. Christ's act of obedience better than animal sacrifices (vv. 5-10)
       c. Christ's offering of himself is adequate and ultimate (vv. 11-18)

II. The Superiority of Jesus' Ministry as Exemplifying a Perfect Life of Faith (10:19-13:25)

   A. A CHALLENGE TO PERSEVERANCE (10:19-39)
     1. Enter the way with confidence (10:19-25)
     2. Apostasy to be avoided (10:26-31)
     3. Endurance needed now (10:32-39)

   B. FAITH EXEMPLIFIED IN THE FATHERS (11:1-40)
     1. The paradox of faith (11:1-3)
     2. Antediluvian witnesses (11:4-7)
       a. Abel (v. 4)

      b. Enoch (vv. 5, 6)
      c. Noah (v. 7)
   3. The Hebrew patriarchs (11:8-22)
      a. Abraham (vv. 8-10)
      b. Sarah (vv. 11, 12)
      c. The significance of these witnesses (vv. 13-16)
      d. Abraham and Isaac (vv. 17-20)
      e. Jacob and Joseph (vv. 21, 22)
   4. Witnesses during the exodus (11:23-31)
      a. Moses' choice (vv. 23-28)
      b. Faith at the exodus and conquest (vv. 29, 30)
      c. At Jericho (vv. 30, 31)
   5. Later Heroes and Heroines (11:32-40)
      a. They witnessed to the faith (vv. 32-38)
      b. These witnesses less privileged than we (vv. 39, 40)

C. JESUS STILL LEADS ON (12:1-3)
   1. We also need to persevere (12:1)
   2. Jesus is our example (12:2)

D. FURTHER APPEALS TO FAITH (12:4-29)
   1. Chastening promotes holiness (12:4-11)
   2. Holy living calls for diligence (12:12-17)
      a. Holiness should be sought (vv. 12-14)
      b. Holiness may be lost (vv. 15-17)
   3. The superiority of the present dispensation (12:18-24)
      a. The former dispensation inspired fear (vv. 18-21)
      b. The present dispensation inspires confidence (vv. 22-24)
   4. Final warning and appeal (12:25-29)
      a. Refusal means rejection of God (vv. 25-27)
      b. Grateful acceptance is demanded (vv. 28, 29)

E. FAITH EXHIBITED (13:1-25)
   1. In the Christian's relationship to others (13:1-6)
      a. In brotherly love (v. 1)
      b. In hospitality (v. 2)
      c. In sympathy (v. 3)
      d. In chastity (v. 4)
      e. In contentment (vv. 5, 6)
   2. In loyalty to leaders (13:7-17)
      a. Imitation of their faith (v. 7)
      b. The unchanging Christ (v. 8)

      c. Sound doctrine important (v. 9)
      d. The two altars (vv. 10-16)
         (1) The Old Testament system (vv. 10, 11)
         (2) Sanctification provided outside the camp (vv. 12-14)
         (3) Acceptable sacrifices (vv. 15, 16)
      e. Obedient to leaders (v. 17)
   3. Conclusion (13:18-25)
      a. Prayer requested (vv. 18, 19)
      b. Benediction (vv. 20, 21)
      c. Postscript (vv. 22-25)
         (1) Final appeal (v. 22)
         (2) Personal greetings (vv. 23, 34)
         (3) Invocation of grace (v. 25)

Introduction

The title of this exposition, *The New and Living Way,* not only focuses on a key phrase of this epistle (10:20) but also reflects an awareness of the contemporary concern with what is new, fresh and vibrant, rather than with what is static, dead and irrelevant. Before Jesus' disciples were called Christians (Acts 11:26) they were known simply as those of "the Way" (Acts 9:2; 19:9). The theme or motif of "way" pervades this epistle. The readers are regarded as like the ancient Israelites in that they have left the bondage of sin but have not arrived at the promised land of "rest" and hence are pilgrims in transit. Their leader is the new Joshua who is leading them into the very presence of God (4:8-14). Like Abraham and other Old Testament saints the readers are viewed as setting out, not knowing where they are going except that they are discontented with the status quo and are in quest of a "better country" and a city whose maker and builder is God. Like their exemplar Jesus they are exhorted to "run the race" to its conclusion and to "press on to perfection." The danger is arrested growth (5:11-14) and the need is for continued progress.

Those in the "main line" churches, as well as those in the charismatic movement, the Jesus movement and the holiness movement, do well to "consider" with this author the portrait of Jesus so winsomely presented here. In no other New Testament writing is the relationship between the old and the new in divine revelation more intriguingly and creatively presented than by this author. Presented herein is *both* "the man for others" *and* our great High Priest.

In pursuit of this goal the author with great originality and clear grasp of the Scriptures shows Jesus Christ to be superior to angels, to Adam, to Moses, to Joshua and to Aaron both in status and effectiveness. Moreover, Jesus is represented as the High Priest of all humanity with clarity and the boldness matched by no other early Christian writer.

In no other New Testament book is both the humanity and the deity of Jesus Christ presented so fully and emphatically. He is described as being of the same nature as the Father and yet as having learned obedience by the things which He suffered.

No other New Testament book presents so effectively both the continuity of the old and new covenants. In Paul's writings the contrast between the two covenants is stressed; here both the similarities and the differences are kept in balance.

No book of the New Testament reflects the background of Hellenistic thought as much as this one, yet no New Testament writer is as dependent on the Old Testament for support of his views. In the Gospels the *person* of Christ is stressed; in Paul's letters the *work* of Christ is paramount. Here, however, both the person (chapters 1-7) and the work of Christ (chapters 8-13) are kept in balance. No other New Testament book—not even Romans—goes so throughly into the subject of the underlying rationale of the atonement, especially as the fulfillment of the sacrificial system. But this book is the most challenging when it repeatedly calls upon us to "consider" Jesus as our Apostle (3:1), as our High Priest (7:4), and as the one who ran successfully the race set before Him, as we must also do if we are to reach the goal.

Most other writers of the New Testament address themselves to the conditions and consequences of salvation; this writer is chiefly concerned with progress *after* the fundamentals of the faith have been experienced. Others viewed divine revelation as developing in historical process; this writer shares this view but in addition sees the old and new as existing contemporaneously as shadow and substance, as phenomenal and epiphenomenal, as material and spiritual.

But basically the main lines are in agreement with the rest of the New Testament. The treatise complements the writings of the apostles. They use diverse instruments but all play the same tune: all focus on the work of Christ.

PART ONE

The Superiority of Jesus' Person

CHAPTERS 1-7

1

The Superiority of Jesus' Person as Son (1:1-2:18)

The reader of this anonymous letter is arrested at once by the sonorous balance and rhythm of the opening words which welcome him like a narthex of a great cathedral. At first the reader may blink in perplexity at the emphasis on angels, the involved arguments concerning Melchizedek, the dire warnings against apostasy and the repeated admonitions to "press on." But as the windows of a cathedral reveal their mysteries to one who attentively lingers, so the formidable aspects of this letter recede and its lasting values become increasingly apparent to the reader.

Here one finds many things "hard to be understood," but he can continue his study in the assurance that "access to the inner sanctuary of Holy Scripture is given to those who come to worship." Where else would one find so precise a definition of the relation of Father to Son as is expressed in the opening paragraph—"the effulgence of his glory, the express character of his substance"? Where else would one find so great an emphasis on Jesus' capacity to share the experiences of His "brethren"? Where could one find equal assurance of a high priest in the present ministry of constant intercession? Where is the Christian life more winsomely presented as a pilgrimage to a "better country"? Where else would one find so creatively set forth the similarity and contrast between the temporal and the eternal, the material and the spiritual as in this brief letter? For these reasons and many others the Christian Church has correctly insisted that this treatise be a part of the New Testament.

In this "word of exhortation" a final appeal was made "to the Hebrews," probably just before their temple was demolished and its priesthood permanently abolished. To them it brought the good news that the daily sacrifice was no longer needed, that the temple ritual was now replaced by "a more excellent ministry" which performs what the other only promised. The measure of this letter's excellence is that it serves equally well not only "Hebrews" but all who find in the person and work of Christ the answer to their deepest needs.

Vv. 1, 2. God . . . has spoken. In this passage the author gathers up in one comprehensive sentence the essential message of the entire Bible and places it in perspective. The basic assertion is that God has revealed himself. All else is a derivative from this central truth. In its brevity and inclusiveness the claim is both majestic and breathtaking. The prologue resembles that of John's Gospel (1:1-18); in both there is a highly concentrated resumé of what follows, expressed in deliberate simplicity and power. This prologue also resembles the introductions to the Gospel of Luke and the First Epistle of John in that its style is more formal than the remainder. In each of the four introductions named the style is much more formal and precise than the remainder of the discourses.

This introduction differs from all other epistles of the New Testament (and of contemporary secular letters) in that there is no mention of the author or the recipients of the letter. Although in some Bibles the title attributes the treatise to Paul, this is not in the original. Thus, we have here the only anonymous book in the New Testament. It is a testimony to the intrinsic merit of the book that it was included in the canon in spite of the fact that it does not claim apostolic authorship. It was the experience of the early church that God speaks through this letter by His Spirit. God still speaks therein. Christians today concur with the judgment of the early church that the contribution of this letter is so important that it is indispensable.

"This is ultimately the most important vindication of its place in the canon of the New Testament." [1]

The style is quite unlike the simple sentence structure of Hebrew literature. By contrast this opening statement is so involved that it defies grammatical analysis. Reduced to its elemental parts the sentence reads, "God . . . has spoken. . . ."

A. Jesus is superior to the prophets (as Revealer of God) (1:1-3)

1. In time

a. Then—"of old time"

The author makes effective use of contrasts as the following analysis indicates:

DIVINE REVELATION

In the Old Covenant		*In the New Covenant*
	Mode	
In many varied ways		In one complete way
	Amplitude	
Fragmentary and incomplete		Final
	Recipients	
Our fathers		Ourselves
	Time	
In the past		In the present "last days"
	Media	
In the prophets		In a Son

The author thus indicates his appreciation of the Old Testament together with his greater appreciation of the culmination of this revelation in Christ. Several things are evident from this one sentence.

b. Now—"these days" (vv. 1, 2)

The author believes in a *progressive* revelation. The earlier disclosures of God's nature and purpose were adequate in their

---

1. A. M. Stibbs, "Hebrews," *The New Bible Commentary* (Grand Rapids: Eerdmans, 1953), p. 1088.

time but incomplete and imperfect in the longer perspective. The author does not believe merely that man progressively grew in apprehension of divine truth, that man's discoveries were the means of an evolving concept of God. The initiative rests with God. There is a hint here that the end was seen from the beginning; that revelation, even when incomplete and partial, was nevertheless deliberate and progressive, anticipating the climactic revelation in Christ.

The author believes that the revelation was completed in Christ, that no further revelations are to be expected. Man's understanding of the finished revelation in Christ, however, can increase. In this sense also "God shall cause more light to break forth out of His Word," as Pastor John Robinson in Holland advised his parishioners as they left for New England in 1620.

The author is enthusiastic about the freshness and relevance of this newly completed divine disclosure. This enthusiasm is sustained throughout the epistle. It is much more than emotion however; it is emotion based upon thought. The subject matter of the message is such that it calls for acceptance with ardor.

The author's thought is Christ-centered. His theology is predominantly Christology. This is not only already in evidence in the opening verses but becomes increasingly apparent as the argument proceeds. In this respect this author is remarkably like many contemporary theologians in stressing the culmination of divine revelation in "the event of Christ." Unlike many contemporary theologians, however, this author stresses not only the incarnation but the vicarious atonement as well.

2. In finality (1:1, 2)

The fact that God gave a special revelation to the Hebrews is the most precious element in the spiritual heritage of Jew and Christian. In this Jews and Christians heartily agree. God spoke to the fathers in "propositional truth" as conservatives emphasize. God also spoke in "mighty acts" as the "neoorthodox" correctly emphasize. Current interest in the modes of divine inspiration has revived discussion as to the mode and extent of divine relation to "the fathers." The biblical records indicate a rich variety of means used by the Almighty to communicate with men.

a. Then—by diversity (prophets)

There is a "general revelation" to all men: In this general divine self-disclosure the means include "the music of the spheres" (Ps. 8:1-4; 19:1-6), providence in daily life (Ps. 104), phenomena of nature (Ps. 29:3-9; Rom. 1:20), and conscience (2 Sam. 24:10; Rom. 2:15). The foregoing suffice to refute the Barthian insistence that there is no "general revelation" to all men in nature. Kant is nearer to the Scripture in recognizing divine revelation both in "the universe without and the moral law within."

Under the category of "special revelation" the Old Testament indicates that God has spoken: in dreams (Gen. 20:3; Jud. 7:13; Job 4:12-16), by a dumb brute (Num. 22:28), by soothsayers (Num. 23:5), by angels (Gen. 22:11), by visions (Job 33:15; Amos 8:1; Ezek. 1:4-28), by the inspiration of the Spirit of God—the most common method (Jer. 1:4; 2 Sam. 23:2), by the ephod (1 Sam. 23:9; 30:7, 8), by the Urim and Thummim on the vestments of the high priest (1 Sam. 28:6; Ezra 2:63; Neh. 7:65), by writing (32:16), by audible words (Luke 3:22; 9:35; John 12:28, Acts 9:4), by wise men (Prov. 1:2-6; 1 Cor. 7:25), by music (II Kings 3:15, cf. 1 Chron. 25:1; 1 Sam. 16:23), by conference (Acts 15:1-31; Gal. 2:1-10), by theophany (Jud. 13:22; Hab. 3:3-15), and by Christophany (Rev. 1:12-20). These are among the multitude of ways in which God spoke in times past. The culmination of all the divine revelation was in the Word of God incarnate (John 1:14-18). This revelation by the Spirit of God was finalized and made easily communicable by the Word of God written (Jer. 36:4; 2 Pet. 1:19). It was a great moment in history when a German teacher risked his life by declaring before the Diet at Worms:

> Unless I am refuted and convicted by testimonies of the Scriptures, or by clear argument, since I believe neither the pope nor the councils alone, it being evident that they have often erred and contradicted one another, I am conquered by the passages of the Holy Scripture I have quoted, and my conscience is bound to the Word of God. I cannot and will not recant. . . . Here I stand. I cannot do otherwise. God help me. Amen!

By this kind of "bondage" Martin Luther found freedom, both from the guilt of sin and from ecclesiastical tyranny.

To the fathers indicates the author's awareness of continuity in the divine revelation. Each of the New Testament writers was eager to show that the gospel was not a radical departure from preceding revelations in the Torah. They insisted that it was both new and yet an unfolding of the old. None faced this more realistically than Paul when he said the relationship of the new to the old is comparable to that of the pedagogue who leads the pupil to the teacher, as in today's world the bus driver hauls the children to the teachers (Gal. 3:25). The orthodox church, represented by the New Testament *corpus*, found the middle ground between the reactionaries, who refused the "new light" by rejecting the gospel, and the ultra liberals like Marcion and the Gnostics who rejected most or all of the Old Testament. The remarkable thing is the ease and readiness with which Gentile converts, to whom the Old Testament was unfamiliar, accepted it *in toto* without reservation.

In the prophets was the customary manner in which both Jews and Christians referred to the Old Testament authors. To the Christians, especially, the prophets were the main source for revealed truth. But the Jews also followed a correct instinct when they designated even the historical books of the Old Testament as the work of "the early prophets." All inspired men were considered prophets—the patriarchs, David and Solomon, Ezra and Mordecai, in addition to those who bore the name prophet—forty-eight prophets and seven prophetesses according to rabbinic lore. [2]

b. Now—completely (a Son)

V. 2. In a Son. Throughout this treatise the author shows the superiority of the Son by contrast with the prophets, angels, Adam, Joshua, Moses, Aaron and the fathers. He proceeds to show in this preview capsule, with which he introduces the letter, the Lord's superiority in both His *person* and His *work*. One wholesome emphasis in contemporary theology is its stress on the culmination of divine revelation in Jesus Christ.

---

2. G. F. Moore, *Judaism* (Cambridge, 1946), I, 237.

3. In person

The contrast of the Son to the prophets is also indicated in Jesus' parable of the wicked husbandmen who beat the messengers sent to collect the rent. Since they "got by" with that, they decided to kill the son and make themselves the heirs of the vineyard (Mark 12:1ff.). In the Orient especially a man's choicest possession is his firstborn son or only son. When Paul said that God (like Abraham offering Isaac) "spared not his own son, but delivered him up for us all" (Rom. 8:32), he was expressing in superlative terms the generosity of God. The author boldly continues the analogy by saying that the Father gave His entire inheritance to His only Son. This inheritance was the entire cosmos, all creation, the universe. The emphasis is not so much on space as on time (not *kosmos* but *aeon*). Christ is King of the ages (1 Tim. 1:17, ASVm), the same "yesterday, today and forever," as this writer later makes clear (13:8). The same idea is repeatedly stressed in the Apocalypse in one of the titles given to Christ— "he who is, and who was, and who is to come" (Rev. 1:4, 8; 4:8). The Gnostics, whose influence was at a maximum at the middle of the second century of our era, did not believe that God made the world because the divine Spirit could not be in direct contact with matter without being polluted. They believed that creation was effected by a series of intermediary beings of which Christ was one. This writer excludes all semidivine beings as does Paul, and knows only one mediator between God and creation—the Son of God. It has recently been said that we need a new Christology for this space age. It is doubtless true that many need a better Christology, but there is no need for some to invent or evolve a better one. The "Christology for the space age" is clearly and emphatically set forth in the New Testament, especially here and in Colossians where Paul says, "In him are ye made full, who is the head of all principality and power" (Col. 2:10).

4. In creative work

The creation of the world through the Son is the same interpretation of the Genesis account as is expressed in John's Gospel (1:1-2). In the fourth Gospel, and probably here also, the literary source for this appears to be Psalm 33:6 where it is stated, "By the word [*logos*] of the Lord were the heavens made; and all the host of them by the breath [spirit] of his mouth" (cf. Heb. 11:3). John noted the term "word" (or Logos in the LXX) and read "Jesus Christ." Also the personification of Wisdom in Proverbs 8:22-31 includes the statement "I was by him, as a master workman." It is understandable that Christian readers interpreted such statements as indicating that the Christ, the Word of God and Son of God, shared in creation. Paul also believed that the world came into existence through the agency of the Son of God. In the great Christological passage of Colossians 1:9-23, Paul declares "In whom [the Son] we have our redemption . . . who is the image [*eikōn*] of the invisible God, the firstborn of all creation; for in him were all things created, in the heavens and upon the earth, things visible and invisible . . . all things have been created through [*dia*] him and unto [*eis*] him." The incipient Gnosticism, which was then appearing in the Church, emphasized that God created the world through many intermediary beings. Orthodoxy rightly insisted that the Son of God is the *only* mediator between God and the *sole* agent in creation.

5. In relationship to God (1:2, 3)

V. 3. **The effulgence of his glory** is a more literal rendering of the Greek than "reflects the glory of God" (RSV). The Phillips rendition is good—"radiance of the glory of God." The New English Bible agrees with the ASV—"effulgence of God's splendor." The term translated "effulgence" means a "shining forth" or outshining. It is "light out of light" as the Athanasian Creed expresses it. The author is struggling to convey the idea of the closest possible relationship between Father and Son without complete identification. In Latin nomenclature the Son is "consubstantial" with the Father. The term "reflection" fails to indicate the intimacy of the relationship. The moon is a lifeless body which merely reflects the glory of the sun and is of quite different "substance" and far removed in space. The sun possesses a "corona" which is visible during a total eclipse. This "corona" consists of "solar prominences" or gaseous flames leaping up approximately 50,000 miles from the surface of the sun. This "corona" is the "effulgence" of the sun's glory, distinct from the sun itself and yet of the same "substance." The relation of Father to the Son is analogous to the relationship between sun and sunlight (cf. John 1:14, 18).

The RSV has an accurate rendering of the second affirmation of verse 3, "bears the very stamp of his nature." The "exact-expression" (HEM), or "very stamp" (RSV), or "very image" (ASV), or "express image" (KJV), or "flawless expression" (JBP) are all fairly accurate attempts to convey in English the force of *charaktēr*. Originally the term designated a cutting agent, later the impression made, especially on a coin (and which determined the value or nature of the coin). The relation which the Son sustains to the Father is that of the stamp and its impression, of the matrix and the casting, of the mold and the object molded thereby. Thus it is that Christ can say, "He that hath seen me hath seen the Father" (John 14:9). Jesus' fitness to reveal God is based upon a "community of nature" (EGT).

6. In His service (1:3)

After taxing the resources of the Greek language to indicate the closeness and yet the distinctness of Father and Son, the author moves from the essential being of the Son to a consideration of His work. His major work was not creation but re-creation, not the fabrication of the planets but the disposition of the sin problem. Our author indicates that the work of the Son in behalf of the sinner is now finished, hence His present posture. He is seated; the "session" of the Son is indicative of a task completed. This aspect of the work of Christ is elaborated at greater length later in this epistle (1:13). Implicit here is the idea that the superiority of the Son of God is both something intrinsically His by nature but also something acquired by merit. Such an idea becomes explicit later (Heb. 2:9, 10; 5:8).

Most of the emphasis in this epistle is devoted to the work of Christ rather than to His person. But the efficacy of Christ's work is dependent upon His personal character. Christians should appreciate His person more than they usually do. A poet has caught this emphasis in these stirring lines:

> I'd sing the characters He bears,
> And all the forms of love He wears,
>   Exalted on His throne;
> In loftiest songs of sweetest praise,
> I would to everlasting days
>   Make all His glories known.[3]

B. Jesus is superior to the angels by nature (1:4-2:18)

After comparing the Son to the prophets, he now proceeds to show by contrast the superiority of the Son to other agents of divine revelation—the angels. The author's driving purpose throughout is to convince the readers that if they have Christ, they have God's best and all they need for salvation. In so doing he hopes to assure their continuance in loyalty to Christ and His better way.

Why is it that in this epistle so much attention is given to angels? Was there danger that angels would be regarded with a reverence that belongs only to God the Father and God the Son? The fact that he emphasizes the contrast between Son and angelic beings indicates that angelology held a prominent place in the thinking of his readers. How much of this is due to the influence of the Bible? How much was due to extra-biblical sources? To what extent were angels media of divine revelation in canonical literature? In Stephen's speech before his execution, he stated that the Law was given by means of angels (Acts 7:53), and Paul notes that the Law was "ordained by angels" (Gal. 3:19). Apparently this author has the Sinai covenant in mind when he refers to "the word spoken by angels" (Heb. 2:2). Does the Old Testament credit angels with the giving of the Law? The view that the Sinaitic covenant was mediated

---

3. Samuel Medley, "O Could I Speak the Matchless Worth," *Hymns of the Living Faith* (Winona Lake: Light and Life Press, 1951), p. 146.

by angels perhaps originated in Deuteronomy 33:2, "The Lord came from Sinai . . . with ten thousands of saints" (cf. Ps. 68:17). Angels were regarded as ministers in the court of Jehovah and as serving a variety of functions including a minor role in communicating the divine revelation to man. [4]

During the intertestamental period angels were regarded with increasing veneration, especially in the numerous apocalypses of the period. This was especially true of Alexandrinian Judaism. There is also evidence that in Asia Minor angels were esteemed so highly as to border on worship. While writing to the church at Colossae, Paul was at pains to emphasize that Jesus Christ is the *only* mediator between God and man and to warn that competition in this area is to be rejected (Col. 2:3, 8-10, 18). He specifically condemns the "worshipping of angels." It was in Egypt later that the Gnostic systems of Basilides and Valentinus came to full flower with a hierarchy of as many as 365 intermediary semidivine beings. [5] For the Jew this was a serious challenge to monotheism. For the Christian it challenged the uniqueness of Jesus Christ, the Son of God. The fierceness of the conflict is attested by the vast amount of writing by the church fathers in condemnation of these and other heretical teachings. Out of the conflict orthodoxy was defined in the first four great ecumenical councils of the church.[6] Since this author knew the prestige of the angels, especially in Alexandrinian Judaism, he took pains to show Jesus' superiority to them. His main concern was not to compare Jesus with angels, but rather to exalt Jesus by contrasting Him with angels.

1. In name (1:4-7)

V. 4. God's Son is said to have a better (*kreitton*) name than the angels. "Better" is the key word of this epistle. Jesus Christ is here presented as better than the angels; He is a

---

4. G. F. Moore, *op. cit.*, I, 403.

5. Irenaeus, Adv. Haer. I. xi. 1-5. A. Roberts and J. Donaldson, editors, *The Ante-Nicene Fathers* (New York: Chas. Scribner's Sons, 1903), I, pp. 332f.

6. These major councils were held at Nicea in 325, at Constantinople in 381, at Ephesus in 431, and at Chalcedon in 451 A.D.; with their conclusions both Catholics and Protestants agree.

better priest than was Aaron (7:7); in Him we have a better hope (7:19); He mediates a better covenant (7:22; 8:6) which is established on better promises (8:6). In addition He provides better sacrifices (9:23), and an inheritance far better than earthly possessions (10:34). In Christ the believer is a pilgrim in quest of a better country (11:16). He will experience a better resurrection (11:35), something even better than what the Old Testament saints experienced (11:40). While Abel's sacrifice was pleasing to God, that of Christ is far better (12:24) and also higher in quality (1 Pet. 3:17). By "better" he means more useful and more serviceable (1 Cor. 11:17; 12:31; 2 Pet. 2:21). Thus the author drives home to even the most casual reader his conviction of Christ's superiority to the best in revealed religion. He intends that his enthusiasm for Christ's superiority will be contagious, and it is.

The **name** stands for His nature. It is more than a label for identification. It means His rank, His status, His standing, His very being. Prayer in the "name" of Jesus means that the personal endorsement and prestige of Jesus sanctions the request. Sometimes the person's name means the same as the person. The "Name" is sometimes the equivalent of God, as when one blasphemed "the Name" (Lev. 24:11-16). It is an awesome privilege and responsibility to bear the name of Jehovah, or Yahweh, i.e., to be associated with the Great God (Isa. 43:7; 44:5).

a. Called a Son (Ps. 2:7; 2 Sam. 7:14)

V. 5. In the following passage our author stresses the superiority of the Son by calling attention to the fact of His sonship in contrast to angelic creatures. The question implies a negative answer: angels, in the singular, were never regarded as sons of God. The second Psalm was originally written with reference to David and his heirs. This Psalm is quoted also in Acts 4:24-26; 13:33; Revelation 12:5; 19:15 and again in Hebrews 5:5; it is a messianic Psalm which exerted a profound influence upon the early church. Linked with it is the reference to Jehovah's covenant with David in which it is said, "He shall build a house for my name, and I will establish the throne of his kingdom for ever. I will be his father, and he shall be my son . . . my lovingkindness shall not depart from him" (2 Sam. 7:13-15). The nation of Israel was sometimes referred to as God's son in a figurative sense (Hos. 11:1). Within the nation those who really embraced the covenant were called "sons" in a more personal, spiritual sense (Isa. 43:6; 45:11; 56:5; Hos. 1:10; cf. 2 Cor. 6:18). Sometimes angels were collectively referred to as "sons" (Job. 1:6; 38:7), but "Son" in the singular had a definite messianic connotation, as here, and was recognized as such by both Jews and Christians. The writer's task here is to convince his readers that these messianic predictions are fulfilled in Jesus of Nazareth.

The central affirmation here is the deity of Christ. This is the central truth of the Christian religion. This is recognized by the World Council of Churches, a group of Christians who are united in one central affirmation that Jesus Christ is both "God and Savior." This excludes Unitarians and others who refuse to acknowledge that Jesus of Nazareth is the unique Son of God. While many who refuse this are labelled Christians and are in the fellowship of Christian churches, it is certain they would not be included in any New Testament church. On the other hand, anyone who could sincerely confess Christ as Son of God and personal Saviour would certainly have been given the right hand of fellowship (Rom. 10:9; 1 Cor. 12:3; 1 Tim. 2:5; 3:16). It is not stated *explicitly* that these scriptures are prophetic of Jesus Christ; they are cited only as not applicable to the angels. *Implicitly*, however, they are clearly applied to Christ.

b. Angels commanded to worship the Son (Ps. 97:7)

V. 6. Instead of being the objects of worship the angels are commanded to render worship to the Son of God, thus clearly indicating the contrast between Creator and the creature. The tendency to worship the creature rather than the Creator is extremely widespread. Paul recognized and condemned this in his general indictment of the Gentile world (Rom. 1:20-25). Idolatry persisted in the people of the Covenant until after the Exile. Probably the last words to be penned in what is now our New Testament comprised an exhortation, "Keep yourselves from idols" (1 John 5:21). In the early church the worship of saints, the Virgin Mary, and martyrs was introduced at an early age and persists to this day. The worship of angels was practiced in the early church but was specifically condemned (Col. 2:18; Rev. 22:8, 9). In modern life idolatry in the form of worship of the self has been vigorously condemned by Rheinhold Niebuhr and others. In this passage the writer urges the worship of Christ to the exclusion of the veneration of all other creatures; He alone is worthy of worship.

c. Angels created to be servants (Ps. 104:4)

V. 7. If angels are not to be worhsipped but instead are commanded to worship the Son of God, what is their status and function? They are to be **servants** (*leitourgikai*), not doing the menial tasks of a household slave (*doulos*), but as courtiers in public service comparable to that of the priesthood or a minister of state. Their primary service is to the Father and the Son, as indicated here; their secondary service is that of assisting Christians v. 14). The words are taken from Psalm 104:4 with its poetic description of creation. In the parallelism the angels are comparable to wind and flashes of lightning. As here used the passage denotes the statues of angelic beings as ministers to the Creator, comparable to swift courtiers about a monarch. However distinguished these creatures are for their unique relationship to God, they are still created beings and need to worship Christ. In paganism little distinction was made between great men and the gods. Men were quite ready to worship not only the gods but the representatives of the gods, both inanimate (Acts 17:23) and animate (Acts 14:15). While in India the writer was told by a bright young Indian industrialist, "Gandhi is now dead and we worship him; when Nehru dies we will worship him." With great difficulty Christian leaders taught their converts from paganism that all worship except that of the Father and Son is strictly interdicted (1 Thess. 1:9). Both angels and men therefore are to join in the worship of Him whose "name is above every name" (Phil. 2:9; cf. Rev. 7:9) to the exclusion of all others.

2. In character (1:8, 9)

a. Stability

V. 8. Our author's gaze shifts alternately from the unique Son of God to the angelic beings around His throne (cf. Rev. 5:6-14). Now he concentrates on the Son again: **thy throne . . . is for ever and ever.** In this connection he speaks of the permanence, the righteousness and the joyousness of the Son's reign. The source of the quotation is a Psalm celebrating the marriage and enthronement of the crown prince (Ps. 45). The basis for the prediction of permanence is the covenant with David and his dynasty (2 Sam. 7). The fulfillment of the prediction, as in many of the messianic predictions, is not in a strictly literal sense (no descendant of David now occupies a throne) but in a spiritual sense—in David's greater Son—in the Messiah. Thus the writer applies it here. David's "throne" endures because it deserves to, because it possesses "survival value." It deserves to because David was a man "after God's own heart" and because these qualities of godlikeness are expressed in Jesus the Christ. The same truth is affirmed later in this epistle where Christ is referred to as being "the same yesterday, today and forever" (13:8; cf. Rev. 1:18). In contrast to man, God alone is unchanging (Ps. 90.); to be unchanging is a quality possessed by deity alone. Devout men often pray,

> Change and decay, in all around I see,
> Oh Thou who changest not, abide with me.[7]

b. Righteousness

As envisioned in the prophets and actualized in Jesus Christ, the Messiah is characterized by righteousness *par excellence.* This is another case of a twofold fulfillment of Scripture. The dynasty of David was characterized by a relative righteousness —a righteousness like that of King Saul. But the dynasty became corrupt; the nation was then corrupted and failure ended with the Exile, never to regain its former status. Out of the broken idealism of the kingdom period and the Davidic dynasty was born the messianic hope of a ruler who could be truly described as righteous (Isa. 11:1ff.).[8] The desire of the nation, expressed through the

---

7. Henry F. Lyte, "Abide With Me," *Hymns of the Living Faith* (Light and Life Press, 1952), p. 39.

8. H. W. Perkins, *The Doctrine of Christian Perfection* (London: Epworth Press, 1927), p. 50.

prophets, was not fulfilled therefore in the Old Testament. But the hope lived on and focused on Jesus Christ the Righteous One (1 John 2:1). In no respect is the uniqueness of Jesus more unchallenged than with respect to His sinlessness and righteousness. Ullmann's *The Sinlessness of Christ* is a classic study, setting forth in detail the miracle of the Master's sinlessness. Most would agree with E. Stanley Jones that if one can believe in the miracle of Jesus' character, he would have no difficulty in believing in the miracles He performed.

It is significant that the Son of God both loved righteousness, and hated iniquity. One cannot truly love holiness without detesting sin. He need not hate the sinner, but he cannot avoid hating the sinfulness which characterizes the sinner. The assumption that love for humanity necessitates a bland acceptance of evil-doing as merely "human weakness" reflects a view of righteousness that is deficient.

c. *Joyousness*

Righteous character and actions are rewarded by divine vindication which brings true joy. The natural accompaniment and consequence of rectitude is a deep, exhilarating and abiding joyousness. Old Testament history demonstrates that when the Israelites repented and experienced spiritual renewal they rejoiced. This was evident at the close of the revival under Hezekiah's leadership (2 Chron. 30:23), the victory under Jehoshaphat (2 Chron. 20:27), at the dedication of the second temple (Ezra 6:16), and at the renewal of the covenant to keep the Law (Neh. 8:12).

The same motif is seen in the New Testament. Although Jesus was described as "a man of sorrows and acquainted with grief," He was also the possessor of joy in the Lord. He was intoxicated with the joy of doing the will of His Father (John 4:34). He was filled with joy at the Father's methods of making His will known (Luke 10:21). In rabbinic thought the Messiah was regarded as characterized by joy. Indeed they believed that the Holy Spirit would not rest upon a person of sad countenance. The Apostle Paul was outstanding for his capacity for suffering. One of the criteria for his apostleship was the extent of his suffering for the gospel. And yet it was Paul who always rejoiced in the Lord, as his Corinthian and Philippian epistles in particular eloquently testify. The true Christian today will rejoice as he chooses and pursues the will of God.

3. In permanence (1:10-12)

From describing Christ as King our author now turns to view Him as the Creator. The words originally addressed to God the Father are here by implication addressed to the Son of God. Beginning with the account of beginnings in Genesis, the Psalmist reflects upon God's creative power and turns from that to his permanence, in contrast to the perishable and transient character of all things created. By including heaven as well as earth in things created the poet includes all things in the universe. He spoke more wisely than he knew, for the universe includes much more than the Psalmist could realize.

Stability and permanence are qualities which finite man always associates with the divine. This conviction is nowhere more eloquently expressed than in the Psalmist's words, "From everlasting to everlasting, thou art God" (Ps. 90:2). When a healthy, vigorous young man or woman is suddenly cut off by accident or by an assassin's bullet, one is forced to recognize how fragile and brief is his claim to physical life. In such crises the man of faith finds relief in the recognition that his God is unchanging—"the same yesterday, today and forever." Such a person finds that by his commitment to God through Christ, his own life takes on the quality of the eternal. Is not this the basis for "eternal life"?

The quality of the eternal which characterizes Christ and His disciples is illustrated in the life of Sequoia, the Cherokee Indian who gave his people a written language and who is the only American Indian represented at the hall of fame in the Rotunda of the Capitol Building in Washington, D.C. The story is told that Sequoia was employed by a group of trappers as a guide to the West. He was a Christian and did not partake of their cursing, gambling, drinking and other forms of vice. They came to recognize and appreciate the superior quality of life which he lived daily among them. When they arrived on the Pacific Coast and saw with amazement the tall, majestic and "ever-living" Redwood trees, they decided to call these trees Sequoia because, like their Indian guide, they seemed to possess something of the eternal. [9]

V. 11. All of creation is compared in a bold simile to a garment which is laid aside after it is worn out. There is a hint of eschatology here. The same idea is conveyed in another striking simile in Revelation 6:14, "The heaven was removed as a scroll when it is rolled up." The biblical writers were sure that the physical universe that seems so permanent really is not. The Lord reigns supreme, all else being subject to change. Such a faith stabilizes a person during the vicissitudes of life; it gives poise.

V. 12. But thou art the same; with infinite relief the authors (Psalmist and evangelist) look to the Lord as the One who changes not. It echoes the affirmation of verse 11—"thou remainest"—and clinches the thought of the permanence of God's rule. The soul that is unreservedly committed to Christ finds thereby the stability that is necessary in the stresses and vacillations of life. The life "hid with Christ in God" alone has "survival value." It is probably a sense of impermanence and hence insecurity which has bred a "beatnik generation." The motto of "eat, drink and be merry," to use a biblical phrase, or "live it up," to use a modern phrase, is the antithesis to the sense of permanence, stability and worth which the believer experiences in Christ. The more positive the commitment to Christ, the greater the poise and the power. If one's commitment is made in times of peace when deliberation is possible, "the anchor holds" when the stress comes.

4. In honor (1:13, 14)

V. 13. The angels are not at God's right hand. The picture is that of an oriental court. The king is seated and the king's

---

9. Cf. "Sequoia," *Compton's Pictured Encyclopedia* (Chicago: F. E. Compton Co., 1950), XIII, 102. "It has been generally assumed that Endlicher, who gave it the name *Sequoia sempervirens*, had in mind the Cherokee Indian, Sequoyan . . . ." "Sequoia," *Encyclopaedia Britannica* (Chicago, 1959), XX, 339.

son and heir is also seated in the place of authority. The fact that they are seated is evidence that their power is not threatened. The son is not in the field of battle defending his authority; that question is settled and his rule is unchallenged. The author emphasizes the contrast between the Son in the place of authority as Heir-apparent, and the angels—heavenly courtiers whose function is to serve the wishes of the Son.

V. 14. The nature and function are here spelled out more specifically: they are attendants, standing ready to carry out any order requested by the King of kings, the Son of God. The beneficiaries of the service of angels are not only God but those human beings who are recipients of the grace of God. In both Old and New Testaments, this ministry of the angels is set forth consistently. These tasks are varied. Angels ministered (*diēkonoun*) to Jesus *after* His temptation (Matt. 4:11). The belief that children have "guardian angels" is probably based on Matthew 18:10. Angels announced the birth of Jesus (Luke 1:26; 2:9-15) and also His resurrection (Matt. 28:2-7; John 20:12). An angel effected the release of Peter from prison (Acts 12:7-10) and directed Philip in personal evangelism (Acts 8:26). The work of the Holy Spirit and that of angels was complementary, as in the case of Philip: a message from an angel initiated the mission to the pilgrim from Ethiopia; then the Spirit gave further direction and effected Philip's departure (Acts 8:26, 29, 39). In the Apocalypse the role of angels has even greater prominence (Rev. 1:1; 5:2; 5:11; 21:9). In these and many other ways, the angels serve as messengers of the Son of God and as assistants to God's people.

A civil servant of the king need not always be busy; "they also serve who only stand and wait," as Milton reflected during his blindness. The writer recalls a gracious host and hostess in India whose household servant stood just outside the dining room door awaiting orders (cf. Ps. 123:2).

Paul apparently believed that a message mediated through an angel would be even more direct, authentic and authoritative than one coming through a prophet (Gal. 1:8; 1 Cor. 13:1). This is understandable since the habitat of angels is in God's immediate presence. They are deathless creatures whose sole function is that of serving God. These considerations probably explain why this author spends more time pointing out the superiority of Christ to the angels than he does in stressing Christ's superiority to the prophets.

Thus from seven quotations from the Greek Old Testament (LXX), this author builds his case for the superiority of the Son of God to all created beings. He apparently seeks to win those (Jews of the Dispersion) who are more familiar with the Greek version of the Old Testament than with the Hebrew original. Because of this he cites passages which differ from our extant Hebrew manuscripts. Commentators have questioned both the relevancy and legitimacy of several of these Old Testament texts. While acceptable to exegetes of that day, the author's method is not one that would find acceptance today, even in the most conservative circles. Our author does not consider, for example, what meaning these passages had in their respective contexts, or what they signified to the original readers; he is thinking only of their meaning for his own generation (ABB, p. 49). This method of exegesis was widely practiced and none apparently questioned its legitimacy. In this case the author proceeds on the principle that statements which rise above the historical to the ideal are to be regarded as messianic and hence applicable to Christ. Because of their experience of the living Christ, readers in the apostolic age studied their Scriptures (the Old Testament) as a "revised version." They saw much there that they did not see before. The modern scholar can agree with their conclusions but not always with their methods. The same can be said for Paul's use of the Old Testament in Romans and other letters. [10]

Thus, by quotation, by rhetorical questions, and by effective use of contrast, this author decisively demonstrates his central affirmation—the transcendent superiority of Christ to all created beings, prophets, and even angels. This superiority derives from His nature, His status, and His function. It is something which calls not only for reflection but also for commitment.

---

10. Wm. Sanday and A. C. Headlan, *The Epistle to the Romans* (I.C.C.: Edinburgh: T. & T. Clark, 1945), pp. 302-315.

C. A superior revelation demands an eager response (2:1-4)

1. The danger of drifting away is imminent (2:1)

After the extended comparison and contrast between angels and the Son of God in chapter one, our author now concerns himself with Christ's relationship to mankind in chapter two. At the same time the contrast with angels is kept in mind throughout the chapter: in verse 2 the importance of the Old Covenant is underscored by the fact that it was mediated through angels; in verse 5 dominion of the world was not given to angels but rather to man; in verses 7, 9 the Son of man is said to be temporarily lower than the angels; and in verse 16 not angels, but men, are the object of Christ's mediatorial work. Thus angels are recognized only to stress their inferiority, first to Christ and then to human beings. Paradoxically, therefore, they are higher than man in the sense that they are deathless creatures, continually in God's presence, and lower in the sense that they are excluded from the benefits of the atonement.

Most of this chapter is in contrast to most of chapter one. There Jesus' dignity and glory is stressed; here, His humiliation. In chapter one His deity is stressed; here, His humanity. The boldness of this contrast is unparalleled elsewhere in the New Testament.

Chapter one: vv. 1-14	*Chapter two: vv. 5-18*
Son of God (1:2, 5, 8)	Son of man (2:6, 9, 11)
Creator (1:2, 10)	Creature (2:9)
"Very God of very God" (1:3, 8)	"Man of sorrows" (2:14, 17)
Glorious sovereign (1:8, 9, 13)	Inglorious sufferer (2:9-11, 14-18)
Heir of all things (1:2, 8, 13)	Human in all things (2:17)
Recipient of worship (1:6)	Sharer of temptations (2:10, 18)
Better than the angels (1:4)	Beneath the angels (2:9)
Changeless (1:10-12)	Changeable (2:9, 10, 14, 17)
Builder of all things (1:2, 10)	Brother to all believers (2:11-14)
"Thy years shall not fail" (1:12)	"Tasted death" (2:9)[1]

---

1. Delbert R. Rose, *Aldersgate Biblical Series: Leader's Guide to Hebrews,* Heb. 2 (Winona Lake: Light and Life Press, 1961), p. 30.

This paragraph is the first of a series of exhortations with which the author's closely knit argument is interspersed. Of the total of 303 verses in this letter approximately 156 are devoted to exhorting the readers to steadfastness and faith.

Because of the importance of God's revelation through prophets and through His Son and because of the fact that we have been privileged above our predecessors in receiving it, we ought to welcome it eagerly, the argument runs.

The **more earnest heed** means "so much more," or "to a much greater degree," or "far greater, more exceedingly" (2 Cor. 7:15; Heb. 13:19; 1 Thess. 2:17). "We are bound to pay all the more heed" (NEB) is a reading which underscores the obligation. Privilege always brings responsibility. Since we have heard, he argues, we have the greater obligation to respond. Jesus repeatedly urged his hearers to give heed, warning that hearing alone is futile. James likewise urges that one be a doer and not a hearer alone (James 1:22-25). In days of complacency there are not a few who assume that respectful attention to the preacher or teacher is all that should be required. Sometimes they consider that they do the speaker a favor by listening. Ezekiel's congregation consisted of such persons (Ezek. 33:32—"they hear thy words, but they do them not").

2. This better revelation must be heeded (2:2-4)

The **word spoken through angels** reflects the rabbinic doctrine of the function of angels in the revelation at Mount Sinai. In Deuteronomy 33:2 there is a poetic description of a theophany accompanied with "ten thousands of holy ones"; it is not a statement that angels mediated the Torah. Likewise in Psalm 68:17 reference is made to thousands of God's chariots at Mount Sinai. More specifically Acts 7:38, 53 speaks of an angel speaking for God at Mount Sinai and of angels as ordaining the Law. This idea of the Law "ordained through angels by the hand of a mediator" is elaborated in Galatians 3:19, but the mediator is not identified; it was probably Moses. Since angels constantly attend upon the throne and are often dispatched for special revelations (cf. Judg. 13:3; Dan. 9:21;

Zech. 1:9), it seemed natural to stress the importance of the Sinai revelation by noting the means by which it was communicated—the highest created intelligences. The author's point is that the reception of the Decalogue was accompanied by a strict accounting for the way in which it was received. The slightest deviation from it was dealt with by a penalty proportionate to the degree of guilt; one could not evade it. The same principle is at work under the new covenant: privilege begets responsibility. The added advantage of grace over law means that those who neglect the greater boon will be treated with a proportionately more drastic punishment. Thus by the motives of love and fear the author propels and entreats his complacent readers.

V. 3. By **escape** he means evading the consequences of the sin of omission. In contrast to the Sinai revelation, the gospel is spoken by the Lord Jesus Christ, not a mere man like Moses. To remain unresponsive in the presence of such a stupendous revelation of grace is to incur the deepest guilt and make one liable to the severest penalties. Since the privilege is greater, the penalty for its rejection is the greater. This idea is driven home elsewhere in this letter, especially in 12:25-29. The sequence of revelation here is noteworthy: it comes from God through angels and is announced by Jesus, "attested" (RSV) by apostolic witnesses, and further confirmed by miracles and gifts of the Spirit. The manner in which this occurred is well illustrated in the Gospels and Acts. When the apostles went forth to preach, they were able to cast out demons, heal the sick and cleanse the lepers; all these being indicative of the divine source of their witness (Mark 6:13). After Pentecost the same principle is seen even more graphically—the preaching of the Word was often followed (and endorsed) by miracles (Acts 3:7, 16) and by the gift of the Holy Spirit (Acts 2:33; 10:44; 15:8). Thus the divine authentication for the gospel was even more emphatic than for the Decalogue; that was on one occasion in one place while this was repeated many times.

V. 4. God also bearing witness: this was the big factor in Jesus' public ministry. Again and again as reported in the Gospels, Jesus pointed out that the Father corroborated His witness by miracles which leant immediacy and relevancy to Jesus' words and works. To assure John the Baptist, Jesus called attention to the supernatural authenticating marks of the Messiah: "The blind receive their sight . . . the lepers are cleansed, and . . . the dead are raised up" (Matt. 11:5; cf. Isa. 61:1ff.). In apostolic preaching the culminating verification of their witness was the *fait accompli* of the resurrection of Christ (Acts 2:32; 3:15; 4:10; 13:30-39; 17:31). The resurrection of Christ was for the early Christians the supreme evidence of the truth of Jesus and the good news to which they were witnesses. The resurrection was the historical event to which they reverted again and again, much the same as the Old Testament prophets, poets and historians constantly alluded to the Exodus from Egypt. Both the Exodus and the resurrection of Christ were regarded as the most conspicuous examples of "God's mighty acts" through which He revealed His will, vanquished His enemies, and vindicated His people.

From this paragraph we get a foretaste of this author's persuasiveness. Whether written by Barnabas ("son of exhortation," Acts 4:36), or Apollos (Acts 18:22-28), or someone else, this "word of exhortation" (Heb. 13:22) contains several salient points: (1) The readers are partakers of the heavenly calling; they are committed Christians. (2) There is a real possibility that they by sheer negligence may lose the grace of God. (3) This need not happen and will not if they persevere in their faith and loyalty. (4) The gospel is no less rigorous than the law in dealing with rebels; indeed the greater privileges call for a more severe penalty to rebels. (5) The New Covenant is backed up by Jesus, the apostles, by the Spirit, and by God himself.

In what way can a modern reader **drift away** from basic Christian commitment? He may do so consciously or unconsciously in a number of ways:

(1) He may lose his "first love" (Rev. 2:4)—that is, he may become less fervent in his devotions and in his zeal for service. This loss may first become apparent in his times of secret prayer. There will be less fervency and fluency, less of a "burden" for souls, less of a feeling of love and gratitude for the Lord. Prayer may become perfunctory and a duty, or it may be neglected entirely, crowded out by activities more acceptable to the "the flesh."

(2) The drifting may also be indicated by a loss of a "passion for souls." One's love for Christ will be in proportion to his love of those for whom Christ died. This may result in less activity in behalf of the salvation of one's neighbors, less evangelistic zeal, less concern for missions, less emphasis on sacrificial giving.

(3) One may "slip away" in the realm of doctrinal belief. Students reared in an evangelical home and church and educated in thoroughly Christian schools may later, either in higher institutions of learning or in professional associations, become in their own estimation "emancipated" and leave "the foundation of repentance . . . and of faith toward God" (Heb. 6:1). This happens repeatedly, both among laymen and among those preparing for full-time Christian service.

(4) With many Christian workers the "drifting away" may be reflected in a professionalism in which one may have "a form of godliness, but denying the power thereof" (2 Tim. 3:5). Form then replaces fervency. The religious functionary finally persuades himself that religious forms and acts have an intrinsic value apart from the attitude of the ministrant.

(5) One may detect this "drift" when, for example, security is preferred to freedom, conviction yields to convenience, expediency seems preferable to principle, when precedent impedes progress, when prejudice becomes tolerable and when complacency becomes habitual. The danger of such "slipping" is omnipresent. This epistle shows the way to avoid this danger. Pope's description of apostasy has become classic:

> Vice is a monster of so frightful mien,
> As to be hated, needs but to be seen:
> Yet seen too oft, familiar with her face,
> We first endure, then pity, then embrace. [2]

After taking "time out" to exhort his readers, the author resumes his argument concerning the superiority of Christ and His claim for allegiance.

---

2. Alexander Pope, "Essay on Man," in W. A. Briggs, edit. *Great Poems of the English Language* (New York: Tudor, 1933), p. 269.

D. Jesus is superior to the angels in dominion (2:5-18)

In Hebrews 2:14-18 we encounter the most explicit statement in the New Testament concerning the philosophy of the Christian plan of salvation. The author here goes beyond the *kergyma*, beyond the proclamation of the plan of salvation to an explanation of it, its philosophy, its rationale. He deals with the question "Why?" Similar approaches to this rationale are seen in Luke 24:26, "Was it not necessary that Christ should suffer these things and enter into his glory?" (RSV). Paul has some moving passages describing the humiliation and exaltation of the Christ (Phil. 2:5-11; 2 Cor. 8:9), but he makes no attempt to explain *why* this method was appropriate, seemly and becoming, or *why* it behooved God to work in this way. In this passage the author explains that the incarnation with its suffering was necessary in order to make the grace of God accessible through a high priest who is both deity and a fellow-traveller, a fellow-sufferer. The two cardinal doctrines of the Christian faith are the incarnation and the crucifixion-resurrection of Jesus Christ. The resurrection proves that the grace of God is adequate; the incarnation makes it available. Later this author deals with the death of Christ and its consequences; here he concentrates on the incarnation. In so doing, he compares and contrasts Christ with Adam and his descendants, showing that mankind rather than angelic beings is the object of the redemptive work of Christ. However, his concern is no longer with angels as such. Here he concentrates on the "Author of our salvation."

1. Angels not given dominion (2:5)

V. 5. For not unto angels. With these words the author resumes the argument of 1:14 after the intervening "word of exhortation." Since the angels are only ministering spirits to serve God and man, they are not rulers of the world. This dominion has been given to mankind. **The world** (inhabited earth) **to come** could mean the world over which Adam was to have dominion, i.e., the present age or the Golden Age of the Messiah (Matt. 19:28) or life everlasting on an earth renewed in righteousness (Rev. 21:1). In the light of the context the probability is that the reference is to the present world; only over this world could Adam possibly have had any jurisdiction. The author's point is simply to indicate that at creation the inhabited earth was not placed under the jurisdiction of angelic beings but human beings. Having thus disposed of the angels he now focuses attention on man—his nature, his needs, and his Saviour.

2. Adam (man) failed to dominate the world (2:6-8)

V. 6. One hath somewhere testified is a reference to a passage of scripture familiar to the author and his readers. "The vagueness proceeds not from ignorance, but is simply a characteristic of the oratorical style which disdains pedantic accuracy in minutiae" (ABB, p. 69). The quotation is from Psalm 8 with a parallel in Psalm 144:3. In both cases the poet is impressed by man's frailty and brevity of life. In Psalm 8 the statement is occasioned by a gaze at the starry heavens above and meditations arising therefrom. Plato said that philosophy begins in wonder. The same may be said for religion. Certainly in this case the poet's contemplation of the vastness and beauty of the heavens leads him to worship and to marvel at God's handiwork (cf. Ps. 19:1-6; 104:1-34).

What is man . . . ? Some commentators believe that the Psalmist was impressed with man's finiteness; others believe that he stresses man's dignity. Rather, does he not stress both? There is no contradiction here although there is a paradox. How can the Psalmist in the same instant be both humbled and exalted? After contemplating the starry heavens he is impressed by man's insignificance. Man can see about 6,000 stars with the naked eye, a tiny fraction of the number in space. The Psalmist could not know, for instance, that while it takes eight light minutes to travel the 93,000,000 miles from the sun to the earth, the distance across the Milky Way galaxy is so vast that it takes 100,000 years for light to cross from one edge to the other. He could not know that one star (Betelgeuse) in the Constellation Orion is larger than the orbit of the earth around the sun. He could not know that in addition to the Milky Way galaxy, some 75,000,000 others are in existence, 50,000 of them in space the size of the bowl of the Big Dipper (Ursa Major). He did not realize that while it takes light four days to cross from one edge of the solar system to the other, some stars are so large that it would take ten years for light to traverse the diameter of one star. He could not grasp the fact (nor can we) that some stars are 10,000,000,000 light years (the distance light can travel in one year at the rate of 186,000 miles per second) distant.[3] Such facts simply accentuate the words of the Psalmist who, while acquainted with fewer facts than we about the starry heavens, was quick to praise his Maker.

Son of man is a Hebrew parallelism, echoing and emphasizing the thought of the preceding statement. Parallelism in Hebrew literature refers to the habit of saying the same or similar thing twice, a phenomenon recognized by Robert Lowth a century ago. In some parallelisms the second member is identical with the first; in others the second statement adds something to the first. In the Hebrew original the author apparently used a synonymous parallelism, the second member being the same as the first. Here, our author uses it as a progressive parallelism, the second member adding a messianic connotation to the thought of the first. Thus he goes from the first Adam in creation to the last Adam in redemption. Doubtless he has in mind Adam as an individual to whom, the Genesis account says, God entrusted the administration of the earth and mankind in general (the Hebrew "*adam*" means "man" or "mankind," a generic concept).

Vv. 7, 8. In what respects has man "conquered" the world over which he was delegated to keep order and make subservient?

In the physical realm man's gains have been rather impressive. Man has "progressed" from a wooden club to atomic missiles so "sophisticated" that by pressing a button in Colorado he can destroy Moscow. In his conquest over space he can now travel around the earth in outer space in much less time than it would take to walk fifty miles. In communication, man has progressed from smoke signals and sign language to color television, and from continent to continent via an earth satellite in space. In the harnessing of nature to serve his needs, he has progressed from the discovery of fire to cook his food to the use of gas to heat his home automatically. In the realm of inner space (the

---

3. "Astronomy," *Encyclopaedia Britannica* (Chicago: 1959), II, 577ff.

atom) and in the realm of outer space, his achievements in the last quarter century have been almost incredible. But in the realm of human relations his lack of achievement has been fantastically slow. The ants and the bees behave better toward each other than do humans. Science has enabled man to gratify his diabolical desires for revenge and greed without sanctifying or directing those desires. Science has served to make genocide an actuality for the first time in human history. Nazi scientists who perfected the means for mass destruction of other human beings gave no evidence of moral scruples about the propriety of their actions.[4] Among the things "not yet subject to man" are death, the weather and sin. To the problems of sin and death the author now turns.

3. Jesus (Son of man) alone given this dominion (2:9)

V. 9. But we behold him. This is one of several places in this letter where the author calls for a consideration of Jesus. Similar expressions occur in 3:1; 7:4; 12:2, 3. The author's preoccupation with Jesus is characteristic of this epistle. The relationship of these verses to the preceding (vv. 6-8) is one of contrast. While Adam was made but little lower than the angels with reference to place, Jesus was made lower than the angels with reference to time. Thus the "lower" of verse 7 is applicable to both the first and last Adam. When was Jesus "crowned with glory and honor"? Was it prior to His incarnation (Rendall), or at His baptism, or at His transfiguration (A. B. Bruce), or after the resurrection and ascension (Delitzsch)? The latter view seems more probable because it is in harmony with this writer (e.g., 12:2) and with the New Testament generally (cf. Phil. 2:5-11; John 7:39; 12:16, 23; 1 Pet. 1:11; 4:13). Phillips' rendering of this complicated construction is clear and helpful: "Jesus, after being made temporarily inferior to the angels (and so subject to pain and death), [is] . . . now crowned with glory and honour." This places the events in their proper temporal and causal sequence. The tasting of death is to experience it with the horror of separation from

---

4. Wm. L. Shirer, *The Rise and Fall of the Third Reich* (New York: Simon & Shuster, 1960), pp. 782, 834 *et passim*.

the body and a venture into the unknown, experienced most poignantly when Jesus prayed, "Let this cup pass from me," in the garden, and on the cross when He cried, "My God, my God, why hast thou forsaken me?" In this epistle, there is considerable emphasis on "tasting" (*geuomai*) and its synonyms "sharing" (2:14) and "partaking" (3:1).[5] All these are designed to stress the homogeneity between the incarnate Christ and believers both deceased and living (cf. Heb. 12:1, 23). The connection between Christ and the believer is much more intimate than that between Christ and the angels (2:12; cf. 12:22) even though angels are presently higher in status and function. The concept extends to partaking not only in experiences of persecution with other saints (*koinōnoi*) but also of sharing (*metalambanō*) in God's own nature (12:10; cf. 6:7). The writer is eager for his readers to grasp the idea that as believers in Christ they are already participants in the divine life shared by Father, Son, and other saints. To forfeit such a relationship by carelessness, neglect (2:1), or unbelief (3:19) would be a tragedy more terrible than what befell the rebels in Sinai (3:17) or to shortsighted Esau (12:16).

4. The rationale of the Cross (2:10-16)

a. The means was appropriate to the end (v. 10)

V. 10. It became him. Here the author launches into the rationale of the passion of Christ. Most people, including even the Hebrews familiar with the Old Testament, did not associate suffering with holiness. The pioneer voices in Job and Isaiah 53 were like voices crying in the night with no one to heed. Even Jesus' disciples were wholly unprepared to envision a Messiah who would suffer (Mark 8:31-33).

The typical attitude among both pagans and Jews would be more like that of Homer. He has Juno say to his son Vulcan,

---

5. "To partake" (*metechein*) occurs in Heb. 2:14, 5:13; 7:13—references to sharing, humanity, nourishment and family. The noun "fellows" or "partakers" (*metochos*) occurs in Heb. 1:9; 3:1, 14; 6:4; 12:8. A study of these terms in their respective contexts underscores the author's constant stress upon the Christian life as a sharing in the life of Christ and of the saints (cf. Gal. 2:20).

"Dear son, refrain: it is not well that thus
A god should suffer for the sake of men." [6]

The problem of Jesus, and later that of apostles and apologists,
was to convince men that vicarious suffering was not only biblical
but also appropriate (cf. Luke 9:22; 24:26; 1 Cor. 1:23). To the
Gentiles it appeared absurd; to the Jews it proved a hindrance
to faith. The rabbis taught that the Lord's anointed was a happy
soul, not a suffering servant. But it is at this precise point that
we encounter what is the most distinctive thing about the Christian
philosophy of salvation. In Buddhism suffering is something to
be endured, not welcomed as redemptive. In Plato suffering was
an insoluble mystery to be endured in the realization that the
suffering of the part is sometimes necessary for the good of the
whole. [7] In Japan misfortune is accepted with stoic fatalism—
"shakatagonai" ("what is to be will be"). Islam denies any
vicarious significance in the death of Christ. The Essenes at Qumran knew of a "Teacher of Righteousness" who founded their sect
but nothing of a leader in whose vicarious death they found life. [8]
In Christianity alone is suffering purposeful and redemptive. It
is in the passion, death, and resurrection of Christ that Christian
theology is most unique. This is both the scandal and the glory
of the Cross.

To make the author (*archēgos*) **of their salvation** (sotērias)
perfect (*teleiōsai*). The **author** is the title given to Christ here
and also in 12:2. The title is that of a leader, ruler, prince or
chief, one who begins or originates something; a founder, or
instigator (Acts 5:31; 2 Clem. 20:5). This is similar to the claim
of Christ in Revelation 1:17 that He is the "first and last" and
to the concept of Christ as a "pioneer" (Heb. 3:1), conducting the
saints into the promised land or **into glory.**

Salvation is another important word in this letter. Negatively
it is salvation from sin to be experienced in this present life (Heb.

---

6. Homer, *Iliad*, xxi, pp. 379, 380.

7. Plato, *Laws*, X, p. 903.

8. Some authorities think no one individual is indicated by this expression, only
"the right way," e.g., T. H. Gaster, *The Dead Sea Scriptures* (Garden City: Doubleday, 1956), pp. 19, 26.

2:3; 2:10; 6:9). Positively it is the blessed state of the righteous to be experienced later (Heb. 1:14; 5:9; 9:28; cf. 11:7).

Perfect (*teleiōsai*) is applied in this treatise to both Christ and the believer. At least twenty times in this epistle reference is made to perfection or a kindred topic; fourteen of these instances uses *teleios* or a cognate form. In four instances perfection is associated with Jesus, three instances it is related to things, and the other times it refers to men. Indeed, the idea of completion, fulfillment and perfection is the "central feature" of this epistle. [9] In his application of moral perfection to Jesus, this author is bold and independent. Jesus is said to be the "perfecter" of our faith in the sense of carrying it on to completion. In 7:28 Jesus is said to be "perfected forevermore" in an eschatological sense, in the sense of resurrection and ascension (cf. Heb. 12:23). In two instances Jesus is said to have acquired perfection by way of discipline (2:10; 5:8, 9). Although He was in fact the Son of God, yet He "learned obedience" or acquired spiritual maturity through the discipline of obedience and suffering when other alternatives were available. If Jesus could not have sinned and thwarted God's plan, as a real man, His temptations would not have been real. This does not mean that He had to be sinful in order to be tempted since temptation is not necessarily an appeal to unholy desires. Temptation is rather an appeal to the unlawful gratification of a lawful desire.

Seen in this light, Adam, Eve, and Jesus could be tempted without any prior sinful inclinations. With Jesus the temptation to turn stones into bread was the perversion of a commendable desire to provide food in abundance. So it was not with reference to sin that Jesus was perfected. It was rather in the addition of experience as a true representative of sinful tempted humanity that He "learned obedience" or became "perfect." If one should wonder how Jesus could "learn" or "become" without being changed, and how being changed can be consistent with Hebrews 13:8, one answer could be, "Great is the mystery of godliness" (I Tim. 3:16).

---

9. Alan Wikgren, "Patterns of Perfection in the Epistle to the Hebrews," *New Testament Studies*, January, 1960, p. 159.

Another more satisfying answer could be found in considering that the incarnation enabled the Son of God to acquire the "consummation of that human experience of sorrow and pain through which He must pass in order to become the leader of His people's salvation" (MRV, IV, 402). This gave Him further qualification both as priest (Heb. 2:17; 5:7-9) and judge (John 5:27; Acts 17:31).

There are more references in this treatise to "the days of his flesh," i.e., to the humanity of Jesus, than in other portions of the New Testament outside of the four Gospels.[10] At the same time no writer places greater stress on Jesus' deity. There is a paradox here but not a contradiction. It took four major church councils to reach a general agreement as to what the church understands concerning Jesus' divine-human nature. In the New Testament is the rugged theology which the speculative theologians must patiently try to assimilate and harmonize. This author affirms both Jesus' full humanity and full deity without the perils of doceticism (limiting His humanity) or humanism (limiting His deity).

b. Jesus' incarnation made salvation available (vv. 11-15)

V. 11. All of one ("have all one origin," RSV). The reference here is to those who share in common the experience of sanctification. The stress continues on the reality of the incarnation. This was a crucial issue when the Johannine Epistles were composed toward the end of the first century, so much so that those who denied the incarnation were specifically denounced as "antichrists" (2 John 7). Christians are in unity with Christ because both are from one source or from a common origin (*ex henos*), i.e., literally "out of God." He who knew no sin does not disdain to be classed with sinful human beings. Jesus was scandalized "in the days of his flesh" because He was often seen in the company of "sinners." This was not in harmony with the pharisaic concept of holiness. In contrast to theirs, the Master's concept of holiness was evangelistic rather than ascetic and exclusive. The incarnation was evangelism. Jesus was willing to "risk" His own sanctity

---

10. Wikgren, *op. cit.*, p. 161.

in order that sinful humans might be enabled to share in His sanctity. Had there been no risk there would have been no real temptation (v. 18).

He that sanctifieth and they who are sanctified (*ho hagiazōn kai hoi hagiazōmenoi*). This important term occurs more frequently in this epistle than in any other New Testament book (9 out of 29 times).[11] In the light of these nine instances and their respective contexts, it appears that the term designates those who are separated from the world and from sin and are united to God by faith. It probably designates in general those who are saved, since all true Christians are sanctified in the sense of being set apart (1 Cor. 1:2; Rom. 1:7). The extent to which the term connotes freedom from sin in this writer's usage is debatable. But it seems clear that the terms for "perfect" as used here clearly contain an ethical thrust, a call to purity of heart and life. This is seen most emphatically in the fact that the call to sanctity is a call to the life shared by God and His Son Jesus Christ (cf. 5:5-10; 12:10; 13:12).[12] The author does not elaborate, however; he continues the emphasis on the real humanity of Jesus.

V. 12. Words used by the Psalmist to describe his rapport with his contemporaries are here attributed to Christ to denote His relationship to mankind. The source (Ps. 22:22) is one of the most messianic of the Psalms, one in which the sufferings of the Psalmist are detailed with amazing relevance to the crucifixion of Jesus. Of this Psalm Delitzsch says, "The Spirit changes the hyperbole into prophecy." Much of the Psalm (vv. 1-21) is descriptive of suffering such as Jesus experienced; from verse 22 to the end the language is more appropriately applied to the resurrection or at least to the One delivered from the previously described sufferings. It is therefore not surprising that our author found his text in this messianic Psalm.

V. 13. The words **I will put my trust in him** are not found in exactly this form in extant copies of the Septuagint. A phrase

---

11. Moultou and Geden, *Concordance to the Greek Testament* (Edinburgh: T & T. Clark, 1897), p. 10. See Heb. 2:11; 9:13; 10:10, 14, 29; 13:12.

12. Wikgren, *op. cit.*, p. 160. R. N. Flew, *The Idea of Perfection in Christian Theology* (Oxford University Press, 1934), p. 89.

similar in form and identical in meaning (*pepoithōs esomai ep'
autōi*) occurs three times (2 Sam. 23:3; Isa. 8:17; 12:2). In the
citation of Isaiah 8:18—**I and the children**—the prophet's identification with his people during their time of trial is brought out in
the context. The prophet is directed to give his children names
prophetic of the fate of his countrymen. They all—the prophet,
his family, and his countrymen—are to be fellow sufferers. Later
the prophet, his children, and his disciples are to experience a
very intimate fellowship at a time when the nation is undergoing
judgment and Jehovah's presence seems remote (Isa. 8:16-22).
It is not surprising that the author of Hebrews was reminded
of this passage when he was meditating on Jesus "in the days
of his flesh." In those days Jesus cried out, "My God, my God,
why hast thou forsaken me?"—underscoring Paul's words, "He
who knew no sin became sin for us" (2 Cor. 5:21). Jesus shared
not only our humanity but also, in a representative and vicarious
sense, shared our sinful humanity as well.

V. 14, "Since therefore the children share in flesh and blood,
he himself likewise partook of the same nature" (RSV) is a
rendering somewhat closer to the Greek. The repetition of the
word **children** links this statement with the preceding quotation
and marks its application to humanity in general. Noteworthy
is the emphasis upon the identification of Christ with human
nature as seen in the words "likewise" and "same" as well as
the synonyms "share" and "partake." "Share" (*koinōneo*) and
"partake" (*metechō*) appear to be synonymous as stated by
Ellicott (on 1 Cor. 10:17) and defended by Moulton and Milligan.
The former in particular "is used specially of the closest of all
human relationships," such as marriage, consanguinity, or of
mystical identification with the gods, e.g., "fellowship with
Zeus." [13]   It was necessary for Jesus to become involved with
humanity in the closest possible way, to become sympathetic as
judge and priest, and to overcome the effects of the sin in the
area where defeat had been experienced.

---

13. Epict. ii. 19. 27, cited in Moulton and Milligan, *op. cit.*, p. 351. cf. Acts
2:42; 2 Cor. 13:13; Phil. 2:1 and especially 1 Cor. 10:16, 17.

c. *Jesus' death makes salvation adequate (vv. 15, 16)*

The view that death is a friend that ushers the soul into immortality is a view more pagan than Christian. The biblical viewpoint is that eternal life is not a natural endowment of the soul but that it is a gift of God. Life is not man's by right but is contingent upon grace. Death is an enemy in the biblical viewpoint, many Christian funerals to the contrary notwithstanding. The fear of death is not to be overcome simply by welcoming it as a "friend," or as an open door to immortality, but rather by recognizing it as an unnatural enemy and find victory over it in Christ. It is only as death is faced with Christ that it loses its terror. Only then can one triumphantly challenge death with the words, "O death, where is thy sting?" (cf. Isa. 25:8; 1 Cor. 15:54, 55). All of this is conditioned upon the historical accuracy of the report that Jesus rose alive from the dead. The battle was fought out in the spiritual realm, and the empty grave and the "physical" appearances of Jesus were the visual evidences of the victory. This passage constitutes another evidence of the importance of Jesus' resurrection in the theology of the New Testament. Because of Christ's victory over sin and death, Christianity is a buoyant, joyous, triumphant faith. Christian songs are written in a major key, not in a minor key as is so much non-Christian music (including "the blues"). In Christian funerals death and the grave are not viewed with finality but only as a temporary and transient experience. By experiencing physical death and overcoming it, Jesus gives hope to His "flesh and blood" that they share in His triumph—now by faith and later in actuality.

As further evidence that men rather than angels are the objects of Christ's redemptive work, the author underscores the fact that the "help" he extends is limited to **the seed of Abraham.** By particularizing mankind in this way perhaps the message would have a greater appeal to those with Hebrew background. To Gentiles the **seed** would have to be interpreted in a spiritual sense to make it relevant. Abraham is the spiritual "father" of all three of the world's monotheistic religions—Judaism, Christianity, and Islam. Many times when the unbelieving Jews justified their rejection of Christ by appealing to Moses, the Christians appealed "over the head" of Moses to Abraham. This is seen in Paul's letters (Rom. 4, Gal. 3, 4) and to a less extent in the Gospels (cf. Matt. 5:21-48; John 8:39-58). This was because Moses was associated with the works of the Law and hence honored by the Jews while Abraham was associated with faith and hence honored by the Christians.

5. Jesus' oneness with humanity qualifies Him as high priest (2:17, 18)

The chapter closes by the introduction of the concept of high priest as applied to Jesus Christ. Hebrews is the only place in the New Testament where Christ's work is described as that of a priest. The term "priest" (*hierus*) or "high priest" (*archierus*) occurs 30 times in the treatise, and in 15 instances the reference is to Christ. To this author therefore we owe the concept of Christ as high priest in Christian theology.

In the word behooved (*opheilō*, "to owe money, be in debt for, to be under obligation, to be bound by duty of necessity"; or "it behooves one, one ought"—JHT), our attention is called to verse 10—it became him (*prepō*).[14] In the former reference the author emphasizes the *appropriateness* of the incarnation, and in the latter he places stress on *obligation* which the desired end imposes.

It is not easy to convince men that their God and Saviour should suffer and be humiliated and die in order to achieve the worthwhile goal, especially if that goal is man's welfare. The Old Testament passage with the greatest insight in this respect (Isa. 52:13-53:12) encounters skepticism and derision at the announcement, "Who hath believed our report?" (Isa. 53:1). Peter had the same reaction at the announcement of the Messiah's passion, "This shall not be unto thee" (Matt. 16:22). The idea of an important leader being humiliated is even more repellent

---

14. The verb *prepō* means (1) "to stand out, be conspicuous, eminent" or (2) "to be becoming, seemly, fit" (1 Tim. 2:10; Tit. 2:1; Matt. 3:15; 1 Cor. 11:13). (JHT).

in the status-conscious Orient than in the more democratic Occident. Even the Greeks considered it "foolishness" (1 Cor. 1:
23) To the Jews it was an outright scandal, a stumbling block
to acceptance (1 Cor. 1:23). It still runs contrary to all man-made standards of propriety. But to those with Spirit-instilled
insight there is an inner beauty and sense of oughtness, a "sweet-reasonableness" which causes one to exclaim with Paul, "How
unsearchable are his judgments, and his ways past finding out"
(Rom. 11:33).

Vs. 17, 18. One of the most distinctive features of the Epistle
to the Hebrews is its emphasis on Jesus Christ as our high priest.
In the Gospel according to Matthew and in the Apocalypse, Christ
is presented as king. Elsewhere His prophetic role is stressed,
but here He is presented as priest. It is debatable whether or not
the readers this writer is trying to reach are disillusioned with
the priesthood, as were the Essenes at Qumran. The scanty evidence suggests that the readers did appreciate the Aaronic priesthood. It is not because they are hostile to the priesthood that this
"word of exhortation" presents Jesus as priest. Rather, because
they appreciate the priesthood and temple service, this author says
that in Christ we have all of the virtues of the Aaronic priesthood
and none of its limitations. However, while they doubtless valued
the priestly ministrations, it would not be surprising if at times
they were impressed by its aloofness from the common man. Jesus
pictured the priest and Levite as "passing by on the other side,"
ignoring human need and remaining cold and unsympathetic (Luke
10:31, 32). Jesus' gentle irony must have struck some responsive
chords among the "laymen." Here the author boldly presents a
different kind of priest, one who is a fellow-traveller, a fellow-sufferer, one who experiences the same kind of temptations as do
other people.

The priests of that day were descendants of Zadok. This ancestor, who lived in the days of David and Solomon (I Kings 1:8;
2:27) and was the only legitimate priest, probably gave his name
to his descendants, the Sadducees. The Sadducees may be seen
through the eyes of the Gospels and of Josephus as a small but
influential group of aristocrats. From this sect of the Jews came
the priests and temple functionaries. They were conservative,
as is customary with those with vested interests, and yet pos-

sessed a political astuteness and opportunism which enabled them to work with the Roman occupation authorities effectively. How effectively they were in this was demonstrated by their success in getting Pilate to condemn Jesus to death. As aristocrats the priests had little personal contact or sympathy with the common people, whom they were inclined to regard as ignorant and inferior.

Against this background the letter to the Hebrews presents a different kind of priest, one who lives on the same level as the people to whom he ministers and hence is in a position to share their perspective, grieve with them in affliction (John 11:35, 36), and rejoice with them when appropriate (John 2:1). In Byzantine art of the fifth and sixth centuries A.D., Christ was normally portrayed as a stern and distant judge as seen, for example, in the ancient monastery at Daphne, near Athens. Because the early orthodox churches stressed the deity of Christ, often at the expense of His real humanity, the intercession of martyrs and of the Virgin Mary was often sought. In the epistle the author boldly affirms the real humanity and approachableness of Jesus Christ in the hope that his readers will recognize that He is as accessible and sympathetic as any other human being, only more so.

Jesus Christ is here characterized as both **merciful** and **faithful**. He is *merciful* in dealing with men and *faithful* in dealing with God. He has sympathy for man in his finiteness and sinfulness, but He does not permit this to lessen His insistence on truth, holiness, and Godlikeness. Because He is *faithful*, He does not tolerate sin.

The contrast between a parish priest who is like Jesus and one who is not is seen in two widely appreciated poems, both of which distinguish between the hireling priest and unselfish servant of God. The parish-priest who was not touched with the feeling of his parishioners' infirmities is thus described by Timothy Dwight, president of Yale:

> There smiled the smooth Divine, unused to wound
> The sinner's heart with hell's alarming sound.
> No terrors on his gentle tongue attend;
> No grating truths the nicest ear offend.
> That strange new birth, that methodistic grace,
> Nor in his heart nor sermons found a place.

Most dantily on pampered turkeys dined,
Nor shrunk with fasting, nor with study pined;
Yet from their churches saw his brethren driven,
Who thundered truth and spoke the voice of heaven. [15]

In contrast the good pastor is thus delineated by Chaucer:

The parson of a country town was he
Who knew the straits of humble poverty;
But rich he was in holy thought and work,
Nor less in learning than became a clerk.
The word of Christ most truly did he preach,
And his parishioners devoutly teach.

. . . .

Wide was his parish, scattered far asunder
Yet none did he neglect in rain, or thunder,
Sorrow and sickness won his daily care;
With staff in hand he travelled everywhere. [16]

Or Oliver Goldsmith's description of the Village Parson:

Thus to relieve the wretched was his pride,
And e'en his failings leaned to Virtue's side;
But in his duty prompt at every call,
He watched and wept, he prayed and felt for all.
And, as a bird each fond endearment tries,
To tempt its new-fledged offspring to the skies,
He tried each art, reproved each dull delay,
Allured to higher worlds and led the way. [17]

The picture thus drawn of Jesus Christ as the One superior
to Adam, who chose to identify himself with mankind rather
than with angels, thus making possible sinful man's reconciliation
with a holy God, is sketched with exquisite insight and power.
In the term **propitiation** (*hilaskesthai*) or "expiation" (RSV) is
found a twofold meaning. When the stress is placed upon expiation,
attention is drawn to the sacrifice itself, on the basis on which
reconciliation is possible. When the stress is placed upon pro-

---

15. Timothy Dwight, "The Smooth Divine," in Carolyn Hill, edit., *The World's Great Religious Poetry* (New York: Macmillan, 1938), p. 369.

16. Chaucer, Trans. by H. G. Leonard, "The Good Parson," C. Hill, ed., *op. cit.*, p. 363.

17. Oliver Goldsmith, "The Deserted Village," C. Hill, ed., *op. cit.*, p. 371.

pitiation, the end result of the process is to render favorable and reconcile. The expiation makes possible the propriation. "My God is reconciled, his pardoning voice I hear; he owns me for his child, I shall no longer fear" (Charles Wesley).

Thus the author introduces the concept of Jesus as priest and prepares the way for a full development of this theme in chapters 5-9. Meanwhile he turns his attention again to the condition of his readers and makes another long and emphatic "word of exhortation."

2

The Superiority of Jesus' Person as Apostle (3:1-4:16)

A. Jesus is superior to Moses (3:1-6)

1. He is fully equal to Moses (3:1, 2)

The "wherefore" directs our attention back to the preceding verses (2:17, 18) in which the role of high priesthood for Jesus was introduced. The epistolary nature of the book comes out in his direct address to his readers as "holy brethren" (*adelphoi hagioi*). The term occurs also in the texts which lie behind the KJV at 1 Thessalonians 5:27. Elsewhere in this letter he simply refers to his readers as "brethren" (3:12; 10:9; 13:22), as is customary in the Epistle of James. The usual designation for Christians in the New Testament is "saints" (*hagioi*), a term which occurs some sixty times in the New Testament (e.g., Heb. 13:24; Eph. 1:1; Rom. 1:7; 1 Cor. 1:2). It designates all those who are "in Christ" and not necessarily those possessing special sanctity. In other words, any true Christian is a "saint," a "holy one" in the New Testament sense. The passage gives further guidance as to the readers he addresses. They are those who have heard and responded to the gospel (2:1, 3) and hence are "**partakers** (*metachoi*) **of the heavenly calling.**" They are "brethren" who have been united with the Sanctifier and hence are said to be "sanctified" or possessed of the sanctity of Christ (Heb. 2:11).

The sanctity that believers thus acquire is both imputed and imparted. It is imputed in the sense of being sanctified positionally (by being united to Christ) and actually (as a result of the transforming energy of the Holy Spirit).

The brethren are now urged to "**consider**" Jesus in the dual role of **Apostle and High Priest.** The verb **consider** is characteristic of this epistle; it occurs also in 7:4; 10:24; 12:3 and 13:7. One term here translated **consider** (*katanoeō*) occurs only once elsewhere in this letter (10:24; cf. Matt. 7:3; Luke 6:41; Acts 7:31; Rom. 4:19). It means not only to "look up" but also to "catch the *significance* of" what is seen, to "ponder carefully" the implications of the phenomena. Moses not only saw the burning bush but also "investigated" (Acts 7:31), and a revelation of God resulted.

The author's introduction of Jesus as **Apostle** is original and unique—it is not found elsewhere in the New Testament, although Justin Martyr used the designation about 150 A.D. (*Apol.* 1:12, 63). The term *apostolos* as applied to Jesus "shows the fresh creative genius of the writer and the unconventional nature of his style" (A. B. Bruce, p. 131). An *apostolos* is one sent—in this case, one sent from God such as John (John 1:7) or Jesus (John 17:3). He has the authority of an ambassador who represents his country. When Antiochus Ephiphanes of Syria was about to invade Egypt during the first quarter of the second century B.C., Rome was already a power to be reckoned with. Rome sent a delegate named Popillius with a message advising Antiochus to return home. Although Popillius had no army or even a bodyguard, the fact that behind him lay the authority of Rome was sufficient to make the haughty Syrian abandon his plans of conquest at once. Jesus' words should be heeded since in reality they are God's words.

V. 3. Worthy of more glory than Moses: the theme of "better" dominates this epistle throughout. Not content to show that Christ is superior to the prophets and angels, not content to prove Him *equal* to Moses, our author now proceeds to demonstrate His *superiority* to the Hebrew lawgiver. He does so by the analogy of building and builder. Implicit here is the idea that the community of God's people is the result of God's creativity executed through the agency of Jesus Christ. Jesus is the Son and Creator, while Moses was only the servant in a situation brought into being by Christ. This role of Christ in the Exodus is likewise reflected in Paul's words to the church of Corinth—"the supernatural Rock which followed them . . . was Christ" (1 Cor. 10:4, RSV).

2. His glory exceeds that of Moses (3:3-5)

V. 5. Moses was faithful. The quotation is from Numbers 12:7 in the context relating the complaint of Miriam and Aaron that Moses was assuming a monopoly on divine revelation. The Lord defended Moses in these words. In what respects was Moses' fidelity expressed, and how does it compare with the faithfulness of Christ?

(1) Moses was faithful in choosing to identify himself with his own people rather than to enjoy the luxuries of the palace (Heb. 11:25, 26; cf. Ex. 2:11). In a sense this was comparable to the incarnation of Christ, "who . . . counted not the being on an equality with God a thing to be grasped" (Phil. 2:5) but rather identified himself with His "brethren" (Heb. 2:14) in their humanity and bondage to death.

(2) After the revelation of Yahweh at the burning bush, Moses was "not disobedient to the heavenly vision" but courageously confronted the Egyptians in behalf of the Hebrew slaves. Jesus likewise faced the temptations of Satan and the hostility of evil men in carrying out His God-given mission.

(3) Moses withstood the suspicion, malice, and jealousy of the people he was helping, even to the rebellions of his closest associates and kinfolk (Num. 12:1-15; 14:1-10; 16:1-3). In spite of their lack of appreciation he chose to remain with his people even when the Lord asked him to withdraw his allegiance to Israel and promised to make another great nation of Moses' own posterity (Ex. 32:10). Jesus likewise made the plight of His people His own.

(4) Moses was faithful as an administrator in the appointment of associate justices (Ex. 18:25), in bringing order out of the chaos of fleeing refugees (Num. 2:1ff.) and in giving purpose to the pilgrims seeking "a better country." Jesus appointed twelve "that they might be with him" and carry on His work.

(5) Moses was faithful as the official medium of divine revelation through "mighty acts," through the giving of the Decalogue and in times of emergency. When Moses was with them, the people could be assured that the divine revelation through Moses was authentic, because God spoke to him "face to face" (Deut. 34:10; cf. John 1:18). The same was true of Jesus—"he that hath seen me hath seen the Father" (John 14:9).

(6) Moses was also faithful as a **servant** (*therapōn*) of God, not a household slave (*doulos*). The term connotes one who ministers by caring for, waiting upon, or healing a "servitor" (NEB). It was applied especially to ministrants in the temple of Asclepius, the god of healing (M-M) (from this come the words "therapy" and "therapeutic"). Moses, therefore, was a servant of deity, not so much in menial household tasks but in supervision of God's dwelling place. Jesus also assumed the role of a "servant" (Luke 22:27; Phil. 2:7).

The author does not concentrate long on Moses; his gaze remains fixed upon Jesus, and Moses is cited only by way of comparison and contrast. Jesus was equal to Moses in His fidelity to His God-given task; He surpasses Moses, however, in His nature and status. For Christ is not a *therapōn* ministering in the temple; nor is He the temple; He is rather the divine *builder* of the temple. "House" is normally used in the Old Testament to refer to both a building and a dynasty. When David resolved to erect a "house" or building for Yahweh, the Lord in turn promised to erect for David a "house" also, meaning a dynasty (2 Sam. 7:1-17).

3. He has the higher claim on our allegiance (3:6)

V. 6. Always this author insists on "considering" Jesus and then moving to the application. His constant concern is for the *relevance* of the message.

B. Jesus is superior to Joshua (3:7-4:11)

1. In the accessibility of His rest (cf. 4:3)

V. 7. The Holy Spirit says reflects the author's view of the Old Testament. The human author is relatively unimportant; the real author is the Holy Spirit of God who inspired the writing. Does this imply a "dictation theory" of inspiration—that the human author acted only as a stenographer? Hardly; this appears to have been a conventional way of introducing an Old Testament passage (cf. Acts 2:17; 4:25). The expression simply emphasizes the divine authorship and hence authority of the words quoted.

a. Accessibility contingent on obedience (vv. 7-19)

The passage is quoted from Psalm 95 and follows a long and eloquent call to worship (Ps. 95:1-6). The verses which follow and which are quoted here show the reason *why* the call to worship should be heeded and show the consequences of refusing the call. This exhortation is a solemn reminder that even "the sheep of his pasture," who have experienced the grace of God may refuse to follow any further and become apostates. This dreadful contingency is held before the readers of this letter from chapter two to the end of the epistle, with far greater emphasis than can be found anywhere else in the New Testament.

(1) It was so in Joshua's day (3:7-11)

The Psalmist has in mind the experience of the Israelites who found the pessimistic report of the ten spies more convincing than the optimistic report of Caleb and Joshua. The quotation is altered by substituting **provocation** for Meribah and **trial** for Massah (cf. Ps. 95:8). The event referred to is the rebellion at Rephidim, occasioned by the lack of water. A similar crisis arose at Kedesh in the wilderness of Sin (Num. 20:2).

Added emphasis is leant to the warning by the emphasis on **today.** It is in line with such exhortations as "Behold, now is the acceptable time; behold, now is the day of salvation" (2 Cor. 6:2). The Scriptures are replete with exhortations to be an "opportunist," in the best sense of the word. The emphasis here is on decision, immediacy, the necessity of promptness in obedience.

Four elements in the exhortation from the Psalm are noteworthy:

(1) Opportunity brings responsibility. They *heard* God's voice, they were recipients of divine revelation; henceforth they were

responsible for their reaction. Jesus repeatedly stressed the importance of not only hearing but taking heed to act accordingly (Matt. 7:24-27; Mark 4:23, 24). James emphasized the same point, "Be ye doers of the word and not hearers only" (James 1:22).

(2) The *peril* of hardening. The danger of becoming lax, slow to respond and eventually impervious to God's commands, is constantly kept before the reader of the Scriptures. "Light obeyed increaseth light; light rejected bringeth night." In this instance the Israelites presumed on the mercy and patience of their God. Because of His great mercies they put Him to the test by skepticism and disobedience. But God's patience was finally exhausted.

(3) *God's* angry *reaction.* The anger of Yahweh was not sudden, impetuous, and petulant; it was slow to gather, calculating, tender, firm and redemptive. But it was relentless and purposeful. With it came a sad appraisal of the Israelites' capacity for obedience—"**they always go astray.**" This chronic tendency to apostasy is the theme elaborated at length during the period of the judges and in the later kingdom period. In the time of the judges especially the usual sequence was a formal adherence to the covenant, a breaking of the covenant—usually in the form of idolatry, then heaven-sent affliction followed by repentance, divine deliverance, and "rest." Then the cycle would start again and repeat itself. This continued until the destruction of Israel in 722 B.C. and the exile of Judah in 586 B.C. This characteristic hard-heartedness of the Israelites was lamented in the later prophets, in the Psalms, and in the literature of the intertestament period. When Stephen thus characterized his ancestors, it was a generalization that all acknowledged (Acts 7:51).

(4) The *penalty* announced was permanent exclusion from the promised land. Even Moses and Aaron were not exempt from this punishment. In a larger sense sin always brings exclusion from God's presence and isolation from the good.

The severest type of punishment apart from execution is soliary confinement, a punishment that sometimes results in mental derangement. Hell, as Olin Alfred Curtis points out (*Christian Theology*), is permanent isolation from God, the sinner being granted his desire to have God let him alone. The worst thing that can happen to us is for God to let us alone, for us to pursue our own way. Our greatest boon is to have "the Hound of Heaven" pursue us in our perversity until we are "defenseless utterly" and surrender to his love.[1]

(2) It is also so in our day (vv. 12-14)

V. 12. The **take heed** is an exhortation comparable to "we ought" (2:1), "consider" (3:1), "exhort" (3:13), and "let us" (4:1, 11, 14). The problem is here identified as **an evil heart of unbelief.** In Ezekiel it was designated as a "stony heart" (Ezek. 36:26), a heart impervious to the softening influences of God's Spirit. Matching this negative warning about something to avoid is the positive emphasis on something to be done; hence, **exhort one another.** The latter term means also to strengthen or encourage as did Barnabas the believers in Antioch (Acts 11:23). This is the important "follow-up" designed to confirm young converts in their faith as Paul sought to do with the believers in Thessalonica (I Thess. 3:13). This writer realized that it is not enough to get people converted. His purpose here is similar to that of Paul in writing to the Galatians, and the author's eagerness matches that of the apostle; the crucial issue in both instances is the confirmation of the converts, not only in sound doctrine but also in a vital relationship to the Father through Christ.

The conditional nature of salvation is constantly stressed in this passage. The practice of each Christian of exhorting one another is set forth as the alternative to apostasy. The early Methodist Class Meeting was an institution designed to give implementation to this exhortation. The Class Leader's responsibility was to exhort and to watch over the souls of the dozen or so believers entrusted to his care. These "cells" were a very effective instrument in the establishment of immature but earnest Christians.

V. 14. "For we share in Christ, if only" (RSV). Here the conditional nature of saving grace is again underscored. These believers are still on probation and the author again emphasizes the importance of holding fast (*katechō*, cf. 3:6) the original commitment, confession or understanding (*hypostasis*). They are al-

---

1. Francis Thompson, "The Hound of Heaven."

ready sharers in Christ's merit; they are fellow-travellers or partners (*metochoi*) of the Saviour (cf. 1:9; 3:1; 6:4; 12:8). The contrast is between the beginning and the end of their faith. The good beginning is of no value until there is a good ending, and the latter depends not only on the adequacy of Christ but also upon their adherence to the covenant by belief and obedience. The big word in this verse is the "if (*eanper*—"if it be that," or "if at all events"—cf. 3:6; 6:3), connecting as it does initial salvation with final salvation.

(3) An object lesson for us (vv. 15-19)

Vv. 15-18. Again the experience of the Israelites is held up as a solemn object lesson. In most biblical allusions to the events of the Exodus the emphasis is on the grace and power of God that resulted in the birth of the nation. This author stresses human responsibility in this series of historic events. The lesson stresses that deliverance from bondage is in itself no assurance of entrance into the promised land. The basis for assurance is twofold: the experience of initial deliverance *and adherence* to the covenant of grace, i.e., adherence to Christ.

What does this do to the doctrine of assurance? Does it make salvation a matter of uncertainty? Is the believer to be deprived of a "full assurance of faith" and of salvation? Not at all. Nothing can separate the believer from Christ (cf. Rom. 8:35). No alien power or combination of them can come between the Father and those who are converted (John 10:29), depriving the believer of divine life. The only conditional factor is the believer's own constancy. The peril faced is that of presumption, of failure to realize that disobedience is dangerous.

How appropriate is the use of Old Testament history in Christian experience? Allegory is often carried too far by enthusiastic preachers and expositors. It lends itself to fanciful and irresponsible imagination. But used with self-discipline it is helpful. Paul used it in illustrating justification by faith (Rom. 4, Gal. 3, 4). He also justified the appeal to Old Testament precedents by saying, "They were written for our admonition" (1 Cor. 10:11). Hebrew history is used most effectively when cited as historical precedents that may be repeated in the life of a nation or of an individual. Jeremiah used the precedent of Shiloh as a warning to Jerusalem. Because Jerusalem did not heed the warning, the temple and city suffered a catastrophe like that at Shiloh. Because Paris was saved during the first World War by "the miracle of the Marne," it was widely assumed that the city would come through World War II inviolate. Such was not the case. The eighteen-inch guns at Singapore encouraged a false sense of security that was shattered when the Japanese approached from behind —from inland. George Adam Smith said that Great Britain's besetting sin at the end of the nineteenth century was complacency. To "afflict the comfortable" by warning against presumption is this author's God-given task; into this task he pours all the ardor of a well-stocked mind, an eloquent pen, and fresh creative insights. His warning culminates in the reminder that unbelief persisted even after the miracle of deliverance, and that unbelief deprived their ancestors of the benefits of their emancipation; they died outside the promised land. It could happen again but it need not. To see that it did not, our author summons all the learning and eloquence at his command.

The chapter closes with a series of rhetorical questions in the typical manner of the diatribe (cf. Mal. 2:14-17), and closes with the brief summation of verse 19—unbelief deprived their ancestors of "rest." To believe or not to believe God is now the alternative; believing Him leads to life; not believing Him leads to sterility and death (cf. Deut. 28-30). The two basic exhortations of the chapter are **consider** (v. 1) and **take heed** (v. 12). In short, as the author points out, if one keeps his gaze fixed on Jesus as a greater than Joshua and "rethinks" his position, he is likely to be alert to the danger of unbelief, and will no doubt persevere in the initial faith that led to his deliverance.

In this age of scientific "miracles" many moderns find it difficult to have faith in God's saving grace and even in the efficacy of prayer. Anne Bronte thus testifies:

> While Faith is with me, I am blest;
> It turns my dearest night to day;
> But while I clasp it to my breast,
> I often feel it slide away.

Then, cold and dark, my spirit sinks
To see my light of life depart;
And every fiend of Hell, methinks,
Enjoys the anguish of my heart.

What shall I do if all my love,
My hopes, my toil, are cast away,
And if there be no God above,
To hear and bless me while I pray? [2]

To prevent this, our author in this chapter urges some important considerations. *Realize* that by faith you are now a sharer in the grace of God through Christ (vv. 1, 14). *Recognize* that the privilege of belonging to Christ is even greater than of belonging to Moses (vv. 3-6). *Profit* by the example of Israelite unbelievers (vv. 7-12). *Give daily attention* by mutual exhortation to the matter of establishment in the faith. *Cultivate a healthy fear* of unbelief, recognize its early stages and hold fast your God-given assurance of salvation.

b. Access to rest now to those who heed (4:1-3)

The thought that dominates our author's mind, in the passage which begins at 3:7 and continues through chapter 4, is that there is a spiritual privilege before his readers that they are in danger of missing. In the words of Andrew Murray, there are "two stages in the Christian life." He continues, "There are the carnal, and there are the spiritual; there are those who remain babes and there are those who are full grown men."[3] Like the author of Psalm 95, this author is gripped by the realization that his ancestors in the Sinai desert had the opportunity of entering Palestine, following the report of the two faithful spies, Caleb and Joshua; instead they listened to the pessimistic view of the majority and because of that unbelief spent their lives wandering in the desert. The promised land was before them; the only reason they did not enter in was their own unbelief. Again this author, quoting the words of the Psalmist and supplementing them by his own, urges

---

2. Anne Bronte, "The Doubter's Prayer," in Carolyn Hill, Editor, *The World's Great Religious Poetry* (Macmillan, 1838), p. 186.

3. *Holiest of All*, Revell, n.d., p. 141.

his readers to recognize the seriousness of the choice that is before them. They can elect to remain either where they are, having experienced initial deliverance but still stopping short of the promised rest, or they can press on by faith and inherit the promised land. The awesome sentence decreeing that the doubters would die in the wilderness was first expressed at Kadesh (Num. 14:28-35). The first time this land was called "rest" appears to be in Deuteronomy 12:9, "For ye are not as yet come to the rest and to the inheritance which the Lord your God giveth you." The Psalmist regarded this lesson as not simply of antiquarian interest but something with comtemporary relevance. After appealing to his contemporaries to come and worship, he warns them of the consequences of refusal. The writer to the Hebrews continues this spiritual emphasis, but now makes the alternatives far more vivid and demanding.

(1) It is possible to come short of this rest (v. 1)

V. 1. There are at least three kinds of rest mentioned in this lesson. The term "rest" occurs at least twelve times in this passage. In all but one instance (4:9) the Greek term is *katapausin*. From it comes the meaning of "down" (*kata*) and to "cause to cease" (*pauō*). Thus the word means to give rest, to desist (Acts 14:18), to lead to a quiet abode (Deut. 3:20; 5:23; 12:10; Sir. 24:11). It also means to take rest (Heb. 4:4, 10; cf. Gen. 2:2; 2 Macc. 15:1; Acts 7:49).

The concept of rest as it is used here has four recognizable facets: (1) The promised land of Canaan (Deut. 12:9; Ps. 95:11; Heb. 3:11; 4:3, 5); (2) the rest following creation (Gen. 2:2; Heb. 4:4, 9); (3) gospel blessings now (4:1, 3, 8, 10, 11); (4) heaven hereafter (4:11, 14). It is noteworthy that the second and third shades of meaning really merge into one. It is also noteworthy that heaven as a place, in the eschatological sense of the term, is not stressed here. Even in 4:14, with which should be compared 4:11—"give diligence to enter into that rest," it is set in a context of a present possibility. In other words, since Jesus as our greater-than-Joshua has preceded us into God's presence in heaven, we may feel free to approach also, entering with boldness to the very throne itself (4:16). Thus the author's constant stress is not an eschatological destination of the soul so much as it is a spiritual experience available now to the obedient.

The entire chapter is characterized by exhortation. He says, "Let us hear" (4:1), "Let us give diligence" (4:11), and "Let us draw near" (4:16). The fear of which this writer speaks is not the morbid fear that harasses and paralyzes or immobilizes. It is rather the recognition of a danger which should spur one to alertness and diligence.

(2) The Word must be believed as well as heard (v. 2)

V. 2. We have had good tidings preached unto us. As has been well stated, "It is not the hearing of the gospel itself that brings final salvation, but its appropriation by faith."[4] Both the Gospels and the Epistles stress the necessity not only of hearing but also of heeding the good tidings. Jesus emphasized the necessity not only of listening to the good news, but also of acting upon it (Matt. 7:21-27; James 1:22). But Bruce continues, "If that faith is a genuine faith it will be persistent." In this epistle the writer appears convinced that a genuine faith is not necessarily persistent. He has been stressing that not only the Israelites who were ready to enter Canaan by faith but also those who were unwilling to because of lack of faith, all had a common experience of deliverance from Egypt (Heb. 3:16). The difference between the unbelievers who remained in the wilderness and the believers who finally entered rest was not the genuineness of their deliverance but the continuation of that faith. The dividing line came *after* deliverance, and the issue was not between a genuine and a false faith, but rather between a genuine faith which *continued* and a genuine faith which turned to doubt. The same volition that made faith active can also lead to its death as long as the believer remains a free moral agent. In the mind of the author, it is this element of contingency that lends to this exhortation the urgency and relevance.

(3) Rest conditioned on obedience (v. 3)

It is true that two alternatives lie open to the interpreter

---

4. F. F. Bruce, *Commentary on the Epistle to the Hebrews* of (*The New International Commentary on the New Testament*), Eerdmans, 1964, p. 73.

of this passage. He can regard the original readers of this epistle as those who have been exposed to the gospel but not converted, or he can think of them as those who have been genuinely converted but are in danger of abandoning this faith, or at least becoming complacent and letting things drift (chap. 2:1-4), an adverse development that is brought out more clearly later. The latter seems to be the situation with which our author is concerned. He is not writing merely to auditors urging them to repent and believe. He is writing rather to believers who are in danger of failing to persevere in that faith.

2. Christ's rest superior (4:4-10)

a. *The rest involves a cessation of self-effort (vv. 4, 5, 10)*

(1) God "rested" on the Sabbath after creation ceased (v. 4)

Our author now turns to another Old Testament quotation on which to base his argument. He is making the transition from rest as a geographical location to a spiritual condition confronting his readers. Our author now brings in a second quotation on the subject of rest. Appealing to Genesis 2:2 he speaks of a cessation of labor following the six creative days. Philo interpreted this as meaning not pure inactivity but "an energy devoid of laboriousness, devoid of suffering, and moving with absolute ease." [5] There is thus a paradoxical quality about this rest in that it is activity but freedom from labor. Another school of interpreters regarded this seventh day as prefiguring an age of righteousness which follows six ages of sinfulness. [6] This interpretation, that thinks in terms of history divided by six periods, followed by a seventh epoch comparable to a millennial reign, has little support.

(2) Believers also may now have "rest"

The author's concern here is practical. He continues to dwell

---

5. Philo, *De Cherubim*, 26, cited by Moffatt, *Epistle to the Hebrews* (International *Critical Commentary*), p. 53.

6. *Epistle to Barnabas* XV. 5 (*The Apostolic Fathers*, ed. Kirsopp Lake, *Loeb Classical Library*). (New York: E. P. Putnam's Sons), I, p. 395.

on the comparison between rest in the promised land and a spiritual rest now available to God's children. The concept embraces both rest in God's presence in heaven (Rev. 14:13) and also a gospel privilege available to believers now.

b. This rest more real (vv. 6-10)

V. 6. Andrew Murray points out two types of rest in God's relation to His work: that which was a cessation of activity regarding creation, and that in which God rejoiced over His creation and watched its life develop. [7] Whether the text will bear this interpretation is debatable. It is certian, however, that our author has in mind two stages in Christian experience: that of deliverance from bondage, and that of spiritual rest which follows complete committal—a rest of faith. It is, in Murray's words, "ceasing from self-effort and yielding up oneself in full surrender of faith to God's working."[8] The writer makes the passage more relevant by emphasizing the word "today" in the Psalmist's passage; thus the ancient exhortation becomes relevant to his readers and to us. The "today" of the Psalmist and of the letter to the Hebrews underscores the timelessness and relevancy of the exhortation, especially when it is seen as a rest available now to those who believe and act.

V. 8. This author like many other ancient writers was obviously intrigued by the similarity between the name Joshua and Jesus. Both come from the same root; both mean "savior." The Septuagint used the term *Iēsous* and the KJV follows this precedent here and in Acts 7:45. The newer versions correctly render it as Joshua as demanded by the context. [9] From the fact that the Psalmist used the word "today," our author argues that Canaan rest is only a type of a better, more spiritual, more important rest. This Joshua did not provide. This is left for a greater-than-Joshua who has already provided it. Bible interpreters have pointed to Jesus as a greater-than-Joshua with reference to His guiding to the land of rest. He is also regarded

7. Murray, *op. cit.*, p. 152.
8. *Ibid.* p. 146.
9. Compare Barnabas 6:8; Justin, *Trypho* 113, 132.

as Joshua's successor in administering a superior circumcision
(Jos. 5:2-7) that corresponds to the "circumcision of heart"
(Deut. 30:6; Acts 7:51; Rom. 2:29; 2 Cor. 3:6). Jesus has also
been regarded as a greater-than-Joshua-the-high-priest. After
the exile the high priest's name was Joshua (Hag. 1:1; Zech.
3:1; 6:1).[10]

V. 9. Because of the rare emphasis upon "today," the author
concludes that there is a rest now for the people of God. Calvin
correctly defines the Sabbath rest as union with God. This is
realized in its fullest degree in heaven; in fact, the whole drama
of redemption, as revealed in the Bible, reaches its climax
in Revelation 21:3, "Behold, the dwelling of God is with men. He
will dwell with them, and they will be his people" (RSV).
This is Emmanuel, "God with us." It is the atonement (at-one-
ment). But the concept of heaven does not exhaust the meaning
of this term. "Before one can get into heaven," as Billy Sunday
expressed it, "heaven must get into us." In other words, there
must be the rest of faith now before there can be the complete
rest of the next life. The believer does not have to wait for
this rest until he gets to heaven; it begins the moment he ceases
from his own self-effort, from the self-life, and reckons himself
to be dead indeed unto sin and alive unto God (Rom. 2:6-11).[11]
This verse and the following one emphasize that this rest is
available now. The force of the repeated exhortations is that
this type of spiritual rest is not merely a distant goal but an
immediate and available spiritual condition.

Rest implies completion and victory. The fact that Jesus
is seated at the throne of God implies His victory over sin
and completion of His work (Heb. 1:3). In a similar manner
potentates in the Orient are normally pictured as comfortably
seated and free from anxiety. The war lords of medieval Japan
are normally pictured seated with flowing robes and a fan.
Their position is secure; they are at rest. As the saints of the
ages have known, there is available to all Christians, on the
basis of submission and faith, a peace of soul, a fullness of
joy, a rest of faith, a victory that Christians must appropriate

---

10. See J. R. Harris, *Testimonies*, ii (Cambridge, 1920), pp. 51ff.
11. Andrew Murray, *op. cit.*, p. 158.

in order to experience. While the sinner *surrenders* before becoming a saint, a saint must *commit* before there is rest at
the inner citadel of his soul. The first calls for a ceasing from
sin; the second calls for a ceasing from the self-life so that
the Holy Spirit not only witnesses to his adoption but comes
in with His fullness. Seen thus, the discussion as to whether
this rest occurs at death or after the general resurrection becomes
somewhat irrelevant. It is then suggested that perhaps the Old
Testament believers experienced this after Jesus' resurrection
while New Testament believers experience it at death (FFB,
p. 79). Such considerations are rather far removed from this
writer's earnest appeal. He has risen far above the concepts
of Jewish apocalypticism [12] by emphasizing the spiritual nature
of this relationship.

3. The importance of entering God's rest (4:11-13)

V. 11. Let us therefore strive to enter that rest. In this passage
the author has just stated (v. 10) that "whoever enters God's
rest ceases from his labors." Now he urges his readers to strive
to enter. Considered in its context, the striving of verse 11 is
not the zealous multiplying of good works to acquire merit and
to earn heaven, nor is it the manful overcoming of temptation
and other hazards of the narrow way from the present to the
good life in the future. That is included in the overall picture
but is not the focus of attention now. It rather means the self-
examination, the confrontation, the commitment, the decisive
act by which one ceases from his own self-effort, renounces
his self-centeredness, and becomes "dead indeed unto sin, but
alive unto God." This is the foundation on which he enters
God's rest and trusts God to do in and for him what he cannot
do for himself. "It is the ceasing from those works which flow
from our own self-life" so that God can work in us "to will
and to do of his good pleasure."[13]   Paul expressed the same

---

12. 4th Ezra 8:52—"That paradise is open, the tree of life planted, the age
to come is prepared, plenty is provided, a city is built. Rest is appointed,
Goodness is established and wisdom perfected."

13. Wiley, *op. cit.*, p. 152.

paradox when he said, "I am crucified with Christ; nevertheless
I live, . . . and the life that I now live in the flesh I live by faith
in the Son of God who loved me and gave himself for me"
(Gal. 2:20).

V. 12. The word of God is living and active. What does this
author mean by "the word of God"? Does he mean God's
word preserved in the Old Testament? Does he mean primarily
a book, a literary document? The term *logos* used here means
primarily an expressed thought. Its origin can be traced both
to the Old Testament and to Greek thought—especially Stoic
thought. Philo speaks of the *logos* cutting and dividing the universe. [14] But, as Moffatt observes, he uses "Philonic language
but not Philonic ideas." Perhaps closer to the author's mind
is the thought of the words in the Wisdom of Solomon 18:15. [15]
A similar passage is seen in Revelation 19:13:15 where the *logos*
of God is comparable to a sword. In this passage the term
has the connotation of judgment. It is like the hammer that
breaks the rock in pieces. [16] The effect is nothing less than
a confrontation with God himself. This word of God is pictured
as illuminating, dividing and exposing the inmost recesses of
personality. It leaves one feeling like Job who complained because
he could not hide from God. He shrank from God's scrutiny
and constant surveillance (Job 7:19). So overwhelming is the
confrontation that the individual realizes that there is, in the
words of the Negro spiritual, "no hiding place" (Rev. 6:16;
Hos. 10:8). The word for nakedness (*gumna*) is the word
from which comes the word gymnasium, a reminder that in
the Greek *gymnasia* the athletes performed without clothing
and were thus exposed to the gaze of the spectators. Francis
Thompson sensed this and cried out, "My harness, piece by

---

14. Philo, *Quis Div. Rer. Heres.*

15. Thine almighty word leaped down from heaven out of thy royal throne,
as a fierce man of war into the land of destruction, and brought thy unfeigned
commandment as a sharp sword, and standing up filled all things with death;
and it touched the heaven, but it stood upon the earth (Wisd. of Sol. 18:15,
16).

16. Jer. 23:29; cf. Isa. 49:2; 55:11; Acts 7:38; 1 Pet. 1:23.

piece, thou hast hewn from me . . . I am defenseless utterly!" [17]
The term translated **laid open** (*petrachēlismena*) may mean,
first, to throw the head back in wrestling; second, the removal
of hide from animals; third, the practice of compelling a condemned person, by means of a dagger under his chin, to look
up and face the crowd. Needless to say, this author's language
is vivid and arresting. But those whose heart is right with God
do not shrink from divine scrutiny; they rather welcome it.
They are not ashamed of their inmost motives in the sight
of God, man or devils. Those who have found the rest of faith
following complete committal are always ready to welcome the
closest scrutiny.

4. Christ now leads believers into this better rest (4:14-16)

This paragraph is probably the focal or central paragraph
of the entire letter. It gathers up much that has preceded and
anticipates much that follows. The figure of Joshua leading God's
people into the promised land still lingers, but here shadow
passes into substance and the Christian's "Joshua" has passed
through the wilderness of temptations and has entered God's
presence, thus opening the way for His followers to enter. The
important thing, then, is to "**hold fast our confession,**" an
admonition stated before by the author. First we were asked
to consider the apostle of our confession (3:1); having done
so it is time now to hold fast and to follow.

V. 15. He now sums up the emphasis of chapter two with
a further word of encouragement that our High Priest is accessible
and sympathetic. It helps us little if He is accessible but not
sympathetic; nor is it helpful if He is sympathetic but powerless
to help. The point is that Jesus is like us in that He has
been subjected to the same pressure that we experience. He
is unlike us in that He does not yield to them, and this is
our assurance of victory.

V. 16. Let us therefore draw near with boldness. Our song

---

17. Francis Thompson, "The Hound of Heaven," in C. Hill, Ed., *The World's
Greatest Religious Poetry* (New York: Macmillon, 1938), p. 47.

now is to "arise, my soul, arise; shake off thy guilty fears; the bleeding sacrifice on thy behalf appears." The imagery gradually changes from that of a pilgrimage through a hostile environment to the promised rest, to that of a temple with its mercy seat and officiating high priest. Thus the dual role which was announced in 3:1—apostle and high priest—is again brought into view. This will be the dominant theme through chapter ten. Up to this time Jesus' role as apostle and leader has been stressed; henceforth his role as priest is the focus of attention.

How may the believer enter into the rest that remains to the people of God? First, it is imperative that one believe that there is such a rest and that it is presently available. Calvin implied that it is something for the present, and states that we ought ever to strive for it, and yet he also paradoxically states that "it cannot be obtained in this life" (JC, p. 99). The second step is to cease from one's own works, from self-effort, from the self-life, to die with Christ and rise with Him. The third step is to trust Jesus as our greater-than-Joshua to bring us into the rest that remains for the people of God, the rest of faith. The fourth step is to be a follower of them who through faith inherit the promises; in other words, to be obedient. It is noteworthy that the tenderness of this paragraph is in contrast to the austerity of the preceding one. The author alternates between warning and entreaty, between rigor and tenderness. This balance is difficult to achieve and to maintain. When Jesus is presented as exclusively a leader of love and tenderness, it can in extreme cases lead to a liberty which degenerates into license. [18]   On the other hand, Christ has too often been presented exclusively as a distant and stern judge—as, for example, in Byzantine art. Such a one-sided portrayal of Christ encourages people to look to the Virgin Mary, to saints and other intercessors rather than to come to Christ directly. One of the many admirable things about this writer is that

---

18. Cf. Bishop J.A.T. Robinson, *Honest to God* or The Rev. Dr. Frederic C. Wood, Jr.—"premarital intercourse . . . can be very beautiful," "Sermonizing on Sex," *Newsweek*, December 21, 1964, p. 45.

he keeps both emphases prominent and balanced. Because of this he says we may draw near with confidence, not waiting until we are better, but come as we are. Those who do so are assured of finding just what they need in the way of grace and guidance. "Twas grace that taught my heart to fear, twas grace my fears relieved" (John Newton).

3

The Superiority of Jesus' Person As Our High Priest (5:1-7:28)

A. Jesus is equal to the Aaronic priesthood (5:1-6:20a)

1. Qualifications of a good high priest (5:1-4)

The author has just been discussing Jesus as a leader, leading into a better rest than that of Joshua. As noted earlier, chapter 4:14-16 is a transitional paragraph; it concludes the section on Joshua as leader and initiates the section dealing with Aaron as priest. The scholars differ as to whether this paragraph should be attached to chapter four or to chapter five. It forms the conclusion of chapter four with respect to three exhortations: "Let us give diligence to enter that rest" (4:11); "let us hold fast" (4:14); and "let us draw near" (4:16). As Joshua led the Israelites into Canaan (4:8), so Jesus leads the believers into God's presence in heaven (4:14). At that time Jesus is presented for the third time as high priest (cf. 2:17; 3:1). In the next three chapters (5-7) the author focuses attention on Jesus as priest.

The basis for the discussion of priesthood is stated in this paragraph (5:1-10). In keeping with this author's rhetorical and eloquent style, the presentation is arranged in six units as follows: (1) The high priest's mission (5:1); (2) the high priest's sympathy (5:2, 3); (3) the high priest's ordination (v. 5:4); (4) Jesus' ordination (vv. 5, 6); (5) Jesus' sympathy (vv. 5, 7, 8); and (6) Jesus' divine mission (vv. 9, 10).

The first three propositions are relevant to Aaron and the last three to Christ, while the paragraph as a whole states things relevant to the priesthood in general. Note should be taken also concerning the similarity between the verses in chapters 4:15 and 5:2, 3, 7, 8—all of them expressing the note of sympathy of priest for people.

In the discussion of Jesus as high priest, up to this point the author has presented Him as sympathetic (2:17), faithful (3:1), merciful, sinless, and successful (4:14-16). There are few places in the Old Testament where the Messiah is presented in the role of priest; His normal role is that of king. In addition to Psalm 110, quoted by this author, there is in the prophet Zechariah the link between Messiah and priest. There the high priest Joshua, a contemporary of the governor Zerubbabel, is called "my servant, the branch" (Zech. 3:8; cf. Isa. 11:1; 53:2). This link between priest and Messiah is again reflected in Zechariah 6:11-13 where the high priest is pictured as having a throne and carrying the name "Branch." In the New Testament, however, only here in Hebrews is the Messiah presented as high priest. This writer, however, makes up for any lack on the part of others by his extended treatment of this theme. His treatment is the more remarkable as it is unique in Christian literature of the first century.

It should be noted that a priest serves as mediator between God and man. As a representative of man, he appears as an intercessor in the presence of God. In behalf of God he appears to man as one authorized to give assurance of pardon. He is recognized officially by both man and God. He is an authentic representation of humanity because he himself is human. He is also an authentic representation of God because he is divinely chosen for that purpose. Thus God and man meet in the mediating work of the high priest. He is the human instrumentality for the work of reconciliation called the atonement (at-one-ment).

a. He stands officially between God and man (v. 1)

The author speaks here of high priests in general who can

speak to men's condition because they themselves are human. At the same time he is **appointed** by God. The word behind this construction (*kathistami*) means to "place down, to place in charge, to ordain, appoint." Thus, he stands for God. His sphere of operation is not in secular affairs but **in things pertaining to God.** Specifically, he offers gifts and sacrifices on behalf of or because of sins.

The use of the present tense here and elsewhere in the epistle implies the continuing practice of the priesthood in Jerusalem. This argues for a date prior to 70 A.D. when the temple was destroyed and (presumably) sacrifices came to a halt. There are some scholars, however, who believe that sacrifices did continue in the temple area even after 70 A.D. This is hard to authenticate.

b. *He is capable of human sympathy (vv. 2, 3)*

As in chapter 4:15, so here the author stresses the sympathy and approachableness of the priest. Any effective mediator must be accessible to both parties. It is well known that one who can best sympathize with another is one who has had similar experiences. Some people possess far more capacity for empathy than others, but there is no substitute for sharing a kindred experience. The word behind **bear gently** (*metrispathein*) connotes moderation. The term presents a happy medium between a slave-like passionateness and a stoic apathy. It was used by Philo to express Abraham's grief over Sarah, and Job's patience under trial. He describes an attitude neither too severe nor too lenient (FD, I, 229). A good priest can more readily bear gently with the weak and willful largely because he has subjected himself to the same infirmities and temptations. This is the third time this theme has been stressed (cf. 2:18; 4:15). No New Testament writer matches this one in the boldness with which he presents, on the one hand, the full regal deity of Christ and, on the other hand, His full humanity. The early church soon lost sight of Jesus' real humanity, which resulted in the presentation of Christ as a distant monarch or judge, as in typical Byzantine art. On the other hand, this emphasis led to the veneration of the Virgin

Mary as one who would mediate between the penitent sinner and her distant and austere Son.

The cult of the Mother-goddess, prevalent in ancient Asia Minor, is still influential today where excessive veneration is paid to the mother of our Lord. But it is a one-sided picture of Christ. The necessity for sympathy is illustrated by the relative ease with which a reformed alcoholic can approach an alcoholic as compared with the approach of one who has never experienced alcoholism. Normally the best evangelists to sinners are those who themselves have been delivered from similar sins. The person looking for a sympathetic hearing will first seek someone who has experienced something like what he is experiencing. This, of course, can be carried to the extreme or perverted by confusing mercy with condolence. Timothy Dwight, president of Yale College, in his poem entitled, "The Smooth Divine," held up to scorn some parsons who were so sympathetic with their parishioners that they refrained from warning them about the consequences of their sins.[1] Sympathy alone, devoid of the righteousness of the law, is reflected also in a chaplain's advice to college girls, implying that in certain instances sex relationships outside of wedlock are not bad.[2]

The priest here described is **encompassed with infirmity.** The term *compassed* appears in Luke 17:2 as a millstone around one's neck and as *clothed* with a cloud in 2 Clement 11:66. It is used to describe the chain with which Paul was bound (Acts 28:20). A papyrus fragment uses the term with the idea of "an affliction with shortness of breath." The same term appears in Hebrews 12:1 with the witnesses *surrounding* the athlete in the arena. In view of his own needs, the high priest is under the necessity of offering a remedy not only for the sins of others but also for his own. However, the effectiveness of his service is seriously limited by the fact that much of his effort has to go for himself and he is not able to devote his full energy in interceding for others.

---

1. T. Dwight, "The Smooth Divine," C. Hill, ed. *World's Great Religious Poetry* (MacMillan, 1938), p. 369.

2. *Newsweek*, Dec. 21, 1964, p. 45.

c. He is divinely appointed (vv. 4-6)

Important in the author's consideration of Christ is the parallel with Aaron. In both cases the priesthood was not something to be coveted but rather bestowed by God's sovereign will. This is in contrast to the sad performance, during the intertestamental period, of priests who resorted to almost any expediency to acquire this position of honor and power. This was also practiced so much in Europe during the Middle Ages that the purchase of certain church offices was known as simony (cf. Acts 8:18). The important thing here is the divine, rather than the human, initiative in filling of this office. In democratic countries this attitude carries over into politics. Many politicians prefer to be "drafted" rather than actively campaign for positions of high responsibility.

After his remarks picturing the typical or ideal high priest, the author presents Christ as the one eminently fulfilling this role. He not only meets all the requirements that Aaron met, but is actually a vast improvement over Aaron and other priests in that He does not need to offer for himself since He himself is without sin.

The author designates the appointment of Christ as the high priest on the basis of two Old Testament texts. His sonship is based upon the assertion of Psalm 2:7, "**Thou art my Son.**" This passage was recognized in the early church as referring to Jesus Christ (Acts 4:25, 26). The reason for this identification is the Psalmist's designation of the Lord's anointed, i.e., the Christ. The fact that this Psalm may have been directed primarily to Israel's king did not deter the early Christians from seeing in it a prediction of the Lord Jesus Christ.[3] Indeed, the Old Testament became for them a "revised version" as a result of their experience of Christ. Oil was symbolic of the Spirit of the Lord.

The second bedrock on which the author bases his argument is the statement in Psalm 110. This priest is after the order of Melchizedek. Since Melchizedek appears in the Bible long before Aaron, it is presumed that he has the greater authority. Here the author does no more than mention the subject and leaves

---

3. Kings, patriarchs, prophets, priests, and even Cyrus were called the Lord's anointed (I Sam. 26:9; Ps. 18:50; 105:15; I Kings 19:16; Lev. 16:32; Isa. 45:1).

for further discussion the connection between Jesus, Melchizedek, and Aaron.

2. Christ meets these qualifications (5:5-10)

a. *He was appointed by God (vv. 5, 6)*

Having shown that Aaron's role as high priest was not the result of his own ambition, but instead the result of God's sovereign choice the author now states that the same is true of Jesus. Christ also "did not elect himself to the honor of being High Priest" (LB). He was unselfish. His exalted status, far greater than that of Aaron, was, like Aaron's, the result of divine appointment. Repeatedly in the Old Testament God chose His servants after His own counsels and often not as men anticipated. (For example, He preferred Jacob to the firstborn Esau; David, instead of the eldest son; and Solomon in preference to Adonijah, the heir-apparent.)

In support of his assertion of Jesus' supremacy, the author cites two psalms. From the second psalm comes, "You are my son, today I have become your Father" (NEV). This is the messianic psalm to which the beleagured believers appealed during one of the first crises of the early church (Acts 4:25, 26).

The appeal is also to another messianic psalm which contains the only other reference to Melchizedek in the Old Testament. In saying, "You are a priest of the order of Melchizedek, and for ever" (JB), he lays stress upon the limitless tenure of Christ's priesthood. In contrast to Aaron's line, which may then have been functioning in Jerusalem, this priest is so much greater that His ministry is never ending. Thus, in item after item, the superiority of Jesus to Aaron is demonstrated.

The thrust here is that the status of Jesus Christ is established by God himself, not by a recent dream of zealots. Christ's priesthood is not one instituted by the Romans (as were some), nor by a vote of Jewish elders, nor much less as the result of Galilean partisans. It is by God's free choice as proven in the Scriptures.

b. *He was sympathetic (vv. 7, 8)*

Here as in chapters 2:17; 4:15; and 5:2 Jesus is presented

as one sympathetic. The term **in the days of his flesh** is a Hebraism meaning His full humanity. It implies that the incarnation was limited to a certain period of time. The passage is a strong refutation of Docetism, the view that Jesus' humanity was only apparent, not real. It is also in contrast to the typical Stoic ideal of the great man who is dispassionate and relatively free from emotion. The requirement of the priest is set forth in verses 1, 2, 3. The fulfillment is now delineated in verses 7-10. The author probably has in mind the synoptic accounts of Jesus' prayer in Gethsemane and the Johannine portrait of Jesus as being troubled as the hour for His passion approaches (John 12:27-33). A picture of Jesus, perspiring in blood and calling loudly upon His Father in heaven, is designed to bring home to his readers the idea that Jesus is with them, not detached from them. His was not a token temptation; He was "in all points tempted like as we are" (chap. 4:15). Jesus' request was not to be saved *from* death but rather *in* death. He saved others but He could not save himself. At no time did He waver from His purpose of fulfilling the Father's will. But this did not mean that in His real humanity He shrank from the ordeal. His was not a servile fear, but a filial fear of God. It included both awe and reverence. The Aristotelian concept of deity was that of the "unmoved Mover." The biblical concept is quite different. In the Old Testament God is pictured as suffering with His people, "rising up early and sending his prophets." The suffering of the Lord in behalf of His people is best reflected in the prophecies of Hosea and Jeremiah, both of whom are anything but dispassionate communicators of revelation.

c. He was perfected by these disciplines (vv. 8, 9)

More than once in the New Testament Christ is presented as under no necessity of laying down His life. He had divine prerogatives by which He could have exempted himself from suffering and humiliation. His sacrifice, therefore, was not something forced upon Him but freely chosen, "I have power to lay down my life, I have power to take it again" (John 10:17, 18). Christ is described as having forsaken the riches which was His and voluntarily impoverishing himself (2 Cor. 8; 9). In a most eloquent passage He is described as relinquishing prerogatives that were properly His and becoming man. Not only did He become man but as a "slave" He experienced death in behalf of humanity (Phil. 2:6-9). The Oriental mind is especially impressed with its inherited prerogatives. A Christian college of the Far East had as its founder a noted leader whose son aspired to succeed his father as president. Though the son did not exhibit the qualifications that his colleagues deemed essential, he insisted on the presidency because his father had been president. The same theme appears in the Middle Ages in the "divine right of kings." It is in contrast to the concept that leadership is to be determined on the basis of individual merit rather than inheritance. This tension runs through much of the Bible. The eldest of Jacob's sons did not receive the leadership that was associated in the popular mind with the firstborn. The same is true of the children of Joseph (Gen. 48:18). Eli's sons did not succeed their father. The father was succeeded by Samuel, the son of humble and otherwise unknown parents. King Saul's son did not succeed him. His successor, rather, was a devout shepherd lad. David's firstborn did not succeed to the throne. Thus, throughout the Scriptures there is a tension between the type of leader that *man* thinks appropriate because he inherits the position, and the other type of leader that may be described as charismatic—one who is chosen by *God's* sovereign will and endowed with the divine Spirit.

How could Jesus learn obedience and thereby be made perfect? His learning as a youth is indicated in Luke 2:52, "Jesus increased in wisdom and stature." A similar idea is expressed in Isaiah 50:5, "I was not rebellious." Paul describes Jesus as having "become obedient unto death" (Phil. 2:8). He did not learn obedience, through suffering, but rather suffering demonstrated the extent of His obedience, just as Abraham's offering of his son Isaac demonstrated his faith (Gen. 22:16-18; James 2:22-26). His obedience was demonstrated in His Gethsemane prayer, "Not my will, but thine, be done" (Luke 22:42). This discipline of suffering made Him complete and adequate as the Redeemer (Heb. 2:10), by which suffering He was made perfect (*teleiotheis*), i.e., "brought through to the full destiny and position to which God was leading him." [4] Thus perfected, or completed and made adequate, He became the "source of eternal salvation" (NEB, Phillips, Moffatt). This salvation is effective to those who obey. The disciple is not above his Lord. As Jesus obeyed, so must His disciples. The cause of Jesus' obedience is set forth in verses 7 and 8; the consequence is denoted in verses 9 and 10, namely, **eternal salvation** to the obedient.

His relationship to Melchizedek is again set forth, the important word (*prosagoreuō*) being "designated" or "addressed" or "hailed" or "received" or "accepted." The term is used thus several times both in Scripture and in secular literature. The term "designate" seems especially appropriate here (cf. M-M). The author's point in the preceding verses is that, far from losing status by His humiliation and suffering, the Saviour added to His status. The fact that He learned obedience does not mean that at any time He was less than perfect, but rather, His perfection became, as a result, the more readily recognized and confirmed. In line with this Paul emphasized that because of this Jesus has been given the "name above every name" and that all created beings should acknowledge His lordship either voluntarily or of necessity (Phil. 2:9-11).

3. Spiritual condition of the readers hinders instruction (5:11-14)

Before proceeding with the explanation of Jesus' relation to Melchizedek, and hence His superiority to the Aaronic priesthood, the author pauses again to exhort his readers. He resorts to the "carrot and stick method" of alternately persuading and exhorting, of enticing and warning. Few will disagree with the author's statement that what he has to say is "hard to explain" (NEB). The argument is complicated, but the main problem lies in the readers' immaturity. It is here that the author administers his most severe rebuke. The use of milk to connote immaturity is used by Peter in a good sense; new converts need a milk diet (1 Pet. 2:1-3). This is appropriate for "babes in Christ,"

---

4. Anthony Snell, *New and Living Way* (London: The Faith Press, 1959), p. 51.

but growth eventually results in maturity. The time of maturity was supposed to have come for these readers, but they were still not mature. Paul also encountered the same kind of people—needing a milk diet, not yet ready for meat. Paul equated this immaturity with carnality (1 Cor. 3:1-3). There was a widespread tendency in the early church, both among the orthodox and the heretics, to classify men in three categories: auditors, believers, and *perfect* or mature ones (cf. 1 John 2:12-14). The **first principles** are elaborated at greater length in the next chapter. The term itself (*stoicheia*) is also used to describe the material elements of the universe (2 Pet. 3:10-12). It appears metaphorically in the context of occult influences which are to be repudiated by the Christians (Col. 2:20). It appears to have the connotation of pagan superstitions (Gal. 4:3, 9). The term does not appear again in the similar passage of chapter 6:1. Here it refers to the first things they learned about the gospel (cf. 1 Thess. 1:9, 10).

The element lacking in his readers is spiritual discernment. Because they had not been diligent in walking in the light, there is now some uncertainty as to what is the light. The inability to distinguish between good and evil is normally a reflection of apostasy in its advanced stages (Rom. 1:18-32; John 9:39-41). The author apparently has in mind here the responsibility of using one's mind in its quest for truth. This would be in accord with an Alexandrian background. While Job's comforters were convinced that no one by searching could find out God, this author implies that the use of one's reason is important if one is to make such progress in spiritual discernment. Certainly there is no encouragement for the indolent here or for those with mental and spiritual lethargy. Pythagoras, in a similiar manner, divided his pupils into babes (*nēpioi*) and the perfect (*teleioi*), as did Paul (1 Cor. 2:6, JM, p. 71).

Church history is replete with examples of Christian converts who in a relatively short time have acquired an amazing amount of insight and knowledge. There are also numerous examples in institutions and individuals who have shown anything but rapid progress in spiritual maturity. Wesley once said that "to expect the end without the means is the very marrow of anti-nominianism." He was arguing for diligence in the means of grace. This author likewise emphasizes the importance of growth through "exercise." No one can employ the recognized means of grace in any sustained way without growing thereby. One of these major means of grace is diligently studying the Word of God. Should not the earnest Christian spend as much time with God's Word as with the daily newspaper? When Sunday schools are available, should he not find his place among other students of the Word? Any professional person feels the need of constant improvement in his profession if he is to make advancement. Why should a Christian expect to do any less? It follows that there should be more than the habitual or perfunctory attendance at church. Too many people are content to get their knowledge of the Bible from a pastor or teacher rather than going to the original sources. In our day, with its abridgements of the Bible and its multiplicity of Bible versions, from which the archaisms have been eliminated, there is no excuse for neglect of the written Word of God. A woman of German background in the writer's congregation said that before her conversion as a young adult she was illiterate, but soon after her conversion she was able to read the Bible. To say the least, she was a good example of one who was able to leave the *first principles* and go on. Multitudes of professing Christians, however, forty years after their conversion appear to know little more than they did at first.

It cannot be stressed too earnestly that the Christian religion is not merely the attainment of a certain stage, to be followed by a maintenance of the *status quo*. The *status* cannot be maintained unless one is eagerly growing. As growth in nature is the result of several factors, including water, soil, the sun, so spiritual growth is a result of several factors, including study, service, faith, prayer, witnessing and obedience. The person with arrested mental growth is called a moron; a person with arrested physical growth is called a dwarf. Tragic as these are, they are not as pathetic as the normal person who has been grounded in "the first principles of the doctrine of Christ" and then has ceased to grow, thus becoming a "spiritual moron." But to the spiritually diligent, growth and maturity are assured by God's grace. The spiritual mature person is not the one who complacently congratulates himself on his past achievements. Rather, he is the one who is most ready to confess his shortcomings. Such a person does not compare himself with others (and thus becomes either proud or despondent), but compares himself with Jesus. The mature Christian does not consider himself as having "arrived"; instead, his constant aspiration is to "have the mind of Christ" and to be made "in his image or likeness." Charles Wesley expresses the idea in these lines:

> He wills that I should holy be,
>   That holiness I long to feel,
>
> That full, divine conformity,
>   To all my Saviour's righteous will.

4. Maturity is imperative (6:1-3)

a. *"Let us advance" (v. 1)*

As is characteristic of this author the stern rebuke is now followed by a warn and tender entreaty. He has just said solid food is for "fullgrown ("perfect"—*teleiōn*) men," and now he urges his readers to **press on unto perfection** (*teleiotēta*). On the surface it appears inconsistent to say they are incapable of taking "solid food" and in the next paragraph to urge them to do so (FFB). But the rebuke of 5:11-14 is not a rebuke arising from despair at their potential. It is rather an indictment of past performance designed to prod them from their lethargy; it is deliberately provocative, as Paul was when he sought to "provoke to jealousy" the Jews over Gentile acceptance of the gospel (Rom. 11:14; cf. Rom. 10:19; 11:11; 2 Cor. 9:2; Heb. 10:24). Joshua employed the same tactic when he prodded the people to an affirmative response by taunting them with, "You cannot serve the Lord, for he is a holy God; he is a jealous God; he will not forgive your transgressions or your sins" (Josh. 24:19, RSV). As anticipated, they responded, "Nay; but we will serve the Lord."

Actually the writer is challenging his readers in a manner analogous to Paul's exhortation to the Philippians—"forgetting those things which are behind . . . I press toward the mark" (Phil. 3:13, 14). With both writers they were pressing on to "perfection," not so much because the "foundations" were inadequate but rather because maturity is so much better.

In this summons to press on to Christian maturity there is a paradox. Here and elsewhere stress is placed upon diligence, upon human responsibility in this connection. Christian maturity does not come by accident; it is impossible to attain without disciplined aspiration and purpose.[5] On the other hand, the passive force of the verb needs to be kept in mind—"let us be borne on to perfection" (or maturity). "Not primarily of personal effort . . . but of personal surrender to an active influence" (BFW). The paradox between human responsibility and divine grace in this joint endeavor is well expressed in Philippians 2:12, 13, "Work out your own salvation . . . for it is God who worketh in you." This cooperation is what the Arminian theologians called *synergism*—God and man working together.

The central thrust of both paragraphs (5:11-6:3) is Christian maturity or perfection. This text is sometimes used as a prooftext for the early Methodist doctrine of a second crisis experience subsequent to regeneration. Properly qualified, this interpretation is justified on the basis of the contrast in the paragraph between the "first principles," which are to be left behind, and the "perfection," which is needed.

Christian perfection or maturity is too important a theme in the New Testament to be ignored or treated lightly. Broadly conceived it has several facets, as presented in the New Testament as a whole: (1) Maturity (*teleios*), e.g., Heb. 5:14; 6:1; 1 Cor. 2:6; 3:1; Col. 1:28; Eph. 4:13. (2) Blamelessness (*amemptos*), e.g., Luke 1:6; Phil. 2:15; 3:6; 1 Thess. 3:13; 5:23. (3) Wholeness (*katartismos*), e.g., Matt. 4:21; 2 Cor. 13:9, 11; Gal. 6:1; 1 Thess. 3:10; 1 Pet. 5:10; Heb. 13:21. (4) Design of discipline, e.g., Heb. 2:10; 5:9; 12:10; cf. 1 Pet. 2:20-23; 5:10. (5) Final salvation (resurrection), e.g., Luke 13:32; Phil. 3:12; Heb. 12:23; cf. 2 Macc. 7:15. (6) Divine love, e.g., 1 John 4:12, 17-21; 1 Cor. 13:1-13; 14:20; 1 Pet. 4:8. (7) Christlikeness, e.g., Matt. 5:48; Luke 6:36; Rom. 12:2; Col. 3:10.[6]

---

5. E.g., "giving all diligence" (2 Pet. 1:5, 10; cf. Phil. 3:14; Rom. 12:6-11).

6. See also G. A. Turner, *The Vision Which Transforms* (Kansas City: Beacon Hill Press, 1964), pp. 132-142; H. O. Wiley, *op. cit.*, pp. 203, 204; R. N. Flew, *The Idea of Perfection* (Oxford, 1934), pp. 78-91; A. A. Ahern, "The Perfection Concept in the Epistle to the Hebrews," JBL, Aug. 1946, pp. 164-167.

b. *First principles should be "left behind" (vv. 1-3)*

Is this list of **first principles** (*archēs*) the rudiments of an early Christian catechism? How may one account for the omission of such distinctive Christian doctrines as the Eucharist, the Holy Spirit, and the Atonement (cf. 1:3)? By **dead works**, does he mean Jewish ordinances (cf. Gal. 4:3, 9; Col. 2:20) or a life of sin (cf. Rom. 6:2, 13; Eph. 2:1; Col. 2:20-3:4)? Is the reference to Christian baptism or to Jewish abolutions? All of these **first principles** are clearly in contrast with the goal (*telos*). We shall not be far wrong if we accept the ambiguities of the Greek text and agree with the RSV rendering—"the elementary doctrines of Christ"—a reading supported by the larger context. He wants his readers wholly emancipated from Judaism (to say nothing of paganism) and to be established in the Christian life.

The things to be accepted and yet left behind include spiritual qualities—repentance and faith; symbolic acts—washings and the imposition of hands; and doctrinal truths—resurrection and final judgment. Similar progress in the Christian life is stressed in writings attributed to John (children, young men and fathers, 1 John 2:12-15), Peter (2 Pet. 1:5-11), and Paul (Phil. 3:9-15).

Lack of a concern for "pressing on to perfection" is conspicuous in most churches today. What pastor is not distressed over the spiritual immaturity of his members? The spiritual illiteracy of today's professing Christians is appalling. Now that the Christian Church is presented with its most serious challenge (from Communism and secularism) since the Moslem conquest of the Middle East, complacency and stagnation is fatal. The need for Christians who are concerned, informed, committed, and articulate was never greater than today. Communists and cultists are usually more informed and committed to their respective creeds than are nominal Christians.

V. 3. His exhortation concludes with his own example of progressiveness—**this we will do.** He does not weaken determination by the qualifying phrase **if God permits**; it is simply a recognition that the grace of God is essential (and available) for success. It is an expression of dependence on a benevolent Providence, and a corrective to presumption and pride (James 4:15), common to Christian and pagan writings. In short, spiritual advance is imperative. The best safeguard against a retreat is an advance, since a static *status quo* is impossible in Christian living. As Oliver Cromwell's Bible stated, *"Qui cessat esse melior cessat esse bonus"* —i.e., "He who ceases to be better ceases to be good" (cited by JM, p. 73).

5. Failure to "press on" has tragic consequences (6:4-8)

a. Repentance impossible for apostates (vv. 4-6)

According to several scholars in the reformed tradition there are two classes of readers in the mind of this author. The first includes those who have listened to the gospel but have not embraced it (cf. Matt. 7:21-23; Mark 4:15). They have never actually been converted, like some of the Jews addressed by Jesus (John 8:30-39; cf. 6:41).[7] The other class (this view is embraced by Andrew Murray[8]) includes real but immature Christians and other Christians who are going "on unto perfection."[8] Which set of scholars has the correct view? Only a forced exegesis can interpret Hebrews 6:1-8 as referring to a hypothetical case of unregenerate Jews, a situation which cannot be duplicated today. This writer is "not given to setting up men of straw. The warning of this passage was a real warning against a real danger" (FFB, p. 123). The larger context effectively demonstrates the basis for support of Murray's view that these were believers to whom apostasy was a real possibility. This view is sustained by the book as a whole. E. C. Smith[9] notes that these readers were real Christians as evidenced by the following considerations: (1) They were partakers of the heavenly calling (3:1). (2) Unbelievers would not have been exhorted to "hold fast" as in 3:6, 14:14; 10:22. (3) Unbelievers would not have been urged to "love and good deeds," as in 10:24. (4) Unbelievers could not have endured with joy the spoiling of their possessions, as in 10:32-36. (5) They are referred to as "sons"

---

7. Kenneth Wuest, *Hebrews in the Greek New Testament* (Grand Rapids: Eerdmans, 1948), pp. 113-118.

8. A. Murray, *op. cit.*, pp. 203ff.

9. Professor E. C. Smith, of John Brown University, "The Meaning of Hebrews 6:4-6," unpublished essay presented to the Evangelical Theological Society, April, 1963.

in 12:5-8. (6) Would the regenerate have been exhorted to brotherly love (13:1-6; cf. Gal. 5:22, 23; 1 John 3:14; 4:7, 8)? (7) Would unbelievers be urged to offer spiritual sacrifices as in 13:15, 16? (8) Would the writer have asked for prayer support from unregenerate readers (13:18)?

Yet as Christians they were in mortal danger. They were in danger of forsaking the gospel (2:1-4), of losing their Christian profession (3:6, 14; 4:14; 10:23), of lapsing into disobedience (3:12; 4:11; 6:4-6), of falling into mortal sin (10:26-31), of losing heart (12:3), of despising the design of chastening (12:5-10), of forfeiting their blessings—like Esau (12:14-17), of refusing to hear God (12:25, 26), and of being perverted by heresy (13:9). Calvin's argument that God gives even the reprobate some measure of grace and illumination and engraves His word on their hearts appears to rest on dogma rather than exegesis or experience (JC, p. 138).

As Calvin points out, there are two stages in apostasy: lapsing into specific sins, such as breaking one or more of the commandments; and repudiating Christ (JC, p. 136). Here the issue is the repudiation of Christ—renouncing Him, His atonement, and His way of life.

Few scholars doubt that this passage indicates that Christians can forsake Christ and apostatize; those who doubt this do so for dogmatic rather than exegetical reasons. A greater problem concerns whether or not this passage teaches the impossibility of apostates to repent and be restored. Because many leaders in the Western Church interpreted this to mean that restoration is impossible, they rejected this epistle as authoritative. The passage must be interpreted against the background of early church history. Eusebius mentions ten notable periods of persecution during the first three centuries. During the times of persecution there were many defections, especially during the persecution of Decius in the middle of the third century. What were the church leaders to do with those who denied their Lord when the pressure was on ("confess Christ and die, or renounce Christ and live") and later, when persecution ceased, repented and sought readmission to the sacraments and Christian fellowship? As Bruce wisely points out, this writer writes not as a theorist, not as a formulator of theological definitions, but as a practical pastor, an observer of facts (ABB, p. 210). He states the alternatives boldly and without qualification in order to obtain the maximum deterrent. Paul did much the same when stressing God's sovereignty (Rom. 9:11-14), and Jesus did the same when stressing God's care for His own (John 10:28, 29).

The possibility of reprobation, i.e., apostasy with no possibility of repentance, is set forth in several places in the Scriptures. For most of the murmurings in the wilderness experience of the Israelites, sinners were given no opportunity of repentance, and death followed (e.g., Num. 16:31-35; cf. Heb. 10:28).[10]

Jeremiah was forbidden to pray for Jerusalem because the cumulative effect of her sins was such as to make repentance and forgiveness no longer an option (Jer. 11:14; 12:7; 15:1; cf. Ezek. 14:20). Jesus spoke of blasphemy against the Holy Spirit for which forgiveness is impossible (Mark 3:29; Luke 12:10). John referred to a "sin unto death" for which intercessory prayer is futile (1 John 5:16). Against these must be placed the numerous passages that assure pardon to the penitent, including Manasseh and Peter (2 Chron. 33:12-18; Mark 16:7). Here the writer is stating in the strongest possible terms that sin is not to be trifled with; one dare not deny his Lord with the assumption that later, when he changes his mind, divine favor will be assured. This would be tempting God; it would be presumptuous sin, something comparable to the shortsighted, impulsive expediency of a man like Esau, contemptuous of his privileges (Heb. 12:16).

V. 6. The sentence structure of the RSV is more literal than that of the ASV here since it places "impossible" (*adunaton*) in verse 4, as does the Greek, rather than transferring it to verse 6 ("For it is impossible to restore again to repentance"—6:4, RSV). This "impossible" is a strong term. It occurs also in 6:18—"impossible for God to lie"; in 10:4—"impossible that the blood of bulls and goats should take away sins"; and in 11:6—"without faith it is impossible to please him." Instead of "fall away" the RSV correctly renders it "commit apostasy"—a deliberate repudiation of Christ, as the context indicates. The RSV also correctly

10. Only after the last of the fourteen instances of "murmuring" was it possible for the sinner to escape the penalty of his sin (by looking on the brazen serpent, Num. 21:9).

renders the participle by "since" rather than "while," thus making it causal rather than temporal. Obviously one cannot re-crucify Christ and repent simultaneously; the meaning rather is that repentance is impossible because they crucify the Son of God "on their own account." The early apostles soundly upbraided their countrymen for having murdered the Son of God, even though it was done "in ignorance" (Acts 3:17; Luke 23:34). Since it was done "in ignorance" they were able to repent and be saved. But those who know Christ experientially and then repudiate Him, expose Him to ridicule as did His murderers at first. Because they do it not "in ignorance," renewal (*anakainizein*) or restoration is impossible.[11] In the light of the general tenor of Scripture teaching concerning repentance, one concludes that the impossibility is not that God's mercy is withdrawn; rather, apostasy of this nature is so serious that one becomes incapable of exercising repentance toward God and faith toward the Lord Jesus Christ (Acts 20:21).

b. In grace as in nature barrenness brings a curse (vv. 7, 8)

The issue is responsiveness, and/or productivity. The seriousness of apostasy is now emphasized by an analogy from nature. The kinship between God and nature, Creator and creature, is frequently expressed in Scripture. Cain was told that because of his sin the earth would not produce, a result similar to that produced by the sin of his father Adam (Gen. 3:17; 4:12). The Israelites were told that apostasy would result in sterility of the soil (Deut. 28:38). A closer parallel is seen in Isaiah's famous parable of the vineyard (Isa. 5:1-7) where non-productivity incurred the wrath of God. Another parallel passage is Jesus' parable of the barren fig tree; its survival was conditioned upon productivity (Luke 13:6-9). Paul was no less drastic in his insistence upon the importance of the harvest (Gal. 6:7).

Here the soil is described as a recipient of the blessing of rain from heaven (cf. Matt. 5:45). The favorable responsiveness of the land incurs God's favor. When the land responds unfavorably

---

11. For "renewal" cf. Herm. *Sim.* 7:6, 3; 9, 14, 3; 2 Cor. 4:16; Col. 3:10; Rom. 12:2; Tit. 3:5.

as when it produces a crop of weeds, it is burned over to clear or destroy the contamination. Fire destroys weed seeds and thus purifies the soil. In the Bible, fire is often a symbol of divine judgment (e.g., Lev. 10:2; Isa. 4:4; Matt. 3:12).

In this paragraph (6:1-8) the challenge to go on unto perfection is set over against a warning against apostasy. The implication is clear. If one chooses not to "press on" he may find himself rejecting Christ and risking final, irremedial apostasy. It is difficult, if not impossible, for a Christian to refuse the challenge to advance without eventually severing himself from Christ; there is no neutral ground. Growth is the inexorable condition of life, in grace as in nature.

6. The writer's confidence in his readers (6:9-12)

V. 9. We are persuaded better things of you. Here as elsewhere the writer oscillates between stern warning and tender entreaty, between rebuke and encouragement. After emphasizing their susceptibility to apostasy in the preceding paragraph, he now stresses its improbability in view of their past performance. The motive of fear was first used to disturb their complacency—to shock them. The motive of love and loyalty is now employed to assure them. The basis for this assurance is God's righteousness, not their own competence or constancy. By recalling their own "good works" he hopes that their sense of propriety, their desire to be consistent, will strengthen their purpose to continue doing good works. Normally it is easier to get people to *do* than to *be*. So here the writer encourages them to continue doing in hope that they will become spiritually established.

Their service is described as **ministering to the saints** previously and presently. This apparently included hospitality to travellers (13:2), a virtue highly prized among beduoins and others to this day; loyalty to their pastors (13:17); generosity to the needy (13:16); and a good stewardship of time, talent, and treasure. [12]

V. 11. Show the same diligence, i.e., persevere unto the end!

---

12. Cf. Rom. 12:6-18; 2 Cor. 1:11; Acts 11:28-30. Benevolence was conspicuous in the early church, as Harnack has demonstrated (*Mission and Expansion of Christianity*).

Pride, if nothing else, will constrain a person to be consistent; hence the exhortation to be constant in faith.

The writer here becomes personal and direct—**each one of you.** He is the earnest pastor or shepherd of the flock. Like Goldsmith's "Village Parson,"

> . . . in his duty prompt at every call,
> He watched and wept, he prayed and felt for all.
> And, as a bird each fond endearment tries
> To tempt its new-fledged offspring to the skies,
> He tried each art, reproved each dull delay,
> Allured to brighter worlds, and led the way. [13]

The fruitage of good deeds is in striking contrast to "thorns and briars" of the unproductive field mentioned in verse 8.

The exhortation to "press on unto perfection" (*teleiotēta*, v. 1) is now reinforced by the **desire** (*epithumia*) that they persevere in the **fullness of hope even to the end** (*telos*). This exhortation is a repetition of a similar one earlier ("hold fast . . . our hope firm unto the end"—3:6). In both passages **hope** is that which confidently sustains and allures the believer to "brighter worlds." The possibility of failure is implied and the possibility of success is affirmed, hence the urgency of the exhortation. What *ought* to be done, by the grace of God, *can* be done, since "God's commands are his enablings."

7. Hope has a sure foundation (6:13-20)

The theme of this paragraph appears to be hope. The idea is that the readers should imitate saints who persevere and therefore "inherit the promises" (v. 12). The promises are valid because they are made and guaranteed by the veracity of God himself. Furthermore, Jesus, our forerunner, has already preceded us into the very presence of God, and we should follow Him. The sequence runs something like this: promise—vv. 12, 13, 15, 17; oath—vv. 13, 16, 17; hope—v. 18; anchor—v. 19; veil—v. 19; forerunner—v. 20; cf. 4:14. Consistent with the main purposes of this treatise, the author continues to urge his readers to perseverance, this time by stressing the validity of the reward or goal.

---

13. Oliver Goldsmith, "The Deserted Village," in C. Hill, eddt. *The World's Great Religious Poetry* (New York: Macmillan, 1938), p. 371.

a. God's promise to Abraham immutable (vv. 13-15)

After a reference to the spiritual ancestors who were success-ful (v. 12), he mentions Abraham as an example of one who "arrived" because he **patiently endured**. He mentions Abraham in this connection only to drop him with the view of presenting this aspect at greater length later (11:8-19). His main concern in this context is not so much Abraham's example as the *covenant* made to Abraham, i.e., the **promise**.

V. 13. The immediate issue is the *validity* or thrustworthiness of the **promise** (*epaggelia*). Originally it was a guarantee to the patriarch Abraham of a homeland, of posterity, of protection from enemies, and of universal blessing (Gen. 12:2, 3; 15:7-21; 17:1-16; 22:15-18). The use of an oath normally is to give divine sanction to a verbal commitment. Often the taking of an oath included an invocation of a curse from God if the oath be not kept—"may the Lord do so to me and more also" (Ruth 1:17; 2 Sam. 3:35; Job 31:40; Ps. 137:5). Since there is no god higher (or other) than Jehovah God, He swore, or affirmed, or covenanted by him-self, by His own name, His own holiness (Gen. 22:16; cf. Amos 4:2).

V. 14. The RSV omits the Hebraism, preserved in the Greek, which appears in the KJV and ASV, and renders it simply, "Surely I will bless you and multiply you." For the serious Bible student a more literal translation, like the ASV which retains the Greek and Hebrew idiom, has a decided advantage.

V. 15. Stress is placed on the fact that because Abraham **pa-tiently endured, he obtained**. God had the responsibility of ful-filling the promises or the commitments which He had made. Abraham had the responsibility of being faithful, of being per-sistent, of enduring. By implication here and explication else-where, the readers are to do likewise.

b. The validity of God's oath (vv. 16-18)

V. 16. Here the author picks up the theme of verse 13—the fact that God swore. This calls for an amplification of the oath's significance. First the general principle is stated that in human relationships "the oath provides a confirmation to end all dispute" (RSV). Thus God, in making His promise or in announcing His

covenant, accommodated himself to the procedure that would provide additional assurance. Hence, not only does God's own nature
guarantee the trustworthiness of His utterance, but He has, in addition, given confirmation by an oral oath.

V. 18a. Thus God's promise of life eternal is based upon **two
immutable things**: God's veracity and God's confirming oath. This
theme is rather prominent in Hebrews. The fact that God swore
or affirmed or avowed is mentioned six times in this letter.[14]
In these passages the term represents a strong and solemn affirmation. In addition the noun(s) referring to the oath taken are five
in number.[15] Our author is impressed by three solemn oaths which
God made to the Israelites (Gen. 22:16; Ps. 95:11; 110:4), all
of which have validity today. It is his purpose to press home
to the mind and conscience of his readers (then and now) the
supreme importance and relevance of this for daily living.

c. God's promise the basis for our hope (vv. 18b-20)

V. 18b. We may have a strong encouragement: the words evoke
a picture of refugees or fugitives, not planners of a "bold new
world." They are pictured clinging to a rope to which is attached
the **anchor of the soul** which is secure **within the veil**. Because
of this word-picture an anchor was a prominent symbol in early
Christian art. It symbolizes both hope and security. The basis
for the strong encouragement is the character of God. It was
a great personal milestone to J. Hudson Taylor, founder of the
China Inland Mission, when he realized that "faith" is confidence
in God's faithfulness. To him henceforth the emphasis was not
on *his* faith but on the faithfulness of *God*. Here also the writer
is drawing the conclusion to his previous argument. Since God,
with whom we are in a covenant relationship, is dependable, there
is no doubt whatsoever about our acceptance by God because
of Christ. At Mount Sinai when the Torah was given, God was in
mystery and unapproachable. The people were warned not to come

---

14. *Omosō* appears in Heb. 3:11, 18; 4:3; 6:13, 16; 7:21. The first three are
quotations from Ps. 95:11, the last three from Ps. 110:4.

15. In Greek literature *Orkos*, son of the God Eris, punished oath-breakers.
Orkos is seen in Heb. 6:16, 17; its synonym *orkumusias* in Heb. 7:20, 21, 28.

near lest they die (Ex. 19:12, 13). Later in the tabernacle, only the priests had access, and that only to the outer "holy place." But now Jesus, as our high priest, is gone ahead as a forerunner, opening up the way into the inner sanctuary, into the very presence of God, by a "new and living way" (4:14; 10:20). No longer must the God-fearer hesitate in fear; he may come boldly into the divine presence with no mediator needed except Christ. He needs not the intercession of saint, martyr, or Mary—only that of Jesus. The believer may come with the added confidence that this present arrangement is not a temporary expedience, subject to change; Christ is our **high priest forever.**

B. Jesus is superior to the Aaronic Priesthood (6:20b-7:28)

1. Jesus is of Melchizedek's order (5:6, 10; 6:20; 7:14-17)

What follows is a closely knit and involved argument which constitutes one of the most distinctive features of this letter. The thesis here stated and defended is peculiar to this letter. It has seldom been challenged or widely quoted; it stands virtually alone in early Christian literature.

Beginning with the quotation from Psalm 110 this author goes to the original account in Genesis, a narrative which is as impressive for its silences as for what is stated (FFB, p. 137). Indeed its silence concerning Melchizedek's human genealogy lends support to the author's argument because the priest-king is thus surrounded with an aura of mystery and suggests a type of the Christ. The author apparently thinks of Melchizedek and his order as existing eternally while the lesser order of Aaron is temporary and transient.

An awareness of the Philonic and Platonic contrast between the earthly and the heavenly, between the idea or pattern and its phenomenal copy, may be helpful at this point. In the background of this letter is the contrast between the real and the imitation, the shadow and the substance, between the spiritual and the physical, the eternal and the temporal, the original and the copy. This emerges at different times in the letter. While Paul thinks of the old covenant as being superseded by the new covenant (Rom. 5:13, 14; Gal. 3:24; 4:4), the author of Hebrews thinks of them as coexisting contemporaneously in the relationship of reality and image. He finds support for this in Exodus where Moses received the ideal pattern of the tabernacle and was directed to make the structure accordingly (Heb. 8:5). The "pattern" revealed on the mount was to be reproduced accurately in the construction of the building (Ex. 25:40). "The Spirit tends to take to itself a body," said Goethe. The name most often associated with this idea of shadow and substance is Plato. He expresses it thus in *Timaeus* 28, 29, 37, 38:

> The creator . . . looks to the unchangeable and fashions the form and nature of his work after an unchangeable pattern. . . . When the father and creator saw the creature which he had made moving and living . . . he rejoiced, and in his joy determined to make the copy still more like the original; . . . Time . . . was formed after the pattern of the eternal nature, that it might resemble this as far as possible; for the pattern exists from eternity.

Even more famous as a means of setting forth the contrast between pattern and the copy is Plato's doctrine of the cave. In this myth or analogy Plato envisions a group of men in a cave all facing the same direction. Behind them is a fire projecting shadows on the wall in front of them. Unaware of the objects which cause the shadows they become convinced that the shadows are the realities, even when told of their error.[1] This contrast between shadow and substance, pattern and copy, idea and antifact, underlies much of Plato's thought. It is reflected in Philo also and Alexandrinian philosophers generally. This supports the view that this epistle has an Alexandrian origin in thought.

This conception of dualism appears in contrast between the heavenly and earthly sanctuaries (Heb. 8:2-5), the temporal priesthood of Aaron and the eternal priesthood of Melchizedek (7:11-16), heavenly things and copies (9:23), and the "host of witnesses" watching the living contestants below (12:1).

It seems therefore that in his presentation of the priesthood this author has in mind the eternal priesthood of Melchizedek

---

1. Plato, *Republic* VII, 514-516, *Dialogues of Plato*, tr. by B. Jowett (New York: Random House), I, pp. 773-775.

which was functioning both before and after Aaron and Levi. Since Jesus is identified with the priesthood of Melchizedek, it is obvious that His ministry is not only more recent but inherently and intrinsically superior. It does not necessarily supersede that of Aaron in time but simultaneously presents a better choice. Unlike Aaron and his descendants, Christ abides a priest continually.

2. Melchizedek unique (7:1-3)

The unique distinction of Melchizedek is seen in his joint title of priest and king. Far from being a pagan priest, he is said to be a priest of the God whom Abraham served.[2]

Abraham with his 318 household servants had just pursued the captors of Lot and other inhabitants north of Damascus, recaptured the people and property, and returned in triumph. Out to greet the patriarch and congratulate him on his victory, as well as welcome back the captives, was the King of Sodom and Melchizedek, King of Salem.

The absence of genealogy does not mean that the historical Melchizedek had none; it simply was not mentioned. Its omission lends an aura of mystery which accentuates his grandeur.

3. Melchizedek's order superior to that of Aaron (7:4-25)

a. In status (vv. 4-10)

(1) Reception of tithes from Abraham (and Levi) implies superiority

V. 4. Now consider how great this man was. Our author has used this term **consider** (*theōreite*) in several places (3:1; 7:4; 10:24; 12:3; 13:7). Here our author can show that Melchizedek is of a greater order than that of Levi and Aaron. He can also prove that Jesus is a greater priest than Aaron since Jesus is of Melchizedek's order. Abraham is the link in the evidence. He has also noted the mysterious quality of Melchizedek and included

---

2. Described as "God most High," maker of heaven and earth in Gen. 14:18, 22. This does not mean highest of the gods; it rather means the transcendant one, supreme over all creation (cf. Num 24:16; Deut. 32:8; Isa. 14:14). C. Spicq, *L'Epitre aux Hebreux* (Paris: Gabalda, 1953), II, p. 182.

that he is "like unto the Son of God." He now points out the significance of the fact that Abraham paid tithes to this awesome personality. He points out that Levi's sons occupy a position superior to that of their brethren, inasmuch as they accept tithes of the other tribes. This shows the importance of Aaron and of the priesthood. This gives added significance to the fact that Aaron's ancestor paid tithes to Melchizedek, thus acknowledging the superiority of the latter. Our author points out that Levi "was in the loins of Abraham" when Abraham paid his tithe. Thus in a sense Levi also paid tithes. Medieval theologians call this the realistic theory. Historically it is related to Romans 5:12 where, according to the Vulgate and an unfortunate translation of the Greek in the passage, Augustine read "in whom all sinned" *(in quo omnes peccareunt)*. This figured prominently in the doctrine of original sin since it became a proof text for the position that Adam's descendants participated in Adam's act, acquiring not only moral taint but also actual guilt. This theology was reflected in the New England Primer in which the children read:

> In Adam's fall
> we sinnéd all.

It is not necessary for our author here to establish the point that Aaron actually paid tithes. It is sufficient to indicate that one in his same category or status paid tithes to Melchizedek.

(2) Blessing Abraham implies superiority

Because Melchizedek bestowed a blessing on Abraham our author argues his superiority to the patriarch—the less is blessed **of the better** (v. 7). The dispenser of this blessing was one who unlike Aaron had no known genealogy. The implication is that he was more than an ordinary mortal. Our author points out in addition that the one bestowing the blessing and receiving tithes was unlike the sons of Aaron in that he lives. This appears to be based upon the phrase "forever" in Psalm 110:4. Thus, from the standpoint of not having a genealogy like Aaron, of receiving tithes, of living forever, and of administering of blessing, our author in this paragraph endeavors to establish the superiority of Melchizedek's order over that of Aaron. His method of exegesis was not unlike that practiced by the rabbis of that day. It was especially familiar to the exegetes of Alexandria. It is more convincing than the argument used by Augustine and many of his successors as a basis for the doctrine of original sin. The essential thing is not the extent to which Levi participated in Abraham's act of giving tithes. The significance lies rather in the inferiority implied on the part of Abraham and his descendants.

b. In permanence (vv. 11-25)

(1) Levi temporary; Melchizedek permanent (vv. 11-14)

The author's argument in this section is that the fact of another priest (Melchizedek) being appointed indicates that Aaron's tenure was temporary; his priesthood was not designed to last indefinitely. Does **perfection** in this context have the connotation of "spiritual maturity" (JBP), of "perfect fellowship between God and the worshipper" (MRV), or finality and adequacy (TH)? The prevailing idea here seems to be that the Aaronic ministry was inherently provisional and temporary, not final and fully adequate. Its inadequacy to effect a satisfactory relationship between God and man is set forth in greater detail later (9, 10). This teaching is revolutionary. It calls for nothing less than the replacing of the entire Old Testament system of priesthood, temple, and sacrifices. It was the anticipation of this very thing which led some to accuse Jesus of abolishing the "law and the prophets" (Matt. 5:17), and others to accuse the early evangelists of "turning the world upside down" (Acts 17:6). In retrospect they are seen to have been half correct; the outer shell was laid aside but the central core remains in Christian thought and life.

The superiority of the new priesthood is based upon a better hope (vv. 18, 19), a divine oath (vv. 20-22), a better offering (vv. 27, 28), and the power of an endless life (vv. 16, 24, 25, 28). The priesthood of Aaron, based upon the Law, is set in contrast to the priesthood of Melchizedek (and Christ), based upon the oath.

The fact that Melchizedek is said to be priest forever, so the author's argument runs, serves notice on the Levitical priesthood that it is destined to be superseded. The change of priesthood calls for a change with respect to the Mosaic law (v. 12). The

law, which authorized the Levitical priesthood and the old covenant generally, is now replaced by the *oath* which authorizes the
priesthood of Christ and the new covenant (vv. 17, 20-22). The
basic proof text is Psalm 110:4. It may be argued that such a
drastic transition is too much of a burden for one text to carry.
But in the mind of this author one clear declaration from God
is as good as a dozen. God's utterance is decisive and need not
be repeated. The priesthood is changed from Levi (based on the
law) to Melchizedek (based on the oath). The change is confirmed
by the fact that Christ is not of the tribe of Levi but rather of
Judah. The weakest link in the chain of argument is the connection
between Jesus Christ and Melchizedek (cf. 5:5, 6); it rests largely
on the linking of two texts (Ps. 2:7 and Ps. 110:4) with little
effort to prove the connection. But this method of exegesis was
widely practiced and seldom challenged. Moreover there were no
rival claimants for the honor of being priest in Melchizedek's
order.

(2) A hereditary priesthood compared with a personal and eternal one (vv. 15-19)

V. 15. The newer versions are effective here: "The argument
becomes still clearer, if the new priest who arises is one like
Melchizedek, owning his priesthood not to a system of earth-bound
rules" (NEB), but to "the power of an indestructible life" (RSV).
Repeatedly in the Scriptures God shows His preference for leaders
that are "charismatic" or specifically chosen and anointed by
God (like Jacob, Moses, Samuel, David, Solomon, Amos), rather
than leaders that inherit their position (like Abiathar and Reho-
boam).

The older law is superseded because it was "impotent and
useless" (NEB), since it did not bring its adherents into a fully
satisfactory relationship to God (cf. v. 1). It was replaced by
the oath which established a new hope (*elpidos*). The news of
the new covenant is presaged in several passages in the greater
prophets of the exile.[3] Hope, here as elsewhere in Hebrews, ex-

---

3. E.g., Isa. 42:9, 10; 43:19; Jer. 31:22, 31; Ezek. 11:19; 18:31; 36:26.

presses confidence of the outcome (cf. Heb. 3:6; 6:11, 18). It is hope that enables the believer to face the future with assurance. It enables the "man in Christ" to face up to ultimate reality with poise and buoyancy; it is true optimism. This hope facilitates one's approach to God.

(3) Law or oath (vv. 20-22)

This author attaches much significance to the oath, "The Lord hath sworn and will not repent" (Ps. 110:4). He sees this as the personal guarantee from no less than Almighty God, and hence of even higher authority than "the law of a carnal commandment" (v. 16), the Mosaic law that established the priesthood.

V. 20. "How great a difference it makes that an oath was sworn" (NEB). What is the difference? After stating that "the Lord has sworn and will not change his mind" (RSV), the author notes that this was not said of the Aaronic priesthood. For this reason, he argues, the priesthood of Jesus has a strong, divine sanction. Indeed it is guaranteed by no less than Jesus himself (v. 22). "The oath signifies therefore the transition from a provisional and temporary covenant to that which is eternal" (MD, IV, 314). The Greek sentence structure here is quite complicated and is best translated by the use of shorter independent clauses as is done in the modern versions. The author stresses the oath in order to claim superiority for the new covenant and priesthood. But why is the oath more authoritative than the Semitic law? Perhaps it is because "the Law is an expression of the sovereign power of God Who requires specific obedience: the oath implies a purpose of love not to be disturbed by man's unworthiness" (BFW, 188). If so it would be in accord with the emphasis on the new covenant, "I will put my Spirit within you, and cause you to walk in my statutes" (Ezek. 36:27). It appears that God now takes a greater measure of responsibility for the success of the new covenant.

Oaths were an important element in ancient Semitic treaties, both Hittite and Hebrew. They were designed to assure the sanctity and the implementation of the agreements. In this context the Aaronic succession of priests received authority through their ancestors; in the priesthood of Christ, authority comes directly from God.

(4) The continuity of the messianic priesthood (vv. 23-25)

The new priesthood in contrast to the old is better because it has continuity. There is no transition in leadership; the new covenant does not come periodically "under new management." Death interrupted the service of the old regime; freedom from death assures continuity in the ministry of the new. Christ's mediatorial work is constantly available. The above facts strengthen the claim of the full adequacy of Christ as the high priest.

V. 25. Does **uttermost** have a temporal or spatial aspect? Does it mean "completely" or "to the very end"? The RSV rendering supports the latter—"for all time to come." Phillips and NEB support the former; the KJV and ASV are ambiguous. Does it mean both? Delitzsch defines it as "perfectly, completely, to the very end, but without necessarily any reference to time" (FD, I, 371). Here the author stresses the moral superiority of Christ, His divine qualities. Previously he had stressed His humanity. His approachableness, not the emphasis on His otherness and superiority. Both are equally important in an effective mediator. The full adequacy of the Christ is stated in emphatic and unequivocal terms, as is done in Colossians. Christ's intercession on our behalf "is not a mere silent presentation of Himself by the Redeemer before God, but an eloquent intercession . . . in behalf of each individual among His redeemed" (FD, I, 372).

(5) The adequacy and finality of Christ (vv. 26-28)

The contrast between the Aaronic and messianic priesthood receives a summary treatment here, climaxing the discussion. Either explicitly or implicitly the contrasts are these:

The Levitical Priesthood		*Christ*
Aaronic priests	v. 11	"Another priest"
Mosaic Law	v. 12	"another law"
"carnal commandment"	v. 16	"endless life"
unprofitable law	vv. 18, 19	"better hope"
old covenant	v. 22	"better covenant"
priests die	vv. 23, 24	"priesthood unchangeable"
sinful	v. 26	undefiled
with sinners	v. 26	separate from sinners
for own sins	v. 27	for sins of others
daily sacrifices (of beasts)	v. 27	one daily sacrifice (of self)

law	vv. 19, 20, 28	oath
priests with infirmities	v. 28	Son perfected
temporary	v.28	eternal

Prominent in this author's mind is the inherent appropriateness of things. Not content with assertion he penetrates to the *raison d'etre* of things, the inner logic of it all. Thus in 2:11, it seemed appropriate (*eprepen*) for the Father by means of suffering to bring His Son to full adequacy for His task of redeeming men. Likewise in 2:17 it seemed appropriate or necessary (*ōpheilen*) for Christ to be made like "his brethren." Here also "it was fitting" that we have just such a high priest as is here delineated. The supply exactly matches the demand. After stressing our high priest's humanity, sympathy and proximity (2:17, 18; 5:2-8), he now stresses His moral superiority to other priests and to mankind generally. Christ is thus both sympathetic and competent; He is like us in His real humanity, and He is unlike us with respect to righteousness. Because He is our Brother we may come without hesitation; because He is God we may come and be assured of receiving help.

In the Roman Catholic and Eastern Orthodox rites the sacrifice of Christ is repeated in the "Mass," thus changing the Eucharist from thanksgiving for Christ's finished work on the cross to a repetition of that sacrificial offering, a reversion to the Old Testament.[4] The New Testament teaching, and that of the early church as well, makes it clear that the sacrificial work of Christ was "finished" (John 19:30) on the cross and that the Eucharist is a "memorial" (1 Cor. 11:25, NEB) of that event.[5] This is one of the distinctive features of the new covenant in contrast to the old, as stated here (v. 27).

V. 28. For the third time Jesus Christ is said in this letter to be "perfect" (*teteleiōmenon*).[6] This time the emphasis is tem-

---

4. See "Eucharist," *Encyclopaedia Britannica*, (1959), VIII, 795-797 and "The Canon of the Mass," in B. J. Kidd, editor, *Documents Illustrative of the History of the Church* (London: S.P.C.K., 1941), III, 1-3; df. pp. 82-84.

5. Not a perpetual offering in heaven, but a completed offering while on earth (ABB, p. 287).

6. Perfect passive participle; hence "having been carried on to completion, culmination, or climax" into all eternity. Cf. Heb. 2:10—"perfect" with respect to experience and Heb. 5:9—perfect with respect to obedience.

poral; His perfection is eternal because no further change or improvement is necessary or possible.

In the preceding section (chaps. 1-7) our author has pointed out that Jesus Christ, as a revelation of the Father, is superior to prophets, angels, Adam, Moses, Joshua and Aaron. In each of these comparisons the emphasis is not so much upon Christ's work as upon His personal status and character. Henceforth (chaps. 8-10) the emphasis is upon the *work* of Christ. By entreaty, logic and warning, Christ has been presented as "the one altogether lovely," as meriting our exclusive and total allegiance. Both as Son of man and Son of God, He has been presented as human and divine, as being sympathetic and competent to a degree unapproached by anyone else in Hebrew tradition. As such Jesus Christ merits—yea, commands—our unswerving loyalty "unto the end."

> If Jesus Christ is a man,—
> And only a man,—I say
> That of all mankind I cleave to him,
> And to him will I cleave alway.
>
> If Jesus Christ is a god—
> And the only God,—I swear
> I will follow him through heaven and hell,
> The earth, the sea, and the air! [7]

Evangelical churches often stress the work of Christ and neglect consideration of His person. In Hebrews one finds the correct balance between the two important needed emphases.

> O could I speak the matchless worth,
> O could I sound the glories forth
> Which in my Savior shine,
> I'd soar and touch the heav'nly strings,
> And vie with Gabriel while he sings
> In notes almost divine.
>
> —Samuel Medley, 1789

7. R. W. Gilder, "Song of a Heathen," in C. M. Hill, *op. cit.*, p. 323.

PART TWO

The Superiority of Jesus' Ministry

CHAPTERS 8-13

1

The Superiority of Jesus' Ministry as Ministering a More Effective Covenant (8:1-10:18).

A. A better sanctuary (8:1-5)

1. The chief point (8:1, 2)

The writer glances backward in the direction of the ground covered as he turns to a new subject. He has proved that the priesthood of Aaron and his descendants is not the only authentic God-appointed system. God has also recognized Melchizedek as high priest and declared that His Son belongs to this superior order. As such the Son has all the advantages of Aaron in terms of identification with his people and suffering with them. But He has advantages which the Hebrew priesthood could never match: sinlessness, immortality, continuity and competence to deal adequately with sin. In addition he has shown Christ, as revealer and leader, to be far superior to prophets, angels, Adam, Moses and Joshua. The **chief point**, however, is that **we have a high priest**. Our chief priest is not on earth but in heaven, not in a temple made with hands but on the throne with God the Father. Moreover, He is *seated* (cf. 1:3), indicating that His work *as a sacrificer* is completed. Henceforth, He gives His time continually to intercession. Furthermore, He performs His service in a better place than do earthly priests. In contrast to the tabernacle (and later the three temples—Solomon's, Ezra's and Herod's), our high priest serves in God's very presence, in heaven itself. By implication the temple on earth is only a copy of the ideal one "on the mount and in heaven." This "true tabernacle" is not contrasted with a false house of worship but simply with "the material, transient, secondary" (FWF).

2. Comparison with the earthly sanctuary (8:3-5)

V. 3. The offering of our high priest is mentioned here and the **somewhat** has reference to His blood, that is, His own life, as will be developed at greater length later (9:1-10:18). He goes on to point out that if Christ were still on earth, He would not be a priest because He is not of Levi's tribe. But He is a priest as stated in Psalm 110. Therefore His priesthood must be heavenly and superior. The use of the present tense here indicates that the priests continue to minister in the earthly sanctuary in Jerusalem. If the temple were then destroyed, it would have surely been mentioned to reinforce his argument.

V. 5. The inferior order of Aaron, he continues, functions in a situation which is only a shadow, a copy, or an echo of the original "tabernacle" in God's presence. Again the Platonic concept of the contrast between the forms or ideas and their physical counterparts is in the background. Like the author of the fourth Gospel, this writer is the more convincing by the use of idioms and imagery familiar to his readers. The fact that Moses was directed to fabricate the tabernacle in accordance with the pattern revealed in Mount Sinai (Ex. 35:40) is seen as evidence of a heavenly spiritual and eternal counterpart to the temple in Jerusalem. The earthly one is not bad; it is simply inferior. The force of the argument is not that the old is superseded, although that is recognized; it is rather that the old is not the original, primal, authentic and true sanctuary. With Paul the old was regarded as having "weak and beggarly elements" (Gal. 4:9), which may actually be harmful if they are accepted in preference to Christ. For similar reasons some earnest Christians reject the sacraments of baptism and the Lord's Supper because they often are substituted for spiritual vitality. Before Gutzlum Borghlum carved out his heroic figures of statesmen on the granite cliffs of the Black Hills, South Dakota, he made a model. Visitors may see the "copy," then look away to the distant peaks to see the "real" figures. Which was the more "real," the idea in the sculptor's mind or the "copy" on the mountain? Both the model in the museum and the statues on the mountain are copies of the master's idea. The materialist denies the existence of everything intangible. One professor of philosophy declared, "There is nothing here on the Harvard University campus which I cannot split with an axe." He was a materialist. Mark Twain (Samuel Clemens) advised against giving up the realities of this life for the uncertainties of the next. Jesus advises the very opposite. In this epistle also, the things most real and most valuable are the spiritual realities known only through "the eyes of faith." Such is the conviction on which other men and women of faith have staked their lives.

B. A better covenant (8:6-13)

V. 6. Verse six is one of the key verses of this epistle. With a keen sense of timing which is so obvious in the opening verses of this letter, the author here repeats, **but now**; the emphasis is upon change, upon progress, upon improvement. One of the functions of a priest is that of mediating between a holy God and sinful men. Christ mediates a better covenant.

The superiority of the new to the old is threefold: (1) His ministry is **more excellent**. The term translated "more excellent" occurs three times in Hebrews (cf. 1:4; 11:4). Originally the term meant "different" (as in Rom. 12:6); later it came to mean "more excellent" as here. Christ has a *name* more excellent than angels, a *ministry* more excellent than Aaron's descendants, and a *sacrifice* more excellent than that of Cain.

(2) He is **mediator of a better covenant**. The covenant (*berith*) is perhaps the most important element in the religion of the Old Testament. The term **better** (*kreittōn*) occurs thirteen times in this epistle and may be said to be its key word.[1] The "better" things include hope, covenant, promises, sacrifices, possessions and country. This theme or motif running throughout the treatise

---

1. Heb. 1:4; 6:9; 7:7, 19, 22; 8:6; 9:23; 10:34; 11:16, 35, 40; 12:24.

constitutes one of its most unique and winsome characteristics.

(3) The priesthood and new covenant are established upon **better promises,** better even than those given to the patriarchs. In what respects are these promises "better"? The old promised material prosperity to those who were faithful (Deut. 28:1-14); the new promises "spiritual blessing in the heavenly places" both here and hereafter (Eph. 1:3). The former promises were mostly for external security; the "better" promises are for spiritual, inner security. Furthermore, the new covenant owes its validity to an "oath" which is even better than the "law of a carnal commandment" (7:16-21).

1. Inauguration of the new implies inadequacy of the old (8:6-9, 13)

Vv. 7-9. As he did in 7:11 and 8:13 so here the author argues that the announcement of the new amounts to an indictment of the old for its inadequacy. The faults of the old covenant are asserted here without listing the faults. Elsewhere he indicates that the old covenant failed to deal adequately with sin (9:9), that it was more concerned with external letters of the law than with the inner motive life (Matt. 5:17-48), more with the temporal than with the eternal, more with the group than with the individual (Ezek. 18:1-32).

The **old covenant** is a specific reference to the Mosaic covenant at Sinai (Ezek. 19, 20). But this went back to Adam (Gen. 2:16; 3:15-19), to Noah (Gen. 9:9-17), and to the patriarchs (Gen. 12:7 *et al*). It was later reaffirmed to Joshua, Samuel, David, Solomon and others. The failure of the covenant, or rather of the Israelites to abide by the terms of the covenant, is the constant lament of the prophets (Jer. 2:13; Mal. 2:1-17), and was shared by Stephen (Acts 7:51). Failure was not due to the inherent weakness of the law but to the evil propensities in man. This latter fact was dwelt upon at length by rabbis and theologians during the intertestament period. They concluded that most of the trouble for chronic apostasy was due to the "evil imagination" in mankind. Writers of the Dead Sea Scrolls and other authors expected deliverance only in the age of the Messiah.

The attitude of Paul towards the law differed from that of this author:

In St. Paul			In Hebrews		
letter	vs.	spirit	type	vs.	reality
bondage	vs.	freedom	good	vs.	better
works	vs.	faith	faulty	vs.	faultless
command	vs.	promise	old	vs.	new
law of death	vs.	law of life	vanishing	vs.	abiding

"Go thou and work, the law demands,
But gives me neither feet nor hands;
A better word the gospel brings;
It bids me fly and gives me wings."

Also, while the old covenant says in effect, "Do and you shalt live," the new covenant says, "Live and thou shalt do."

The disobedience of the Israelites did not annul or veto the old covenant because men's disobedience does not change the law (Rom. 9:6-8). But a more drastic solution was made necessary because of the prevelance of unbelief and other sins.

2. The characteristics of the new covenant (8:10-12)

Vv. 10-12. The provisions of the new covenant are best summed up in Jeremiah (31:31ff.) and in Ezekiel (36:25-27). The quotation repeated here is the longest in the New Testament. It is taken from a portion of Jeremiah's little "Book of Consolation" (30-33). These chapters of Jeremiah's prophecy were written during the siege of Jerusalem. They are remarkable in that they are the most optimistic portion of the prophecy and yet written in the prophet's darkest hour. In a similar manner Augustine's *City of God* was written amid the ashes of a Rome which had fallen to the barbarians, when the light of western civilization was about to be eclipsed.

The new covenant had four notable characteristics: (1) It was to be in the inner disposition. The contrast was between the external code upon granite plates and the inner renewal of the disposition. (2) There would be a *personal* relationship to God, more individual than the older group or family allegiance. (3) In the new covenant all would have access to an adequate knowledge of God ("upon my servants and handmaids will I pour out of my Spirit"). (4) The new covenant would be characterized by a great-er degree of mercy for the sinner—repentance would be available to all, sins would not only be checked but they would be extirpated (Rom. 6:1-14).

V. 13. The significance of the **new** is its contrast to the old. Because the new is in effect, the status of the first covenant is changed from current to **old**. If old, then *vanishing away*, is the author's logic.

In the Old Testament the covenant (*berith*) was an agreement or contrast, either between men (Jacob and Laban), or between man and God (Abraham and Jehovah). The usual Greek term for this is *sunthēkē*. But the term here for covenant is not *sunthēkē* but *diathēkē*, which is not an agreement between equals but something bequeathed apart from any merit on the part of the recipient. Thus the new emphasis is upon unmerited favor, upon grace. It is the equivalent of a will or testament. For this reason we say "new testament" rather than "new covenant." [2]

After insisting that the Christian serves a different high priest, the author boldly calls for a change from the Mosaic covenant, regarded by the Jews as sacrosanct, to this new covenant announced by the prophets of the exile. To this radical change he brings all of his considerable power of exegesis and eloquence. It is the clearest appraisal of the two covenants to be found in the New Testament.

C. A better sacrifice (9:1-10:18)

1. The inadequacy of the old system (9:1-10)

The writer presses home to his readers the inadequacy of the Old Testament to deal with sin and the adequacy of Christ to do this very thing. Running through his argument from chapters 8-10 is the contrast between shadow and substance, the earthly and the heavenly, the temporal and the eternal, the physical and the spiritual, the copy and the original. He deals briefly with the earthly sanctuary before hastening on to deal with the covenant in particular. He now returns to the tabernacle for more thorough analysis. The main objective of his argument,

---

2. For further elaboration on this important subject see "Covenant" in the Introduction.

however, is to sustain the thesis that the sacrifices under the new covenant are superior to the old. It is not necessary for his argument to assume that the temple is still standing and its priesthood functioning. He bases his argument entirely on the tabernacle preceding Solomon's temple. However, his argument has greater cogency if the Levitical priesthood is still functioning. Readers would contrast *current* temple offerings with Christ's *final* sacrifice. His failure to mention a termination of the sacrificial system would be hard to explain if it had already ceased to exist. There are those, however, who believe that the sacrifices continued even after the destruction of the temple in 70 A.D.[1]

a. The tabernacle plan (vv. 1-5)

The author is obviously intrigued by the arrangement and services of the sanctuary in the wilderness, but he does not permit himself to dwell unduly on the details. This chapter has fascinated many modern commentators who have sought to fathom the significance of these details. Our author pauses on this only long enough to point out the contrast between the old covenant and Christ.

The original tabernacle measured about 15 feet by 45 feet. The holy place measured 30 by 15 feet while the holy of holies was a cube. The pattern seen here is very similar to that of ancient temples which have been unearthed by archaeologists. Examples would be the one at Hazor and another at Bergama. The tabernacle itself stood in a courtyard measuring 75 by 150 feet. The author confines his attention to the contrast between the holy place and the holiest place. In the outer holy place he mentions only the candlestick which symbolized light and would recall to the Israelite the fact that the Israelites were guided through the Sinai desert by a pillar of fire at night. Opposite the candelabra with its seven branches was a table containing the bread of the Presence or the showbread (Ex. 25:23-30; Lev. 24:5-9). This reminded the Israelites that this was the bread of life.

---

1. A view presented by Kenneth Clark of Duke University to the Society of Biblical Literature.

The incense altar which stood in front of the second veil presents a particular problem. Was it a golden censor as in the AV and ERV or a golden incense altar as in ARV, RSV and NEB? There is little ground for doubting that the latter is the correct interpretation. Both the description in the Bible and the incense altars exposed by archaeologists indicate a rectangular altar about a foot square and two feet in height with a "horn" projection on each of the four corners. This altar was only for incense, not for the offerings. The latter were to be offered on the great altar in the courtyard outside. Was this altar of incense in the holy place or the holiest place? The Old Testament description makes it clear that it was in the holy place rather than within the veil. The writer of the Hebrews, however, gives the impression that it was within the inner sanctuary along the ark of the covenant. All of our sources make it clear, however, that the incense altar stood in the holy place of the tabernacle.[2] In addition, it is to be noted that the high priest was to burn incense upon it daily (Ex. 30:7). This would have been impossible if it had been within the inner veil which the high priests could enter only once a year. Still, the altar of incense was regularly associated with the ark of the covenant rather than with the other vessels in the holy place (Isa. 6:66; Ex. 40:5; 1 Kings 6:22). This altar for the exclusive use of burning incense probably symbolized prayer (Rev. 8:3-5).

Within the holy place upon its gold covered table was the rectangular box called the ark of the covenant, surmounted by the mercy seat and the cherubim. The manna within the box was a reminder of divine providence during the forty years sojourn in the wilderness. Aaron's rod was another reminder of that experience; it symbolized the authority vested in the priesthood (Num. 17). By far the most important were the tables of the Law on which the Decalogue was inscribed. Thus the three objects symbolized, respectively, faith in God's providence, respect for authority, and a life of obedience. The chief interest for the

---

2. Exodus 30:6, 7, Josephus, *Wars*, V. 5.5; Philo, *De Victim Offer*. 4.

Christian lies in the mercy seat (German *Gnade-stuhl*). It was here God said He would meet His people. This symbolized atonement as the very term itself signifies. [3]

This mercy seat, overshadowed by the winged cherubim, represents the place where the holy God and sinful man meet in the atonement. "Though sundered far we often meet around one blood-bought mercy seat." It is to this, metaphorically, that the author of this letter continually encourages his readers (4:16; 6:19; 10:19).

b. The tabernacle ministry (vv. 6-10).

The author dwells on the contrast between the holy place, accessible to the priest daily, and the holiest place, accessible only to the high priest once a year. The background is found in Leviticus. When the sons of Aaron undertook to offer unauthorized incense, they suffered instantaneous death by fire (Lev. 10:1-3). This led to strict requirements concerning the holiest place (Lev. 16:1-5). Unless the instructions were followed carefully, the holiest place with its mercy seat would become the scene of fiery judgment. This led to one of the most important days in the Jewish calendar, the annual Day of Atonement. On this occasion, one of two goats was slain and offered as a sin offering (Lev. 16:9). The other of the two goats chosen by lot became the scapegoat or Azazel. [4] By placing his hands on the head of the scapegoat, the priest symbolically transferred the sins of the nation to this innocent goat. This sin-laden goat would then be led away by a man into the wilderness of Judea, south and east of Jerusalem. In later usage the goat was pushed off a cliff and left to die. Holman Hunt painted a memorable picture of this event in his portrait entitled, "A Scapegoat." This dramatic event stimulated the imagination then and now. For the Christian, Jesus Christ became the scapegoat, the innocent, bearing away the sins of the guilty. He was made a curse for us. There is a strong implica-

---

3. Hebrew, *Capporath* or "covering"; LXX, *Hilasterion* or "propitiation."
4. This strange term *Azazel* meant "destruction," although it was a name given to an archangel in Jewish Apocalypses.

tion that the Jewish leaders deliberately planned it thus (John 11:45-53).[5]

The author's purpose in the foregoing description is now apparent. (1) He makes it clear that this is only a copy of the true sanctuary in heaven. (2) The fact that the sacrifices had to be repeated, some daily, others annually, indicated that their effectiveness was short-lived and limited. (3) The fact that the high priest had to offer for himself and for the people indicated that he himself was not free from the sin which he was instrumental in removing. (4) The various repeated ritual offerings and washings failed to deal with the inner source of the trouble. They did not cleanse the conscience. They failed to transform the worshipper's life. After he had gone through the ritual he was no better fitted to cope with temptation than he had been before. Thus he continued to sin and offer sin offerings. (5) Perhaps the most important truth the author is trying to put across is that the way into the holiest place—into God's very presence—was available only once a year to one person. God was a long way off and not readily available. This is, of course, in direct contrast to the accessibility to God's presence now, made possible through the great high priest, as is repeatedly stressed throughout the letter.

It is significant that here and elsewhere, as he speaks of the atonement, this author lays much greater stress upon the objective conditions of the atonement than does Paul. With Paul and many of the prophets, the emphasis is upon repentance, upon the subjective factors in bringing sinful man and a holy God together. Paul, in particular, stresses the circumcision of the heart and the believer's transformation. Here the emphasis is upon the objective grounds of justification, namely, the finished work of Christ. [6]

---

5. Caiaphas with remarkable insight and foresight said that Jesus would die for the nation. It may be that he ruthlessly determined to order Jesus' execution as proof to the Romans of the Jewish leaders' loyalty in destroying their own king. By so doing they would accrue merit in the eyes of the Romans. It is not unusual for wicked men to obscure their own guilt by charging an innocent victim with a crime of which they are guilty and insisting upon his punishment, thus drawing attention away from themselves while professing to be insistent upon justice and righteousness.

6. A. C. Purdy, *op. cit.*, XI, 688.

There may well be here a deeper, practical symbolism in this tabernacle with two rooms. The holy place symbolizes to the Christian the access to God that comes to the believer who enters the first veil, corresponding with his justification or regeneration. This, however, did not "make the worshipper perfect" (9:9). This perfection, this fulness of God's presence, does not come until entrance is effected to the holiest place. The same Holy Spirit who signifies that this is not accessible in the old dispensation makes it equally clear that it is accessible in the new. Thanks to the pentecostal effusion of the Spirit, it is the privilege of every believer under the new covenant to enter into the holiest of all. [7]

2. The effectiveness of the new system (9:11-22)

The argument moves now from a description of the tabernacle with its inadequate service to the contrasting adequacy of the ministry of Christ. The effectiveness of the new system is seen, first, in the fact that it is placed in heaven itself rather than in an earthly copy or imitation; second, that it consists in the blood of Christ rather than that of beasts; third, that it provides an eternal inheritance; and fourth, that it provides forgiveness of sins, an inner spiritual transformation.

a. A better place and sacrifice (vv. 11-14)

Unlike the priests of old, Christ does not function in a building made with hands. This was admittedly the shortcoming of the old covenant. The very idea of monotheism—that God is spiritual in nature, not physical—belied the assumption that He was located in any one building or place. While He chose Jerusalem to put His name there, people of insight recognized that it was only a symbol of His presence (Isa. 66:1, 2; Acts 7:48-50). The problem faced by this author is getting his readers to make a more spiritual conception of their relationship to God. It is by no means an easy thing for people to grasp the truth that "God is a Spirit: and they that worship him must worship him in spirit and in truth" (John 4:25). The constant concern of this author is to help people

---

7. A. Murray, *op. cit.*, p. 388.

"see" the invisible with "eyes of faith." The majority of men seem to demand something tangible, physical, some ritual when they worship. The point of emphasis is that Christ is invisible; He ministers in an invisible sanctuary. There is no sprinkling priest with blood and hyssop to dramatize God's method of dealing with sin. It is probably a concession to this demand for the objective and the visible that a large segment of the Christian church still continues through the "sacrifice of the mass" to objectify the work of Christ. Actually, however, this is retrogression in the direction of the Old Testament and far beneath the spiritual conceptions set forth here. The author's point is that the superiority of heaven to an earthly tabernacle, of Christ to Aaron, or the blood of Christ to the blood of beasts should be obvious.

V. 14. Is **the eternal Spirit** the same as the Spirit of God, the Holy Spirit or the Spirit of Christ? Does it mean Christ is in the Spirit or the Divine Spirit in Him? It probably signifies a sacrifice which was human and therefore could die, and yet divine and hence uniquely efficacious. Says Delitzsch:

> The eternal spirit is that element in the sacrifice of Christ which answers to the animal soul (*nephesh*) in the expiatory sacrifices of the Old Testament. Hence, the medium of his own eternal spirit, i.e., the whole, divine, and human, but more particularly the divine inward being of the God-man, the divine eternal personality which at the resurrection interpenetrated, transfigured, and as it were, absorbed, the *sarx*, so that he is now all together *pneuma* (1 Cor. 15:45; 2 Cor. 3:7; cf. Rom. 1:4; 1 Tim. 3:16; 1 Pet. 3:18).

The eternal Spirit, therefore, seems to unite the physical-temporal with the spiritual-eternal forever.[8]

b. The provisions of the new covenant (vv. 15-22)

(1) It provides "an eternal inheritance" (vv. 15-21)

In this paragraph the author employs the word covenant (*dia-*

---

8. J. M. McFadyen, *Through Eternal Spirit* (N.Y.: Doran, n.d.), pp. 144-146. Interpreters differ widely: "The Holy Spirit," "Jesus' human spirit," "Christ's glorified state," "immortal life," "divine influence" are among the interpretations offered. See Moses Stuart, *op. cit.*, pp. 585-7.

thēkē) in two different meanings. The ASV text reflects this change in verse 16 where the word is translated testament rather than covenant. The difference is this: the Old Testament and New Testament meaning of the term means a contract or an agreement or a settlement, either between man and man or man and God.[9] The meaning of the term in secular papyri of this period means "will" or "testament" consistently.[10] Many authorities agree with B. F. Westcott that the New Testament meaning of the term invariably means "covenant." Other authorities stand with Adolph Deissmann that the meaning is always "will" in the New Testament. This author's usage is probably deeply influenced by the Septuagint. As might be expected, the Septuagint mediates between the Old Testament and the contemporary Greek usage. In the Septuagint usage *diathēkē*, as a translation of *berith*, retains the Old Testament conception of an "agreement" between two parties. It loses the Hellenistic sense of "will" or "testament" since death is not essential to make it operative (A-G, p. 182). Both the Septuagint and the New Testament usage retain the concept of *diathēkē* as an expression of a person's "will" or "purpose" or "decree."[11] In this passage the author skillfully employs the dual meaning of the term to establish his case. This transition in meaning from covenant to testament or will is reflected in the text of the ASV, RSV, and NEB versions. Here our author points out that even under the old covenant the death of the sacrificial victim was necessary. Likewise, under the new covenant the death of Christ makes it operative. The transition is from the older emphasis upon a mutual agreement to the newer emphasis on affirmation of God's purpose, irrespective of the reaction of the other party. This change is reflected in Ezekiel 36:25-27 where God assumes a greater responsibility in that He writes His law

---

9. Eg., between men (Gen. 14:13; Obad. 7; Gen. 21:27, 32; 31:34; Josh. 9:6, 7, 11, 15, 16) or God and man (Gen. 9:9-17; Isa. 54:10; Jer. 33:20, 25). See Brown, Driver & Briggs, *Hebrew and English Lexicon of the Old Testament* (Oxford: Clarendon Press, 1962), p. 136.

10. E.g., a woman bequeathed her home and garden to the goddess Aphrodite (M-M, p. 148).

11. Rom. 11:27; Luke 22:20; 1 Cor. 11:25; 2 Cor. 3:6; Heb. 8:8; 9:15; see Introduction.

in the heart rather than upon stones. In other words, it becomes more subjective; hence, more effectual. The author uses the element of death both to indicate the time factor in which the new covenant becomes effective and also the significance of Christ's death in the new declaration. Under the new covenant, therefore, its validity depends less upon the person's performance and more upon the person's acceptance; it is less objective and more subjective in its working. At the same time its objective basis is far superior inasmuch as the offering of Christ is superior to the offering of beasts. The effectiveness of the sacrifice depends both upon the worth of the priest and the quality of the victim (CS, II, 259).

(2) It provides forgiveness of sins (vv. 15, 22)

The paragraph closes with an emphasis upon a significance and efficacy of blood in the removal of sin. The reader is taken again back to the atonement chapter (Lev. 17). Here one finds the nearest approach in the Old Testament to a rationale for blood sacrifices. An unsophisticated person, seeing blood issuing from wounded beast or man, observes that as the blood leaves, life ceases. He rightly concludes "the life of the flesh is in the blood" (Lev. 17:11). For this reason it was considered a sacrilege to partake of the blood because it represents the life of another. At the same time, this is the reason why certain savages drink the blood of their enemies, thereby seeking to absorb their strength. Blood, therefore, is simply a symbol of life, and the underlying principle in the shedding of blood is the idea of substitution. Sin can be pardoned on the basis of repentance on the part of the sinner and the providing of an acceptable substitute. The sacrificial system is based upon the philosophy that the guilty party may be pardoned if he presents in his stead the life of an innocent victim—the idea of substitution as symbolized by both the Old and New Testaments.

> The idea of sacrifice as applied to the death of Christ cannot be put aside as a merely passing metaphor, but is interwoven with the very weft and warp of primitive Christian thinking, taking its part (if we may trust our traditions) from the words of Christ

himself. What it all amounts to is that the religion of the New Testament, like the religion of the Old, has the idea of sacrifice as one of its central conceptions, not however scattered over an elaborate ceremonial system but concentrated in a single many-sided and far reaching act.[12]

Therefore the significance of the blood of Christ is not that of a gross, materialistic literalism but is rather a symbol of life. The blood of Christ, therefore, simply means the life of Christ given for the guilty. "The center of the symbolism sacrifice lies not in the death of the victim, but in the offering of its life."[13]

3. Summary: a better remedy for sin was necessary and is available (9:23-28)

In this paragraph the author sums up the respects in which Jesus' sacrifice is superior to the old. The vicarious offering of Christ is better than anything provided under the old covenant for several reasons: (1) It is moral and spiritual, not external and ceremonial. (2) It was made by a sinless priest. (3) It is never to be repeated, but is final and hence adequate. (4) It was not a beast but the Son of God. (5) It included both the sacrifice and the sacrificer. (6) It removes deliberate sins as well as sins of ignorance. (7) It cleanses from *sin* as well as ceremonial defilement. (8) It purifies the conscience thus, relieving fear. (9) Christ's sacrifice was voluntary, deliberate and conscious. (10) The emphasis is no longer on law but rather upon love; rather it is the law of love (cf. Rom. 8:2).

In his summation of the preceding arguments, the author notes (vv. 23, 24) that the Old Testament sacrifices were adequate only as the copies of the real. The old sacrifices were good as far as they went. They fulfilled their purpose but they were inadequate for the task at hand. They were national rather than international. They were temporal rather than eternal. They were physical rather than spiritual. They were liturgical rather than moral

---

12. William Sanday and A. C. Headlam, *The Epistle to the Romans* (ICC)(Edinburgh: T & T Clark, 1945), p. 92.

13. Sanday and Headlam, *op. cit.*, p. 93.

or spiritual. They dealt only with the consequences of the sin—the guilt incurred—but did not purify the source from which sins came. They covered the past but made no provision for a better future. They did not deal with the deeper areas of motive from which action springs.

In addition, our author notes that Christ's one sacrifice replaces frequent inferior offerings (vv. 25, 26). There is marked contrast here between the sinner bringing repeated sacrificial offerings and the one complete and final offering made on his behalf by another. The emphasis is placed less upon the sacrificial act and more upon the acceptance of the life and death of the substitute. It calls for faith, love, loyalty, and obedience. It begets a new hope.

Christ's return is to be welcomed (vv. 27, 28). When the high priest emerged from the holiest place on the Day of Atonement, he was welcomed as one who effected forgiveness on behalf of the nation. This author points out that our high priest has entered into heaven itself, there to make full atonement. He will return to His own from the heavenly Father's presence. This time salvation will not only be full but also final. Thus the author here briefly links the high priestly mediatorial work of Christ with His messianic reign as king.

It is noteworthy that this principle of vicarious sacrifice is no longer held by most Jews or by liberal Christians. It is held only by evangelical or conservative Christians. In other words, most "liberals" regard Jesus as only a great teacher and heroic example. The most distinctive part of Christanity, however, is that which sees in Christ's death the basis upon which God can treat the guilty sinner as though he had never sinned. The New Testament viewpoint does not use the blood of Christ as a mere literalism, or in a materialistic sense. Rather it is a phrase typifying the voluntary surrender of Christ's guiltless life as an acceptable substitute for the life of the guilty. It insists, however, that the most distinctive thing in Christian theology is Christ's vicarious or substitutionary death. For this reason the Cross, as a symbol of Christian religion, is not a medieval anachronism but an appropriate symbol of what is most distinctive in the Christian faith.

4. Christ's one offering alone makes the believer "perfect" (10:1-18)

a. The limitations of the law are obvious (vv. 1-4)

The writer here sums up the preceding argument in a climactic statement (10:1-18) before finishing his letter with a lengthy exhortation to steadfastness. He has already demonstrated and now repeats his conviction that the Old Testament law is like a shadow or silhouette cast by the *eikōn*, "true form" (RSV), which is the sacrifice of Christ. His argument is that the ineffectiveness of the old system is evidenced by the fact that the offerings have to be repeated. Each occurrence of offerings reminds the worshipper of their ineffectiveness. It has been suggested that this is like looking repeatedly at a bottle of medicine as a reminder of something that was either effective or ineffective.[14] But the analogy misses the main point of the argument, namely, that repetition *proves* ineffectiveness (v. 2) rather than merely serving as a reminder of ineffectiveness. The author's point seems to be that under the old system the worshippers participated in a "sinning religion"; that is, the offering of sacrifices gave no lasting ease of conscience or victory over sin. Christ, by contrast, makes the believer a new creation; old things pass away and everything becomes renewed (2 Cor. 5:17); he is henceforth "freed from sin" (Rom. 6:7). What Christ provides and the old covenant did not is victory over habitual sin and a renewing of the mind (1 John 3:6). The new covenant not only atones for past sins but also provides spiritual renewal which makes possible victory over sin.

The inadequacy of the Torah or Law was threefold: (1) The old system—including the moral Law (Decalogue), the liturgical law (sacrifices, ablutions, etc.), and the civil law—was seen to be a feeble shadow or reflection of the real atonement of Christ. Under the new covenant the last two were abolished (Rom. 7) and the first implemented by Christ (cf. Matt. 5:17, 18). The law was not bad, was not antithetical or inimical to the gospel; it was inadequate because it was only a shadowy outline of the real. (2) The law was ineffective in dealing with sins; it removed

---

14. Wm. Barclay, *op. cit.*, p. 126.

guilt for past sins but did not renew the nature; sin continued as in the past (vv. 2, 3). (3) The old sacrifices had little intrinsic merit when compared with Christ's (v. 4).

b. *Christ's act of obedience better than animal sacrifices (vv. 5-10)*

The apparent contradiction between the Hebrew and the Greek is not as serious as it first appears. The literal meaning of the Hebrew, "mine ears hast thou bored," is similar to the less picturesque, "mine ears hast thou opened." The Septuagint translators in more than one instance paraphrased instead of translated in order to adapt the meaning to sophisticated readers.[15] It seems likely that the LXX makes the logical transition from the opened ear to a prepared body. Is the contrast between Jesus' body and the bodies of beasts, or is it between sacrifices and obedience?[16] May there not be a double contrast? "First he says, 'Sacrifices and offerings . . . thou didst not desire . . .' and then he says, 'I have come to do thy will.' He thus annuls the former to establish the latter" (NEB). The contrast is between the Levitical offerings and Christ's obedience. In addition, the "body of Jesus Christ" (vv. 5, 10) is in contrast with burnt offerings (vv. 5, 6, 8). In short, instead of an ineffective repetition of animal offerings, the gospel reveals Jesus as obediently offering His own body as a sacrifice. It is a reminder of the Gethsemane prayer, "Nevertheless, not my will but thine be done" (Luke 22:42), just before He gave "his back to the smiters."

Because of this will (v. 10), i.e., the will of God (v. 7), as "the eternal Spirit" (9:14), the sacrificial death of Christ is vested with infinite value. Christ's sacrifice possesses "sanctifying virtue" because it was "a perfect embodiment of Divine righteousness" (ABB, pp. 380, 381).

---

15. E.g., in Gen. 5:22 the Hebrew anthropomorphism "Enoch walked with God" becomes "Enoch pleased God" (as in Heb. 11:5).

16. The superiority of obedience to the bodies of beasts is stated repeatedly in the Old Testament, e.g., 1 Sam. 15:22; Ps. 50:8-14; 51:16, 17; Hos. 6:6; Amos 5:21-25; Isa. 1:12-17; Mic. 6:6-9.

c. Christ's offering of himself is adequate and ultimate
(vv. 11-18)

Briefly the author presents Christ in the role of king as well as priest. He is pictured as enthroned here (v. 12) and in chapter 1:13. His sitting, in contrast to the priests' standing, implies the completion of His task as offerer and offering: "It is finished." His session by the Father's side indicates His royal role as King of kings. But here, as in chapter 1:3, the author does not dwell on Jesus' royal Davidic role at length. The apocalyptists preferred the Davidic role (Rev. 1); Paul and John preferred to link Jesus with Abraham (Rom. 4; John 8); the Pharisees contrasted Him with Moses (John 8, 9), but this writer stresses His link with Aaron and Melchizedek.

V. 14. The summation of verses 11-13 is found here: the **one offering** repeats the assertion of verse 12 (**one sacrifice**) and strengthens the affirmation of finality concerning the work of Christ as priest. Because His offering was adequate it is completed. This is at variance with the doctrine of the Mass, in which the offering of Christ is allegedly repeated. Is it "an assertion of the never-failing efficacy of the supreme deed of Christ"?[17] The verse is in contrast to verse 1 where it says that the old system of sacrifices "can never . . . make perfect them that draw nigh." Here Christ "**hath perfected forever them that are sanctified.**"

We learn what Christ does by learning what the law by contrast failed to do. Previously the author has pointed out that under the old covenant the sin problem was not adequately dealt with (10:4), the conscience was not "made perfect" (9:9); in short, the subjective effects on the worshipper were inadequate. Because the objective grounds (shadowy sanctuary and beasts) of the Old Testament system were inadequate, the subjective effects were inadequate. On the other hand, under the new covenant, because of the objective basis (the real sanctuary and Christ), the subjective change in the believer (pardon and sanctification) is adequate or "perfect."

By **perfected forever** he means "he has put them in the ideal

---

17. R. N. Flew, *op. cit.*, p. 74.

religious relation to God" (James Denney). This apparently designates not moral perfection as such, but the perfectly adequate sacrifice on Christ's part and the perfectly assured forgiveness for men. It has primary reference to the effectiveness and hence finality of the new covenant, as the following verses indicate. [18] The essential thing to note is that Christ has dealt adequately with the sin problem in two ways: First, His one sacrifice provides an adequate objective basis on which God can remove sin (cf. Rom. 3:22-30); and second, so far as the individual is concerned, it completely terminates the dominition and aftereffects of sin in the believer (cf. Rom. 6). The atonement provided by Christ in the new covenant perfectly or completely deals with the sin problem objectively (in the economy of salvation) and subjectively (in the individual believer). In the light of Acts 2:47 and parallel texts (see exegesis), the verse designates "those who from time to time continue to be set apart or sanctified."

The first quotation from Jeremiah (8:8-12) emphasized in its context the transition from the old covenant to the new; this repetition of the quotation emphasizes the effectiveness of the new in contrast to the old (BFW, 329). On this note of finality and adequacy the writer terminates the expositional or doctrinal section of this treatise. The remainder deals almost entirely with exhortation. His whole purpose to this point has been to demonstrate, mostly from the Old Testament, the superiority and adequacy of Jesus Christ both as man and as Son of God. He now concentrates on exhortations, confident that his readers will respond to their Captain in faith and perseverance.

---

18. *Teleioō* here "means giving the worshipper a satisfactory assurance that his sins are forgiven," A. B. Bruce, HDB II, 334.

The Superiority of Jesus' Ministry as Exemplifying a Perfect Life of Faith (10:19-13:25)

A. A challenge to perseverance (10:19-39)

1. Enter the way with confidence (10:19-25)

V. 19. The analogy of the tabernacle is still present in the mind of the author. Once again he summons all the force of persuasion he can muster, urging them to enter into God's very presence with confidence. As Joshua led into the land of promise (4:8-11) and as the high priest entered the holiest place annually (9:7), so Christ, as our Joshua and our high priest, has gone through the curtain into the innermost sanctuary of God's presence (cf. 4:14; 9:12, 24). In what sense is the body of Jesus analagous to the inner veil of the sanctuary? It is perhaps more than a coincidence that when Jesus died the curtain of the temple was rent from top to bottom, revealing the hitherto darkened interior of the holy of holies (Matt. 27:51). In similar imagery Paul speaks of Christ abolishing in His flesh the partition between Jew and Gentile (Eph. 2:14, 15). In both cases the body of Christ is the means by which the dividing barrier is abolished. But why? What is the significance of this comparison? The equation of Jesus' body with the "new and living way" reminds one of the incarnation as the means by which Christ defeated the devil (2:14) (CS, II, 316). In a "daring, poetical touch" the author says that the "veil" (the flesh of Christ) had to be rent in death before effective blood was available to open up the **new and living way to God** (JM, p. 143).

V. 21. In this paragraph there are two sources of encouragement and three distinct challenges. The two bases of encouragement are the fact that a "new and living way" has been opened, and the fact that we have a great high priest presiding over *God*'s **house** (cf. 3:2) or sanctuary. In the light of these accomplished facts the readers are exhorted to **draw near** (v. 23), and to **hold fast** (v. 23), and to "spur one another on" (v. 24), with special reference to corporate worship and fellowship.

In contrast to the cautious circumspection with which the ancient high priest was compelled to enter tabernacle and temple, the way is now wide open for every sincere seeker to come into the throne-room of the Most High God. In the language of the temple, the seeker must come simply with a sincere heart or motive and a cleansed heart and body. The cleansing of the body in preparation for worship is common in many religions of mankind. Before a Moslem enters the mosque to pray, he must wash his feet at the laver in the center of the court yard. Before the Shintoist worships at his shrine, he must wash out his mouth at the fountain in front of the temple. The ancient temple of Solomon had the large laver in front of the temple for a similar purpose. The figurative language here suggests to the Hebrew the ablutions of the temple service. To the Christian it is a reminder of his baptism and of the inner cleansing which it symbolizes.

V. 23. In addition to the approach to God there must be tenacity in adhering to one's confession of faith and hope. The basis for this faith is the faithfulness of God. Abraham "reckoned" that God was able to do what He promised in spite of the circumstances (Gen. 15:1). There is also a warning here against negligence (cf. 2:1-4), a sin of omission. Those who fear the Lord are drawn by a common interest to those of like common faith (Mal. 3:16), resulting in the "communion of the saints" or Christian fellowship, which is so important for growth and stability. St. Benedict and John Wesley were among the first to recognize the importance of fellowship among Christians—the former in a monastery, the latter in the class meeting. As Wesley learned and taught, man is a social being and hence it is well-nigh impossible to be a mature and vital Christian in isolation. Even monks live in communities. There have been periods in history when Christians, due to severe persecution, have been silent and inarticulate. In such times the church has not grown. It has grown, in spite of oppression, when the Christian witness is bold even unto death, so much so that the words "witness" and "martyr" came to be synonymous.

The **Day** is capitalized in the RSV because it refers to the Day of the Lord. Although this epistle is not seriously preoccupied with eschatology, the end of the age is seldom out of the author's thoughts (9:28; 10:30; 12:23, 28).

2. Apostasy to be avoided (10:26-31)

V. 26. The author now reverts to the theme which he so forcefully expressed in 6:4-8. The emphasis is upon deliberate and willful sin. In the light of the context it includes the sin of refusing to follow Christ in the "new and living way." The alternative to obedience is apostasy. In such a case the sacrifice of Christ is without effect. The picture of a fiery judgment is evoked, the imagery suggested by the Old Testament where fire often symbolized judgment both in the law and in the prophets. [1]

V. 28. Note is taken of the death penalty meted out to offenders under the Mosaic law with no opportunity for repentance. The doctrine of repentance did not receive prominence until the kingdom period when it found expression through Amos, Hosea and their successors. The author argues that the greater the sin, the greater the punishment; if breaking the law received the death penalty, how much more certain is the judgment for those who commit the far greater sin of rejecting Christ. The argument here does not stress the impossibility of repentance and restoration; it simply reasserts it. The emphasis is rather upon the certainty and severity

---

1. Evil men and cities were judged by fire (Lev. 10:2; Isa. 4:4; Amos 1:4, 7, 10, 12, 14).

of the punishment. The author's high regard for Jesus makes the rejection of Jesus the more heinous and unforgivable.

V. 29. This needs to be compared with Jesus' statement that blesphemy against the Son may be forgiven but blasphemy against the Holy Spirit cannot be pardoned (Matt. 12:31). This passage at least implies that blasphemy against Christ has no forgiveness. The word "blasphemy" is not used, but desecration of Christ's blood and insulting Christ personally is clearly indicated.

V. 31. The fearfulness of divine judgment is a characteristic emphasis of this letter (12:29; 4:13; 6:8). In this manner the writer seeks to create the greatest possible deterrent to infidelity and apostasy. The appeal is frankly to fear. Is fear a legitimate motive? Fear is a legitimate motive, although it is rooted in selfishness and hence not the most worthy motive. If all higher motives, such as love, loyalty, gratitude and service, fail, then fear or enlighted self-interest should be employed vigorously, as is done here.

3. Endurance needed now (10:32-39)

As in chapters two and six so here stern warning is followed by tender entreaty. The fervent exhortation (vv. 19-25), followed by a stern warning (vv. 26-31), concludes with a message of encouragement (vv. 32-39). He now appeals to memory, the recollection of former days when their faith was new and fresh and their loyalty laudable. The motivation to which he appeals is that of consistency. Why should they now reverse their former position and cast off all that they held most dear before? The situation is similar to the churches of Galatia to whom Paul spoke so frankly and forcefully.

A rather clear and detailed picture of the group of young believers is here presented. (1) They had been **enlightened** or converted and made "partakers of the Holy Spirit" (6:4). (2) They were convinced that their treasures lay in heaven, not on earth. (3) They suffered grievously for their faith by way of abuse and ridicule. (4) They endured a loss of material possessions joyously because of their faith. (5) They had compassion on others who, because of their faith, suffered likewise.

Such afflictions were so common in the ancient church that it is impossible to identify the people or to fix a date for this persecution. Paul reports bitter persecution by the middle of the first century (1 Thess. 2:14) and Acts confirms it (Acts 14:2, 19). The general persecution in the times of Nero (c. 64 A.D.) and a more severe one in the time of Domitian (c. 95 A.D.) is reported by Eusebius. But local persecutions, such as are reflected in this letter, could have occurred at almost any time or place during the first century.

V. 35. The **boldness** (*parrēsian*) for which he pleads is the same term used in the same sense in 3:6—"if we hold fast our confidence." The term occurs also in 4:16 and 10:19 where it means "boldness." The ASV translates the term "boldness" at each of these occurrences; the RSV renders it "confidence" in each case. The term occurs frequently in the New Testament, especially in the Johannine literature where it means "publicly, openly, or plainly." In a persecution context this openness requires boldness. Here it means an open, courageous confession of Christ.

In addition to boldness, the qualities of persistence, perseverance and patience are required. To bolster the exhortation for endurance or patience, the author calls on Habakkuk as a witness to this truth. The text is appropriate because Habakkuk was tempted to doubt and be impatient with God's apparent unconcern over evil. Instead of doubting, however, the prophet inquired and then waited patiently for God to answer or reveal himself. While waiting, Habakkuk determined to live on "naked faith," a faith which did not demand immediate evidence but was content to survive without *obvious* guarantees.

Three things are indicated by the quotation: (1) A confidence is voiced that God will intervene and reveal himself in due time. (2) Meanwhile the prophet will continue to live his life on the conviction that God is in control and that eventually righteousness will triumph. (3) The possibility of "shrinking back" in unbelief or even lapsing into apostasy is held out as a warning. If this occurs, divine displeasure will be forthcoming. The important thing, therefore, is to continue living by faith even if there is no visible or outward encouragement.

V. 39. The chapter concludes with the expression of confidence into which the author brings his readers. He places himself and his readers with the ones that refuse to "shrink back" but rather "have faith and keep their souls" (RSV).

The entire chapter is a summary and restatement of what has been stressed before. The adequacy of the atonement which only Christ provides is reiterated and emphasized. The importance of adherence to Christ and the new covenant is stressed. The danger of failing to hold onto one's faith, and the consequent wrath of God, is again brought into sharp focus. The reward that awaits those who persevere in the espousal of Christ and His way is again held out as motivation and encouragement. Having dealt with doctrine based on Scripture and experience, he is now ready to cite examples of men and women who lived victoriously. What has been done once can be done again, he implies. What ought to be done, by the grace of God, can be done.

B. Faith exemplified in the fathers (11:1-40)

1. The paradox of faith (11:1-3)

Here we find a classic statement as to the nature of faith. What species of faith does this author have in mind? There are several varieties of faith in the Scriptures. One is a confidence that a statement is true either because of or in spite of the visible evidence. Abraham had a faith like this when he believed that God would give him an heir (Gen. 15:6; Rom. 4:3). Another is an acceptance of tradition such as a creedal statement (1 Cor. 15:2; cf. James 2:19). With Habakkuk faith was a confidence in the final triumph of righteousness (Hab. 2:4; Gal. 3:11). With Paul, as with the Protestant Reformers, faith was *trust* in God's mercy for pardon, i.e., "saving faith" (Eph. 2:8). Jesus urged an aggressive, creative, achieving, venturing faith (Matt. 8:10; Mark 2:5; Luke 7:9; 17:5; cf. John 11:40). Faith is often the equivalent of one's entire commitment as a Christian (e.g., Luke 22:32; 1 Tim. 1:2; 6:21; Jude 3; Rev. 2:13). Of these various facets of faith the most prevalent and significant are "nominal faith" (e.g., James 2:19), "saving faith" (e.g., Eph. 2:8), and a confidence in God, as in Habakkuk 2:4 and here. With the writer to the Hebrews, faith is primarily a conviction of the truth and importance of the way of Christ and commitment thereto. It is a paradox in that eternal verities, not accessible to the five senses, are more real and more important than tangible, visible, material objects. The author's presentation of the nature of faith must be seen against the background of his readers who are tempted to doubt the worth and validity of their Christian faith (cf. Mal. 3:14). The contrast between visible objects of inferior value and the invisible truths of superior value is illustrated in Plato's contrast between the eye of the mind and the physical eye, between the visible and the intelligible.[1] Here it is not the eye of the mind but the "eye of faith" which sees the realm that is not less real because it is invisible. The author marshalls an array of witnesses to attest the truth of his position that the real heroes are those who have something "better" than this world offers.

Here faith is equated with the underlying essence (*hypostasis*), foundation of, confidence in, or assurance of the object of one's hope (cf. 1:3; 3:14). The connection between foundation and confidence is obvious; a firm foundation gives confidence. Faith is also said to be the test, proof, demonstration or conviction of invisible realities. This term (*elegchos*) means a rebuke or reproof (2 Tim. 3:16); its verb form means to convict, as when the Spirit convicts the world of sin (John 16:8).[2] To convict means to convince and to rebuke simultaneously. In short, faith as used here means "the conviction of unseen reality" (11:8, 13, 39). This paradox of seeing the invisible is similiar to Paul's paradoxical statement of knowing that which transcends knowledge (Eph. 3:19).

Faith is much more than trusting in the word of another; the word is the vehicle by which the truth itself is apprehended and appropriated. Faith links the person with objective reality—in

---

1. In the *Republic* Plato contrasts the visible (*opōmenou*) world, consisting of objects and shadows, with the intelligible (*nooumenou*) world, consisting of hypotheses (*omōiōthe*) and first principles (*archai*). He concludes that the copy is to the original as opinion is to knowledge. The writer to the Hebrews had a similar contrast between the immediate sensory world and the invisible realm, discernible only by faith. See Plato, *Res Publica*, 510 (Oxford, 1937).

2. See also John 3:20—"reproved," John 8:9—"convicted," 1 Cor. 14:24; Tit. 1:9; James 2:9—"convinced." *Elegchos* means a demonstration "of the existence of the immaterial as though it were actual" (FWF, p. 161).

this case, with God. "The invisible takes the initiative and wakes faith; faith receives the impression and seeks for ever fuller union with it. [3] As Murray notes, a faith that deals almost "esclusively with the word as the ground of faith" tends to be more intellectual than spiritual. Faith, he continued, deals not only with the promises of the Bible but also with "an unceasing spiritual intercourse with the unseen world around us." [4]   Faith includes an element of venture. Abraham ventured into the land of promise, uncertain of his destination (11:8); this calls for holy audacity.

2. Antediluvian witnesses (11:4-7)

a. Abel (v. 4)

Precedence for this imposing array of witnesses to the faith of the fathers is to be found in Jesus Ben Sirach (c. 180 B.C.), who begins his catalogue with the words, "Let us now praise famous men and our fathers who begat us" (Ecclus. 44:1). He began with Enoch and ended with Simon the high priest.[5]

These were selected with one thing in mind—the long-term perspective which looked beyond the present to God and the future. Why was Abel and his sacrifice more pleasing to God than was Cain? Did God's preference refer to the sacrifices or to the sacrificers? Both the Genesis account and the reporting of it here makes no distinction between offering and offerer, "The Lord had regard for Abel and his offering, but for Cain and his offering he had no regard" (Gen. 4:4, 5, RSV). In the Hebrews resumé it appears that it was the offering which God preferred— **a better sacrifice than Cain, through which he obtained. . . .** Was God pleased with Abel because he presented the better offering or was God pleased with the offering because Abel was the better man? Which was cause and which effect? Wesley believed that it was the offering itself which God favored because it testified both of a Creator and a future Redeemer.[6] Calvin believed it was the character of Abel which was decisive. In his words:

---

3. A. Murray, *op. cit.*, p. 422.

4. *Ibid.*, p. 423.

5. Compare also the eulogy of Mattathias (1 Macc. 2:51-60) and that of the mother of seven martyrs (4 Macc. 16:20ff.; 18:11ff.).

6. J. Wesley, *Notes on the New Testament* (London: Epworth Press, 1958), p. 842.

Abel's sacrifice was for no other reason preferable to that of his brother, except that it was sanctified by faith . . . because he himself was graciously accepted. But how did he obtain this favour, except that his heart was purified by faith (J. C., p. 267).

Support for this view is seen in the reason given Cain for God's displeasure: "If you do well, will you not be accepted? And if you do not well, sin is crouching at the door" (Gen. 4:7, RSV). That Abel was more righteous than Cain is indicated also in 1 John 3:12.[7] Spicq, Delitzsch, F. F. Bruce and others conclude that God's preference for Abel and his offering was due to the character of the offerer rather than the nature of the offering. In support of this, Spicq cites Genesis 4:7, "If you do well, will you not be accepted?" (RSV). Delitzsch bases his conclusion in part on the observation that the **through which** (*di'ēs*) of verse 4 refers to Abel's faith rather than to his offering. The ancient interpreters, however, including Puilo and Josephus, follow the Septuagint in finding the relative merits of the offerings decisive. There seems little exegetical ground either here or in Genesis for supposing that Abel's offering was preferred because it anticipated the sacrificial offering of Christ (FFB, p. 285). It is likely that God's acceptance was indicated by sending the fire to consume the sacrifice (cf. Gen. 15:17; Lev. 9:24; Judg. 6:21; 1 Kings 18:38).[8] Is it Abel's faith, Abel's sacrifice, or Abel's blood that continues to witness? Exegesis alone gives no decisive answer (BFW), but it seems likely that it is the faith to which Abel bears witness. Faith best fits the context in this chapter. Abel's blood cried for vengeance (Gen. 4:10), in contrast to the blood of Jesus which pleads for mercy (Heb. 12:24). (JM, p. 104).

b. Enoch (vv. 5, 6)

Enoch, "the seventh from Adam" as Jude describes him, was one of the more influential of the patriarchs, especially to the later apocalyptists. The apocalypse which bears his name

---

7. But envy at God's preference of Abel and his offering would be adequate to account for Cain's murderous act. Also the description of Abel as "righteous" (Matt. 23:35) may be with reference to the total picture rather than to his character *prior* to his offering.

8. So Moses Stuart, *Commentary on the Epistle to the Hebrews* (Andover, 1833), p. 488.

(c. 170 B.C.) had a profound influence on the writers of the New Testament. [9] The translators of the Septuagint, apparently troubled about the Hebrew anthropomorphism—"Enoch walked with God"—transliterated it into something more congenial to the sophisticated reader; it reads, "Enoch pleased God." [10] This is the rendering used by this author. This apparently influenced the language of Hebrews 13:21—"well-pleasing in his sight." This is in the sense of a servant being satisfactory to his master. The "walking" implies fellowship. "How can two walk together unless they are in agreement?" asked Amos (cf. "appointment" RSV, Amos 3:3). [11] The "translation" (*metatithēmi*) means "to change one's position, to convey to another place, to transfer." It was used for the removal of Jacob's bones to his family tomb in Canaan (Acts 7:16; cf. Gen. 50:13). Other instances in Scripture of bodily transfers supernaturally from one locality to another include those of Elijah, Philip and perhaps Ezekiel. Enoch and Elijah are the only ones in Scripture who departed from this life without physical death. This probably accounts in large measure for their influence in popular thought during later generations.

c. Noah (v. 7)

V. 7. Noah was the tenth from Adam and contemporary with Enoch for fifty years. His faith was an exceptionally effective illustration of this author's emphasis on faith as seeing the invisible. Noah heard God's warning and believed it although there was no visual evidence to support it. Noah's contemporaries did not believe the warning and continued their worldly pursuits complacently and with a false sense of security.

In his generation Noah was so conspicuous for righteousness that he was called "perfect" (*tamim*) and "just" (*yasher*). He is cited for righteousness four times in the New Testament: in the Gospels as a protestant in the midst of secularism (Matt.

---

9. See R. H. Charles, *Pseudepigrapha of the Old Testament* (Oxford, 1913).

10. Also Ecclus. 44:16—"Enoch pleased the Lord."

11. Some ancient commentators assumed that God took Enoch away early in life in order to keep him from sin or because of his repentance for past sin. See Wisd. 4:10; Ecclus. 44:16; Philo, *de Abrahamo*, 6.

24:37, 38; Luke 17:26, 27), in the Epistles as a "preacher of righteousness" to a "lost generation" (1 Pet. 3:20; 2 Pet. 2:5), and here.

This author notes four things in particular about Noah. (1) Noah's reaction to God's warning proved that he was a man of faith. As Abraham believed God's promise of blessing in spite of any visible confirmation, so Noah believed God's promise of judgment without visible evidence. Noah was **moved with godly fear,** i.e., "he took good heed" (NEB). His was not a morbid fear that goads and paralyzes, nor a servile fear which brings bondage, but a wholesome fear that leads to constructive action.

(2) Noah's faith found expression in obedience; he built the ark as commanded. In so doing he exposed himself to scorn by his skeptical contemporaries, meanwhile preaching righteousness to them.

(3) He condemned the sin and carelessness of his neighbors. He was apprehensive while they were carefree and complacent "until the day that Noah entered the ark" (Luke 17:27), but then it was too late. This gave further evidence of his rugged individualism with respect to righteousness.

(4) The result of his faith and obedience was to become an **heir of righteousness,** like Abraham. Hence there followed the covenant between God and Noah's posterity (Gen. 9:11-17).

3. The Hebrew patriarchs (11:8-22)

a. Abraham (vv. 8-10)

Abraham is the example of faith *par excellence.* The writers of the New Testament often appealed beyond Moses to "father Abraham." [12] Abraham illustrates faith because he left the security of Mesopotamia with its irrigated farm economy, the family ties of his ancestors, and most of his wealth, for the vicissitudes of nomadic life in Canaan. His going was not because "distant pastures look greener." He did not know his destination; he knew only the command to go and the One who would go with him. He went because of God's command in spite of the fact that he could

---

12. See John 8, Rom. 4, Gal., 4. While Moses stood for *law* and David for *nationalism,* Abraham was the leading exponent of *faith.*

not foresee the outcome. Few have expressed faith in the final outcome of the journey more effectively than Walt Whitman after he had watched the flight of a migratory water-fowl.

> There is a Power whose care
> Teaches thy way along that pathless coast—
> The desert and illimitable air—
> Lone wandering, but not lost.

> He who from zone to zone,
> Guides through the boundless sky thy certain flight,
> In the long way that I must tread alone,
> Will guide my steps aright.[13]

He would have been in full rapport with a New England prophet of faith and hope. Abraham did not know where he was going, but he knew with whom he was going.[14]

> I know not where his islands lift their fronded palms in air,
> I only know I cannot drift beyond his love and care.[15]

Thus he became a true pilgrim, divinely discontented with the *status quo* of his polytheistic surroundings and lured by the lonely, lofty monotheistic faith he now embraced. In so doing he set the precedent for "pilgrim's progress" to all succeeding generations. He did not consider the nomadic life of a beduoin superior to city-life. He simply was discriminating about the city. He left the wicked city of his birth to become a temporary wanderer because he sought a better city (vv. 10, 16). The unseen heavenly city is better because its architect is God and because its foundations are permanent—*no tent-city this!*

b. Sarah (vv. 11, 12)

By faith Sarah was included in this "hall of fame." Abraham was 100 years of age and Sarah was ten years younger when Issac was conceived (Gen. 17:1, 17, 21). Sarah laughed incredulously at this announcement and was rebuked (Gen. 18:9-15). But

---

13. Wm. Cullen Bryant, "To a Waterfowl," in C. Hill, ed., *op. cit.*, p. 266.

14. D. R. Rose, *op. cit.*, p. 107.

15. J. G. Whittier, "I Bow My Forehead in the Dust," *Hymns of the Living Faith* (Winona Lake, Ind., Light and Life Press, 1951), p. 410.

her faith was linked with that of her husband, and the miraculous birth of Isaac occurred. At least twice in the New Testament the birth of Isaac is compared to a resurrection from the dead (Rom. 4:19; Heb. 11:12; cf. Gal. 4:23). Here the parents, long past the age of child-bearing, are regarded as good as dead. Their faith did not stagger in unbelief at this fact, but rather believed that God was able even to bring life from death, even as Christ was raised from His sepulchre.

The basis for Sarah's faith was the character of the One who made the promise. In spite of the human impossibility involved, she believed that what God had promised He was able to perform. The result of Sarah's faith was innumerable posterity. To most people, and to an Oriental especially, a numerous progeny is the greatest imaginable benefaction. With Abraham's posterity, however, the welfare of all mankind was involved. The descendants of Abraham and Sarah were to be channels of blessing, not merely recipients of blessing.

c. The significance of these witnesses (vv. 13-16)

Before completing his catalogue of witnesses, the author injects a bit of interpretation. He stops recording history to do some editorializing. These witnesses had one thing in common: They were free people having an option of returning to their homeland or seeking a better one. As citizens of two worlds they determined to risk alienation from their neighbors in order to secure "that better part." The point the author makes repeatedly is that these saints were commendable because they perceived the unseen verities of eternity. Samuel Clemens (Mark Twain) is quoted as advising against giving up the certainties of this life for the uncertainties of the next, but the view of the Epistle to the Hebrews is the opposite. These "pilgrim fathers" and mothers had a "divine discontent" with the *status quo*; they sought instead a "better country." Like persons of today are exposed to a certain kind of ridicule and perhaps persecution from their "this-worldly" contemporaries. The parallel is obvious. These patriarchs were migrants, not because of necessity but of choice; they could have returned to the comforts of civilization. The readers likewise could turn again to "the weak and beggarly elements" if they chose to do so (Gal. 4:9). The author seeks to deter them from this by shaming them and simultaneously challenging them by the heroic examples of their forebears.

> I'm far frae my hame, an' I'm weary aftenwhiles,
> For the langed-for hame-bringing an' my Father's welcome smiles;
> I'll ne'er be fu' content, until my een do see
> The shining gates o' heaven an' my ain countree.[16]

Far from being **ashamed** of nomads like these, the Lord God is actually preparing an eternal city for them, a city with sure foundations (cf. John 14:2). Beduoins of the Arabian desert today have a stubborn pride and sense of superiority to urban dwellers. This author would like to see a similar *esprit de corps* among Christian "pilgrims."

d. Abraham and Isaac (vv. 17-20)

The command to offer Isaac as a living sacrifice must have been a greater test of Abraham's faith than the promise that he would have an heir through a son of Sarah. This unusual command must have seemed to Abraham not only cruel but quite inconsistent with the former promises of an heir through Isaac. There is no evidence that Abraham hesitated or evaded the issue; instead he promptly obeyed. This author interprets his obedience as attributable to Abraham's belief in the resurrection, viz., that the promise could be fulfilled even if Isaac were slain in his youth. This could only be possible if Isaac were raised from the dead, married and had children. To all intents and purposes, says our author, Abraham did offer his son as a burnt offering. God accepted the consent of the will instead of the deed. By the torture of testing such as this, Abraham rightly bears the title, "Father of the Faithful," the spiritual ancestor of the three monotheistic religions of mankind— Judaism, Christianity and Islam. James points this out as the evidence that Abraham's faith was genuine. Faith was confirmed and demonstrated by an act (James 2:21). From that time on,

---

16. Mary Lee Demarest, "My Ain Countree," C. Hill, edit., *op. cit.*, p. 743.

Isaac was to his parents as one who had been brought back from the dead. The "binding of Isaac" was later cited by Jewish authors as a commendable example of passive obedience on the part of Isaac.[17] It demonstrated utter obedience on the part of both parent and child, and thus demonstrated a faith, a confidence, a loyalty without precedent. It was this farsighted confidence in Divine Providence that enabled Isaac at the close of his long life to "invoke future blessings" on his sons, Jacob and Esau. Isaac had not the strong, independent, creative character of either his father or his son Jacob, but he did have a rugged faith and is worthy to stand in the patriarchal succession as a custodian of the true faith.

e. Jacob and Joseph (vv. 21, 22)

It is rather remarkable that the author does not mention the faith that led Jacob to make a covenant with Jehovah at Bethel. Nor does he mention the faith that enabled Joseph to persevere under the most severe kind of sustained torture in his youth. By faith Joseph endured the betrayal by his brethren, the libelous accusation of his master's wife, and the ingratitude of his beneficiary. But the theme of this chapter is the type of faith that "endures as seeing the invisible." Thus it is that our author selects for special mention the faith exhibited by the patriarchs when they looked to the future and in this confidence bestowed blessings on their respective posterities. Prominent here is a confidence in God's long-range purpose for His chosen people. It marks the origin of a near-mystic conviction of God's purpose for the nation. This sense of corporate mission and divine destiny is still potent for today among the descendants of these patriarchs. To a large extent this accounts for the survival of the Jews and their recent reestablishment of a homeland. The state of Israel bears witness to the persistence of this mystic bond of kindred, faith, land and destiny, even though Zionism is, to a large extent, a secular movement.

---

17. 4 Macc. 13:12, *Ant.*, I, 232; 1 Clem. 31:3—"Isaac, knowing with confidence what was to be, was gladly brought as a sacrifice."

4. Witnesses during the Exodus (11:23-31)

a. *Moses' choice (vv. 23-28)*

The three greatest characters in Old Testament history are Abraham, Moses and David. There are several ways in which the faith of Moses and his parents was demonstrated. (1) Moses parents refused to destroy their baby, not only because of parental love but because they feared God more than they feared Pharaoh. The fear of the Lord often makes one unafraid of anything or anyone else. The soldiers in Cromwell's army were supine in the presence of God and consequently audacious in the presence of their fellow men.

(2) In his young manhood Moses deliberately chose not to be identified with the splendor of the Egyptian court. Instead he identified himself with his countrymen who were despised slaves. His act of self-denial, his identification with his kinsmen, was his great renunciation. Buddha made a similar renunciation. And a greater than Buddha thought "not the being on an equality with God a thing to be grasped, . . . emptied himself, taking upon him the form of a servant and was made in the likeness of men" (Phil. 2:6, 7). Many persons who rise above their environment are content to "enjoy the pleasures" of their superior status with little regard to their origin. Others, like St. Francis of Assissi, lose their worldly lives to find life more abundant. Moses' greatness lies in his basic choice to cast his lot with his people. This passage implies that this choice was determined by faith, the conviction that God would bring deliverance to his tribesmen. His was in part an enlightened self-interest—"he looked to the reward" (11:26, RSV). This author is not asking that his readers give up something for reasons that are not obvious; he simply urges that they concentrate on the best things available. In a sense this letter has to do with values. The writer exhorts in effect, "Don't let the good become the enemy of the best!"

(3) Faith led Moses to leave Egypt. In this idealized reconstruction of the story, Moses is motivated by loyalty to a higher king than Pharaoh. As one paraphrase puts it, "He defied the king's anger with the strength that came from obedience to the

Invisible King" (JBP). Actually Moses left Egypt because Pharaoh sought to kill him after his murder of the Egyptian (Ex. 2:15). In retelling the story, Hebrews emphasizes the faith that guided and sustained Moses during his forty years in exile. The immediate occasion of his leaving Egypt was fear of Pharaoh; the basic reason, however, was faith in a King greater than Pharaoh who in due time would bring a redress of grievances. Josephus, writing about 90 A.D., had a similar perspective: Moses "left the land taking no supply of food, proudly confident of his power to endure." [18] This was Moses' first "exodus" from Egypt; the second was quite different.

(4) Before the Exodus itself the Passover was observed. In this event the Israelites were spared the destruction of their firstborn which the Egyptians experienced. It served also as a reminder of the greatest day in Israel's colorful history. To have slain animals and sprinkled blood upon every doorpost called for real faith, a faith that was prepared to endure curiosity, scorn and derision from skeptical neighbors. It required a faith that was farsighted and unconditioned by outward, visible evidence.

b. Faith at the Exodus and conquest (vv. 29, 30)

The Exodus from Egypt, the sojourn in the Wilderness of Sinai and the conquest of Canaan constitute the most glorious chapters in the colorful history of Israel. The Exodus signifies the birthplace of the "nation under God." The experience of the deliverance from Egypt taught the people that the God of their Fathers was a God who cares and who keeps His covenant. It also taught them that God is all-powerful. During the Sinai experience they learned of God's providence. The conquest confirmed these earlier lessons and emphasized the importance of their obedience in keeping the covenant. Later generations appealed to the Exodus experience again and again to encourage the people to believe that if God intervened once and brought deliverance, He can be expected to do it again. People in distress could look back

---

18. Jos., *Ant.*, II, 254.

to the history of the Exodus and, on the basis of a *fait accompli*, predict that God would intervene again. In this manner apocalpyses came into being. Prophets, recalling God's mighty acts in the past, "saw" that God, consistent with His own nature and record, could be expected to intervene in the future, defeating His enemies and delivering His people (cf. Isa. 64; Hab. 3; Ps. 80). Writers in the Old Testament recalled the Exodus in a manner similar to the use the New Testament writers made of the resurrection of Christ. Both of these miracles served to demonstrate the fact that by God's timely intervention, foes were humiliated and God's chosen vindicated (cf. Ex. 15; Acts. 3:11-26; Rom. 1:4; Eph. 1:17-23). Not only was the Exodus made possible by faith, but it became the main source of faith for generations to come—"unto this day."

The Pharaoh of the oppression was probably Seti I whose elaborate tomb in the Valley of the Kings near Luxor is one of the largest and most ornate in Egypt. The Pharaoh of the Exodus was probably Rameses II, perhaps the most haughty of the Egyptian pharaohs. His tombs and monuments are to be seen all over Egypt, since he was unsurpassed in advertising himself. There is poetic justice in having the most vain of the pharaohs suffer the ignominy of defeat before the God of Israel. Merneptah, the successor of Rameses, reports having a battle with the Israelites in Canaan, the earliest available extra-biblical evidence of their occupation of the "promised land." [19]

c. At Jericho (vv. 30, 31)

V. 30. The inhabitants of Jericho were badly demoralized even before the arrival of Joshua's army. As the spies learned from Rahab, Isarel's victories east of the Jordan were well known and led to a defeatist attitude on the part of the Canaanites (Josh. 2:11). Before the siege, the people of Jericho were isolated within the walls of the city, expecting the worst (Josh. 6:1). Rahab's family had kept the secret of the visit of the two spies so exceptionally well that she was not suspected of giving aid

---

19. "Israel is laid waste, his seed is not." in J. B. Pritchard, ed., *The Ancient Near East* (Princeton, 1958), p. 231.

and comfort to the enemy. Why the march around the city seven times? Was it psychological warfare? It may well have had the effect of added demoralization. But it was also a witness to the faith of the marchers and their leaders. They ran the risk of ridicule if the city had remained intact. Faith often risks derision. But, "nothing ventured, nothing won."

V. 31. Rahab was apparently one of the few professional women in Jericho. In many countries a house like hers is licensed as a "public house." Some think that the lodging of the spies at her house "was not a matter of accident" (BJV, IV, 530). Some early expositors, embarrassed at the thought of including a prostitute among the faithful, translated *pornē* (cf. pornography) as "landlady!" The faith of the Israelite marchers at Jericho was one of audacity. The faith of Rahab was mainly enlighted self-interest. She was convinced that Jehovah was the God to be reckoned with and hence sought to engratiate herself with the coming victors. She did so at the risk of life of herself and her family. Like Jael she took her stand with the people of God rather than with her own kinfolk (cf. Judg. 4:17). Hers was a clear-eyed, farsighted, calculating faith which correctly appraises values, then acts accordingly—exactly what the readers of this epistle are being urged to do. In cases like this, a decision on the basis of faith alone is good sense as well as good religion.

5. Later heroes and heroines (11:32-40)

a. They witnessed to the faith (vv. 32-38)

V. 32. Some of the greatest characters of the Old Testament were women. Among them were Sarah, Miriam, Deborah, Rahab, Jael, Ruth, Hannah, Judith and Esther. Noteworthy here is the omission of Deborah and the inclusion of her less distinguished colleague Barak. Apparently the author has in mind those of the apocrypha as well as those of the canonical scriptures. Verse 35 apparently contains a reference to the widow of Zarephath (1 Kings 17: 23), the Shunamite mother (2 Kings 4:35), and perhaps the mother of seven martyrs of the second century B.C., a woman who believed in the resurrection (2 Macc. 7:29).

The severity of the persecution reflected in verses 35-38 is nowhere better demonstrated than in the decades of the Maccabbean struggle for the survival of the Hebrew faith and nation (B.C. 178-142). From this struggle came the Pharisees who were at that time the most stalwart defenders of the faith of their fathers. The Apocalypse of Isaiah depicts the prophet placed in a hollow log and sawn in two (cf. v. 37). In short this summary of the faithful embraces all of Hebrew history from the patriarchal period to the dark days of the Seleucid persecution. The moral challenge of heroes and heroines is widely used to bolster morale. The example of a martyr is often more effective than a sermon. It was the assurance of a better future which enabled these witnesses to endure the bitter present. [20]

b. *These witnesses less privileged than we (vv. 39, 40)*

What was it that these heroes and heroines lacked that is available to believers now? They had not been permitted to enter into the holiest, into God's presence (9:9, 12). Their consciences had not yet received the assurance of being fully cleansed (9:9-14). What they lacked was "perfection," the "fitness to enter into the holiest" for immediate communion with God." [21] Theirs was a faith which endured victoriously in anticipation of the new covenant and "better things." This assurance begat endurance. For us, however, faith permits immediate access to God through the "new and living way" pioneered by Christ.

In what sense is the perfection of the fathers' faith dependent upon the present generation (v. 40)? The present generation, that is those under the New Testament dispensation, have the responsibility and privilege of demonstrating the validity of the "better promises" which the witnesses of old envisioned and by which they were sustained. If you fail, the author assures his readers, the faith of the fathers will be invalidated. If the fathers could carry on in anticipation of future blessings, how much more should we endure when these blessings are at last available! But, if these two spiritual generations, the Old Testament saints and the Christian believers, are now united in one common fellowship their confi-

---

20. T. C. Edwards, "Epistle to the Hebrews," *An Exposition of the Bible* (Hartford, Conn.: S. S. Scranton Co., 1904), p. 542.

21. *Loc. cit.*

dence will have not been in vain; they will experience fulfillment or be perfected. Then the church militant and the church triumphant will be united; all will be triumphant. The better thing, therefore, is immediate access to God as provided by the "author and perfecter of our faith."

In summary the faith that is defined and exhibited in this chapter has several characteristics:

(i) Faith is paradoxical in that it "sees" the invisible; it is based upon spiritual rather than sensory perception.

(ii) Faith is confidence in God's faithfulness, accessibility, concern and competence.

(iii) The man of faith may not know what the future holds, but he knows Who holds the future.

(iv) Faith fosters perseverance.

(v) The evidence of faith is prompt obedience.

(vi) Faith is the victory which overcomes the world.

C. Jesus still leads on (12:1-3)

In the Christology of this epistle, the superiority of Jesus' ministry is stressed in chapters 8-13. After elaborating upon His role as minister of a more effective covenant (9-10), the author now concentrates on Jesus as exemplar of a perfect life of faith. The example of Christ is best presented here in the opening paragraph of chapter 12. After challenging his readers to the type of faith exemplified in the fathers, the author presents Jesus as a successful runner who has gone before them to victory. Earlier he had presented Jesus as in the tradition of Joshua, the leader who entered into the promised land. Then he presented Jesus as a high priest who entered into the innermost sanctuary and bids us to follow. Now he presents Jesus as one who endured suffering in view of the ultimate goal of His life. In Paul's letters the emphasis is upon Christ as the object of faith. In Hebrews, Christ is often the example of faith (EFS, p. 183). Jesus' example as heroic leader is similar to the emphasis in the Gospels and in the book of Acts.[1]

---

1. E.g., Matt. 11:3-6; Mark 10:45; Luke 10:28, 37; John 13:15; Acts 1:1, 21; 10:38. Finally, He is seen as the sacrificial victim as in Pauline, Petrine and Johannine theology (7:27; 9:12-14, 25:28; 10:10-14).

In this epistle, Christ is not only the example which we are to follow (Heb. 12:1; cf. 1 Pet. 2:21), but He is also leading us into the presence of God and the culmination of our pilgrimage (Heb. 4:8-10, 14; 12:2). Thirdly, He is the perfecter of our faith (Heb. 12:2; cf. Isa. 53:12; Phil. 2:11). Before us in chapter 12 lies "one of the great moving passages of the New Testament" (WB, 194).

1. We also need to persevere (12:1)

This word-picture marks the climax of chapter 11. The author presents a picture of the arena or stadium in which athletes are competing. Authorities differ as to whether in this analogy the emphasis is upon the spectators looking at the contestants or whether the contestants are looking at the spectators and drawing inspiration from them.[2] But may it not be both? The victors of the struggle now in heaven look with interest on the church militant, and at the same time the church militant looks to these examples for encouragement and challenge. This writer is fully aware of the incalculable privilege that the church militant has in being in this tradition. He now draws the appropriate conclusion from the evidence that he has assembled. This he does in a sentence which begins with the term **therefore.** "How much of the history of philosophy is condensed into that single sentence!"[3]

These witnesses, represented by the preceding heroes and heroines, are compared to a cloud (*nephos*, a term used in classical Greek for a vast multitude).[4] As a runner strips for the race, so these believers are urged to dispense with everything that is not essential so that their race may not be hindered. The **weight** (*ogkon*) is a word normally used to denote excess flesh. The readers were well aware that athletes must discipline themselves before a race by a strict diet and training. The successful runner

2. "The idea is not that they are running in the presence of spectators and must therefore run well; but that their peoples' history being filled with examples of a much enduring but triumphant faith, they also must approve their lineage by showing a like persistence of faith" (M. Dods, *op. cit.*, p. 365).

3. J. Fitch, *Educational Aims and Ideals*, p. 28, cited in J. Moffatt, *op. cit.*, p. 193.

4. Homer refers to "a cloud of foot soldiers" (cf. Isa. 60:8).

must not only dispense with that which is bad but also with that which is not wrong in itself but will nevertheless hinder his race. The laying aside of sin which clings so closely (ASVm) is an analogy familiar in the Pauline letters. Paul urges that the old nature should be put off as a filthy garment (Col. 2:9; 3:9). The analogy of a race is a common one in the New Testament (Phil. 3:12-14; 1 Cor. 9:24, 25; 2 Tim. 4:7, 8) because of the influence of Greece and the Olympic games. Every major city in the Middle East had its stadium or arena. This metaphor was familiar throughout the Roman world.

In view of the issues at stake, the race is worth putting forth every effort. We are exhorted to run with fortitude, with persistence, with steadfastness or with "resolution" (NEB). The term translated here **patience** (*hypmones*) is not merely a passive acquiescence to conditions; it has also the positive, active quality of persistence or endurance. It includes determination.

Thus the author's challenge involved recognition of the privilege of having such inspiring precedents, the challenge to follow their example, the necessity of renunciation, and persistence or endurance.

2. Jesus is our example (12:2)

As he has done before, this author beckons his readers to look within toward Jesus (cf. Heb. 3:1). The term for **looking** (*aphorōntes*) represents a turning from looking at the surrounding spectators to a concentration of the gaze in a single direction (FWF, p. 174). Other spectators fade from vision as the runner sees Jesus only (cf. Mark 9:8). Here Jesus is described as the initiator and consummator of our way of life. These terms for Jesus are described in various versions as "the source and the goal" (JBP), "pioneer and perfecter" (RSV). One version paraphrases it, "on whom faith depends from start to finish" (NEB). The meaning is probably best reflected in the terms "originator and consummator" (HEM). It is similar to the Alpha and Omega of the Apocalypse (Rev. 1:8). Jesus is here presented again as the one who both originates and also carries through to a successful consummation the whole panorama of salvation.

What was the joy that was set before Jesus that led Him to

endure the cross? The term for *anti* normally means "instead of" (Luke 9:11; 1 Cor. 11:15; James 4:15). The term is found in several passages dealing with the atonement (Matt. 20:28; Mark 10:45; and here). However in this passage the context seems decisive in favor of the other meaning, "in view of" (cf. Matt. 5:38; 17:27). This interpretation is in line with several other similar passages in which enduring the cross is to be followed by triumph and glory (Phil. 2:8, 9; 1 Pet. 1:11; 5:4; Isa. 53:11, 12). The joy that awaited Jesus was the joy of fulfilling the will of God (A. Clarke). It was customary for the Christians to envision Jesus as seated at God's right hand, having finished the work that God had given Him to do. The word "seated" typifies victory. He is not fighting for His throne. He is simply occupying it (cf. Heb. 1:3).

V. 3. The readers are asked now to consider Jesus in another role, not as a contestant in an athletic game but rather a victim of persecution. The word translated **consider** (ASV) occurs five times in this epistle and is a translation of four different Greek words.[5] Here and in chapter 3:1 the reader is asked to consider or concentrate on Jesus. The term translated **consider** (*analogizomai*) occurs nowhere else in the New Testament. It comes from the same root as our noun "analogy." Whereas the other terms stress vision, this one stresses reflection. As Peter urged sufferers to look to Jesus and thus gain fortitude to endure, so here the writer urges concentration on Jesus' patient endurance of persecution. This should prevent the tragedy of becoming weary of struggle in a manner similar to the fatigue of athletes *after* the winning of a contest (Aristotle). The danger here is that they will give up *before* they finish the end of the contest.

What does one see when he looks at Jesus, as admonished by this author? He sees Jesus as, first of all, the adventuresome and courageous pioneer who goes ahead and shows the way. He is a traveler, not a bystander. He does not merely coach from the sidelines but, like the traditional war hero, personally leads the assault. Second, Jesus is seen as the one who brings

---

5. *Katanoēsate*—3:1; 10:24; *theōreite*—7:4; *anatheorōuntes*—13:7; and *analogizomai*.

the project to a successful culmination. He has finished His work and leaves nothing more to be done. Third, He has suffered patiently as a martyr, setting the example for His followers. He suffered physical pain, both before and on the cross. In addition He suffered shame and ignominy, both before and on the cross. Fourth, he was triumphant and now reigns with God the Father. His victory under circumstances similar to ours is our guarantee of the certainty of the victory if we follow His leadership.

D. Further appeals to faith (12:4-29)

1. Chastening promotes holiness (12:4-11)

The author's purpose in this paragraph is to convince his readers that suffering for their faith is not something to be offended about but to be welcomed and profited thereby. He begins by saying that "it could be worse." They have not had to lose their lives because of their faith. Some souls in the early days did, including James and Stephen. Toward the end of the first century many others paid with their lives because of their faith, as is reflected in the Apocalypse. Hebrews was probably written in the period of time when the fiercest of the Jewish persecution was waning and the relentless Roman pressure had not yet developed. In the earlier chapters the readers' faith seemed to be threatened, not so much by external coercion as by inward demoralization and lack of faith. Here the emphasis is apparently upon external pressure, serious but not sufficiently severe to jeopardize life itself. After persuading them that "it could be worse," the author then proceeds to give them a rationale of suffering. After the analogy of discipline in the home, he argues that chastening or persecution may be interpreted and even welcomed in the providence of God as something that contributes to Christian maturity (cf. Rom. 5:1-5; James 1:2-4; 1 Pet. 1:6; 4:1, 12-14; Matt. 5:11). Consequently, suffering for one's faith can be fitted into the overall view of God's providence and love because of the end result of suffering. Several attitudes toward suffering are possible. First, there is the stoical attitude of admitting no feeling. Second, an attitude of self-pity is possible; third, there is an attitude of resentment toward God and the persecutor; and fourth, there is the possibility of acquiescence mingled with trust.

This latter gives one a certain buoyancy even in adversity. A faith that is tested is like tempered steel that has resilience and is not brittle. Sometimes one with faith can make a loud profession, but it is a bold front and rather brittle. It often breaks when the real pressure comes. Tempered steel, however, has a certain elasticity which permits it to bend a bit but snap back ready for more. For this reason, a strong wind may bend a willow without breaking it, but the "stronger" but brittle white oak is often dismembered by the storm.

The Roman father was notorious for his seemingly absolute power of arbitrary choice. If he chose to commit his son or daughter to death, no one could challenge his right to do so. In Japan a popular proverb reflects the arbitrary rule of the father. The four "natural calamities" in Japan, we are told, "are fire, typhoon, earthquake and father." With this type of father in mind the author states that we do not question the authority of our fathers to chasten us since they do it for our good. How much more appropriate and imperative it is to subject ourselves to the **Father of spirits**.[1] God's purpose is benevolent and beneficent. He designs that we share His nature or partake of His holiness. It is obvious, therefore, that one path to perfection is the path of chastening. We are assured that God permits His children to suffer because He loves them and is eager that they share His divine nature.

The story is told of an American ambassador to Greece whose name was Perifoy, whose son was a spastic but had a good mind. Included among his Greek playmates was the young prince who said on one occasion to the unfortunate lad, "I think you must be Jesus' favorite pupil." The boy was surprised and asked his father about it. His father, an unbeliever, nevertheless professed to agree with the prince's interpretation. The father, however, could not bring himself to reconcile his personal tragedy with the goodness of God. Later the healthy son suffered in a highway accident, but the other son—the helpless cripple—lived. The father finally came to a position of faith and was able to believe in God's goodness even though he could not see it.

---

1. Perhaps the father of angelic beings; cf. Num. 6:22; Job 12:10; 32:8; 33:4; Eccl. 12:7; Zech. 12:1; Isa. 42:5.

The Christian Scientist seeks to ignore pain. The Buddhist seeks to avoid pain by eliminating desire. The philosopher may attribute pain to blind fate. But to the Christian, pain affords him the opportunity to be made a partaker of God's holiness.[2] The emphasis is upon receptivity. Here also the emphasis is upon receiving His holiness. In other words, the purpose of chastening is to make us more like Christ.

2. Holy living calls for diligence (12:12-17)

a. Holiness should be sought (vv. 12-14)

In view of the beneficent effects of chastening, the readers are now summoned to cease from self-pity and resentment and to become active and disciplined advocates of this way of holiness. The summons to straighten up and to help the weaker traveler is an echo of Scripture (Isa. 35:3 and Ecclus. 25:8, 23; cf. Isa. 40:11). As in chapter 6, so here the reader is exhorted to give all diligence to press on the path toward perfection. The emphasis is not upon despising the chastening (v. 5) but rather on despising the allurements of the world. Aquinas and Luther agreed that the only way for the believer to face the world is to despise it. The saints of the past have advised the believer to first, despise the world; second, despise himself; and third, despise the fact that he is despised.[3] The request for holiness or to be well-pleasing to God should be matched by the quest for peace, or to be well pleasing to one's fellowmen. The latter is more difficult than the former. Jesus did not succeed in His quest for peace with all men, but His quest for holiness resulted in hostility from His fellowmen. However, in practical life there are many areas in which the seeker after personal holiness can labor to be agreeable, to avoid giving offense, to be kind and cooperative under all circumstances. If one yields to the temptation to be vindictive or resentful, he will be diverted from the goal of holiness of heart and life. Holiness as seeing the Lord is brought out in Matthew 5:8. "Blessed are the pure in heart, for they shall see God"; 1 John

---

2. Of the three synonyms of "partakers" (*metochos* and *koinōneiō*), the one used here is *metalambō*). It is found also in 6:7.

3. St. Phillip of Neri, cited by William Barcley, *op. cit.*, p. 197.

3:3, "Everyone that hath this hope . . . purifieth himself, even as he is pure"; and "We shall be like him, for we shall see him even as he is." That it is not always possible to have peace with one's neighbors is indicated in Romans 12:18, but it should always be one's goal. Nearly all believe that holiness is necessary to see God or to dwell in His presence. Those in the Catholic church believe that entire sanctification will be realized in purgatory. Most Protestants believe that it will occur at death. Those in the Quaker and Wesleyan churches believe that it may happen in this life, prior to death. Such would seem to be the case here and in Hebrews 6:1.

b. Holiness may be lost (vv. 15-17)

This is the writer's final warning against the danger of apostasy. Here the danger may not come from without in the form of persecution, but from within in the form of a "root of bitterness." The language is apparently taken from Deuteronomy 29:18. This metaphor may refer to the nurturing of resentment over a real or imagined injury. This will eat like a cancer, but should be faced and rejected at once, by God's grace. In Matthew 18:15-20, we are given a specific procedure for such a situation. Instead of complaining to others about unjust treatment, or continuing in silent hostility, we are urged to confront the brother who offends and tell him the situation so that reconciliation may result. If that step is unsuccessful, we have recourse to the committee of other believers. If this fails, the matter can be referred to the congregation at large. If this third attempt at reconciliation is ineffective, the offender can be excommunicated. He can be thrust out from Christian fellowship. We are repeatedly assured that unless we forgive, we cannot expect to be forgiven.

Another danger is secularism typified here by Esau. So little did he appreciate the unseen values of the future, compared with the material gains of the present, that he recklessly bartered away his birthright for a meal. Jewish commentators often regard Esau as a man "utterly sensual, intemperate and vile" (FWF, p. 178). This author may have been influenced by Philo's similiar view of the subject. The main charge against Esau here was his poor sense of values, his acting on the impulse of the moment rather than being farsighted, deliberate and discriminating. His problem was that when he saw his error later, it was then too late to make the change. The Greek text, as translated by some versions, gives the impression that he was not able to repent ("he found no chance to repent"—NEB). The context in Genesis 25:33 indicates that it was not God who did not repent or restore, but rather Esau's father Isaac who would not alter the blessing, once it had been uttered. The solemn warning here is that the believer who squanders and profanes his privileges in Christ may find a subsequent repentance to be too late. It is likely in the case of Esau that his repentance was more a remorse than a real change of attitude. "Remorse is the consciousness of doing wrong with no sense of love; penitence is the same consciousness with the feeling of sorrow and tenderness added."[4] Esau symbolizes the secularist of today who is so preoccupied with material things that he despises, profanes, makes common the precious things of the Spirit. "As Esau lost the temporal heritage which might have been his, so the writer warns Christians that they may lose the heavenly heritage which is theirs."[5]

3. The superiority of the present dispensation (12:18-24)

a. The former dispensation inspired fear (vv. 18-21)

This paragraph has been described as a summary and climax of the whole epistle (M. Dods). It is indeed "a climax of tremendous eloquence and force" (FWF, p. 180).

b. The present dispensation inspires confidence (vv. 22-24)

As Paul contrasted Jerusalem and Sinai to emphasize the contrast between Jew and Christian, so here the contrast emphasizes the superiority of the new covenant. The warning of the previous paragraph is now followed by encouragement, a procedure so characteristic of this author. The Old Testament Sinai was known

---

4. F. W. Robertson, cited in T. Edwards, ed., *Useful Quotations* (New York: G. Crosset & Dunlap), 1933, p. 543.
5. Robert Shank, *Life in the Son* (Springview, Missouri: Westcott Publishers, 1961), p. 326.

as the "Mount of God," for it was here that Moses received the law, and here also that Elijah received a renewing of his own faith (1 Kings 19). This striking contrast between the old and new covenants is dramatized by the analogy of the two mountains. The contrast may be seen in ten different categories.

MOUNT SINAI	MOUNT ZION
(Privilege)	(Privilege)
Terror	Beauty
Danger	Deliverance
Darkness	Light
Word of God dreadful	Word of God redemptive
Unapproachable	Approachable
Exclusive holiness	Inclusive holiness
A blazing mountain	A company of the redeemed:
	Angels
	Saints
	God, the judge
	Jesus, the mediator
(Responsibility)	(Responsibility)
Blood of Abel (vengeance)	Blood of Jesus (mercy)
Voice from earth	Voice from heaven
Removal	Remaining

God's presence and holiness are associated with both mountains. They have much in common, but all the contrasts favor Mount Zion as over against Mount Sinai. Mount Zion, the poetic name for Jerusalem, came to symbolize heaven in many pages of the New Testament, especially in the book of Revelation.[6] It is remarkable that Christians all over the world so readily accept one historic city in Palestine as symbolic of eternal fellowship between God and the redeemed. In addition to the angels, certain persons on earth are enrolled in heaven in the Lamb's Book of Life.[7] Christians consider themselves "the first born" (James 1:18; Rom. 8:16, 29). The expression **just men made perfect** is a reference to those who are now in heaven. They have experienced

6. The term Mount Zion first denoted the Jebusite stronghold of David, later the temple area north and finally the entire city of Jerusalem.
7. See Mal. 3:16; Ex. 32:32, 33; Luke 10:20; Rev. 13:8; 21, 27.

not only full salvation but final salvation. Here, as in several other places, the term **perfect** denotes those who have experienced the resurrection.[8] Last but not least, Jesus, in contrast to Adam, is presented as the One whose blood cries for mercy rather than for vengeance.

> Five bleeding wounds he bears
> Received on Calvary,
> They pour effectual prayers,
> They strongly plead for me:
> "Forgive him, oh forgive," they cry,
> "Forgive him, oh forgive," they cry,
> "Nor let that ransomed sinner die!"
>
> —Charles Wesley, "Arise, My Soul Arise,"
> *Hymns of the Living Faith*, No. 244.

4. Final warning and appeal (12:25-29)

a. *Refusal means rejection of God (vv. 25-27)*

After showing the vastly superior privileges of the new covenant, the author now emphasizes that it brings a correspondingly greater obligation. We are dealing with the same God as the one who was revealed on Mount Sinai but under more favorable circumstances. The alternation between warning and entreaty is again in evidence. The urgency is brought out in the words **yet once more.** This note of urgency was voiced in the term "today" (3:7-49) and the term "new" (8:13). The readers of the Bible are often reminded of the instability of earthly matters (Ps. 102:25, 26; 2 Pet. 3:10; Rev. 20:11; Heb. 1:12; Hag. 2:6). In contrast is the heavenly kingdom which is unshakable (Dan. 2:44; Heb. 1:12; Rev. 21:1). The emphasis on the instability of things temporal is designed to disturb the complacent (Hag. 2:6; cf. Jer. 48:11). The disturbance is often an aid to faith, to the establishment of new patterns of thought and conduct. When the long, peaceful, prosperous reign of Uzziah ended, Isaiah "saw the Lord" (Isa. 6:1). In the Old Testament the periods of greatest prophetic activity coincided with the times of national turbulence. In world

---

8. Luke 13:32; Phil. 3:12; IV Macc. 7:15. See G. A. Turner, *The Vision Which Transforms* (Kansas City: Beacon Hill Press, 1964), p. 141.

history some centuries experienced more change than others. Centuries which have witnessed a more-than-usual amount of change or revolution include the sixth century B.C., the first century A.D., the seventh century A.D., and the twentieth century. The changes within the memory of adults living today are perhaps more momentous than those of any other similar period of human existence. This could and should lead to repentance and renewal.

b. Grateful acceptance is demanded (vv. 28, 29)

God now deserves the same reverence and awe as the God who revealed himself to Moses on Mount Sinai. If the Israelites responded under those conditions and kept the covenant, how much more should we who are more favored respond with gratitude and reverence. The alternative is judgment, no less now than then. God is a **consuming fire**, and fire usually symbolizes judgment (Amos 1:4-7, 12; Lev. 10:2; Isa. 4:4; Matt. 3:12). Thus the author moves to the climax of his exhortation.

E. Faith exhibited (13:1-25)

1. In the Christian's relationship to others (13:1-6)

a. In brotherly love (v. 1)

The badge of Christian discipleship is brotherly love, "By this shall all men know that ye are my disciples, if ye have love one to another" (John 13:35). Later the pagans generalized on the attitude of the Christians, "Behold, how they love one another." After the tornado that swept through Ohio and Indiana on Palm Sunday, 1965, the Amish communities received nationwide attention by helping the disaster victims rebuild wrecked homesteads. The impression this made upon "the world" was similar to the impression made by the early Christians on the pagan neighbors.

Is there a distinction between brotherly love and love of one's neighbor? The former presumably is more intimate and informal because it is directed specifically to another Christian. The love of neighbor is one of the dominant themes of the New Testament (Matt. 22:39; Rom. 13:9; Gal. 5:14; James 2:8); in each of these passages the word for "love" is *agapaō*. The word for "brotherly love" is *philadelphia,* used here and elsewhere in cognate passages.[1] The essential point is that the Christian's relationship to both his fellow Christians and unbelieving neighbors should be permeated with divine love. Sometimes it takes more grace to love an unpleasant Christian than a congenial non-Christian. Sometimes even monks, nuns, clergymen, missionaries and other saints find it hard to tolerate one another at close range; hence the necessity for this admonition. The zealous Paul found it hard to tolerate halfhearted John Mark at first (Acts 13:13; 15:38; cf. 2 Tim. 4:11). The importance of brotherly love is seen also in the numerous passages urging the unity of the Spirit.[2] This quality of *philadelphia* was an important factor in evangelism during the early centuries. It favorably impressed the heathen and facilitated the gaining of adherents. Today practically all churches vie with each other in professing to be "the friendly church." Proper friendship is the ally of evangelism, but it is no substitute for evangelism. The church of Christ is more than a fraternity or a sorority; it is more than a service club, but it could well include the best features of each.

b. In hospitality (v. 2)

Hospitality, even to strangers, is a virtue widely appreciated among non-Christians, especially in the Orient. A well-known story in Japan concerns a humble peasant who was awakened at night by a stranger who wanted shelter. The farmer not only welcomed the stranger but used the only fuel available, his own precious *bonzai* tree, to warm food for his guest.[3] After the stranger's departure the farmer was invited to a large manorial estate to spend the rest of his days in relative luxury. His guest proved to be the lord of the manor; the peasant had entertained an "angel" unawares!

In Greek culture Zeus, the chief of the gods, was the friend

---

1. E.g., add "to godliness brotherly kindness" (2 Pet. 1:7; cf. Rom. 12:10; 1 Thess. 4:9; 1 Pet. 1:22). See also 1 John 3:16f.

2. Eph. 4:13-16; Phil. 2:1-5; 1 Pet. 4:8.

3. The *bonzai* tree is a dwarf planting in Japanese homes, painstakingly pruned to preserve its diminutive size and prized for generations.

of the traveller. Greek legends include instances in which gods were entertained under the impression that they were ordinary men.[4] Among the ancient Hebrews, for instance, hospitality to strangers was regarded as one of the most demanding of virtues. Lot preferred to have his daughters raped rather than have his guests embarrassed (Gen. 19:8). Similarly the old man in Gibeah was more ready to surrender his daughter's virginity than see his guest mistreated, even though his guest was a perfect stranger (Judg. 19:24). It is reported that Saladin the Moslem warrior, after the battle at the Horns of Hattin, had as captives in his tent the two leaders of the Christian armies. He offered a drink of water only to the one whose life he decided to spare; he would not kill a man after showing him hospitality.

Hospitality to strangers was especially important to the early Christians because they travelled much and were usually impoverished. The inns, when available, were often filthy and charged exorbitant prices.[5] Hospitality also provided an opportunity for witnessing to the traveller. The expression of solicitude for travellers was well known among Christians.[6] It was sufficient to call for the mingled admiration and scorn of the pagans.

c. In sympathy (v. 3)

Another aspect of brotherly love was compassion for prisoners. They probably were those imprisoned for their faith. However, it seems quite clear that solicitude was not limited to imprisoned Christians. Compassion is a virtue characteristic of all those who are Christ-like. The writer is here calling for empathy, for the willingness and capacity for entering sympathetically into the situation of suffering (cf. Rom. 12:15). In the recent civil rights movement thousands of white marchers from Selma to Montgomery, Alabama, sought thus to identify themselves with those deprived of citizenship rights. Jesus is quoted as specifically commending the visiting of prisons (Matt. 25:36). Members of the "Holy Club" at Oxford, led by the Wesleys, became distinguished

---

4. E.g., Homer, *Odyssey*, xvii. 485f.; Plato, *Soph.* 216B; Ovid, *Met.* viii. 626f.
5. Plato, *Laws*, XI, 919.
6. Ignatius, *To the Romans*, IX.

for their zeal in ministering to prisoners. Kagawa in Japan and Ghandi in India both gained international fame for their identification with the underprivileged. Such a concern indeed is said to be the hallmark of the Messiah (Isa. 61:1-3; Luke 4:18, 19). An added incentive to this solicitude is the reminder that "you, like them, are still in the world" (NEB).

d. In chastity (v. 4)

The sacredness of the marriage bond is the third area in which brotherly love must be expressed. This concerns both one's spouse and also others, whether married or unmarried. The rabbis considered sex as a necessary evil, as a symptom of "the evil imagination." However there was not in Hebrew religion the aversion to sex which was often seen in Christian asceticism.[7] Sexual irregularity was commonplace among the sophisticated heathen of the first century. The early Christian evangelists would tolerate no deviation from the high standards of the Judeo-Christian heritage, as is seen in the writings of Paul and others.[8] There is reason to believe that the Christian ethic was even more rigorous than the Hebrew (cf. Matt. 5:27-32). At the same time the wholesomeness of conjugal love is set forth positively and negatively in the pages of the New Testament. Jesus' presence at the wedding at Cana implies as much. The avoidance of marriage on religious grounds is condemned as a heresy (1 Tim. 4:3). The Christian ideal is that of a home in which there is love, purity and mutual respect (Eph. 5:22-33; Col. 3:18-25).

In today's world there seems to be a reversion to the lax sex mores of pre-Christian Greece and Rome. Freudian psychology with its preoccupation with sex and self, minus the God-fearing faith of the fathers, is gradually undermining our moral standards which are not products of a morbid Puritanism or prudish Victorianism but have their roots in our Christian heritage. Apostasy and skepticism pave the way to immorality and eventually the disintegration of moral fibre and of civilization itself. The history

---

7. Old Testament texts which may imply the opposite include Ex. 19:15; 1 Sam. 21:4, 5.

8. 1 Cor. 5:1-13; 1 Thess. 4:3-8; 2 Pet. 2:14.

of many nations testifies to the deadliness of this sequence. The headlines and bylines of today's news are constant reminders of the relevance of the issue today. Spiritual revival and moral renewal are the best safeguards to marital fidelity and wholesome sex mores.

e. In contentment (vv. 5, 6)

Contentment is an important Christian virtue which is not sufficiently appreciated. The opposite of contentment is anxiety which Jesus said is unbecoming to His disciples (Luke 12:22-34; Matt. 6:25-33). Paul exemplified the Master's admonitions when he declared, "I have learned, in whatsoever state I am, therein to be content" (Phil. 4:11). As Paul advised Timothy, "Godliness with contentment (*autarkia*) is great gain" (1 Tim. 6:6-8). How can one be free from anxiety over "the cares of this world" and not be complacent and indolent? Where is the "happy medium"? The answer seems to lie in one's scale of values and also in one's confidence in God's providence. The latter will enable one to trust God for the final outcome, even when the prospects are ominous and foreboding. The former—one's scale of values—is the issue in the challenge to "seek ye first his kingdom, and his righteousness, and all these things shall be added unto you" (Matt. 6:33). Materialism and concurrent secularism threatens to engulf and distort one's sense of true values. Most of us need a periodic reorientation in values. Usually one's adherence to "this world's goods" is in inverse proportion to his commitment to the things of God.

Marxist communism, with its materialistic interpretation of history, has many adherents today. [9] But millions who reject communism as an ideology place the highest value on material possessions rather than upon spiritual "treasures in heaven."

---

9. K. Marx, *The Communist Manifesto*, is said to now have a larger circulation than the Bible. According to Marx the most decisive factor in world history is economics. The history of mankind, he says, is primarily a struggle for material wealth, for "things."

2. In loyalty to leaders (13:7-17)

a. *Imitation of their faith (v. 7)*

Not everything in this section is concerned with leadership, but this theme is central in verses 7, 8, 13, 17 and in much of the subject matter between. In contrast to these good examples is the bad example of those who are led astray by false doctrines (v. 9). The leaders referred to appear to be deceased and in the apostolic tradition, perhaps actual apostles (cf. 2:1-4).[10] The importance of loyalty to leaders is often stressed in the New Testament (1 Thess. 2:1-14) and even in later writings such as Ignatius' letters and the *Didache*. The absence of the canonical New Testament in the early decades and the threat of rival heretical leaders made this matter of proper leadership very important. Today, likewise, there are "charismatic" leaders who often attract a large following, especially of believers poorly grounded in the Christian faith. Many are converted to the leader more than to Christ. The task of the pastor or evangelist is poorly done if his converts have difficulty in transferring their allegiance to Christ.

b. *The unchanging Christ (v. 8)*

Having emphasized the necessity of following spiritual leaders, the author now turns to the subject of Christ as the leader of these leaders, the One who does not vacillate.

The term "consider" appears five times in this letter and is one of the distinctive terms of this writer. Readers are asked to consider (*katanoēsate*) Jesus as their great leader and pioneer (3:1) and to consider also one another (10:24) for mutual stimulus. They are also invited to consider (*theōpeite*) or reflect on Melchizedek (7:4), and also to consider (*anatheōpountes*) or appreciate their recent leaders (13:7). They are urged to consider

---

10. These leaders (*hēgoumenoi*) are mentioned also in vv. 17, 24; cf. Clem., 1 *ad Cor.* 1. The term was later applied to bishops and abbots; see B. F. Westcott, *op. cit.*, p. 434.

(*analogisasthe*) Jesus as "author and perfecter" of their faith (12:3). Twice their attention is directed to Jesus as leader, and once to Melchizedek; twice their attention is directed to other Christians. The purpose behind these exhortations is to incite the readers successively to follow (3:1), to inquire (7:4), to stimulate (10:24), to imitate (12:2), and to obey (13:7). [11] Christian growth, stability, and maturity are likely to follow from "considerations" of this kind.

V. 8. This familiar verse gives assurance to any who are disturbed by the passing of the former leaders, mentioned in verse 7. It is consistent with other claims of the eternity of the Christ, "Before Abraham was born I am"; and "I am the first and the last." [12]

A major factor in the frequent apostasies of the people of the old covenant was the transition from one leader to another, or from a trustworthy leader to no leader. After the death of Joshua and the death of his contemporaries, "there arose another generation after them, that knew not Jehovah, nor yet the work which he had wrought for Israel" (Jud. 2:10). The tragic cycles of apostasy dominating the period of the judges resulted. Good leaders like Hezekiah and Josiah were succeeded by kings who were both weak and bad. By contrast, the Christians have in Jesus Christ a leader who does not depart but remains. He does not change in character and competence as did Solomon but remains eternally the same. Christians who consistently obey are assured of His constant presence—even "to the end of time" (*aiōn*)—NEB. The fact gives stability to the individual believer. It is a safeguard against leaders who appear with **divers and strange teachings.** It also assures the continuity and triumph of the Christian community.

c. Sound doctrine important (v. 9)

The hazards to which the infant church was exposed seemed all but overwhelming. In addition to the hostility of unbelieving

---

11. Of these synonyms, "to fix one's mind upon" (*katanoeō*) is the most common—e.g., Matt. 7:3; Luke 6:4; 22:23; Acts 27:39; James 1:23 *et al.*

12. John 8:58; Rev. 1:17; 2:8; 22:13; cf. Isa. 41:4; 44:6; Mal. 3:6.

Jews there were the internal dangers of personal defections, of perversion through false teachings and of factionalism. The latter peril was augmented by the fact that in the early decades there was no generally acknowledged body of authoritative writings. The New Testament, as such, was not universally accepted until the fourth century. [13] The first century of our era was one of unusual intellectual and spiritual ferment. This fact made it relatively easy to launch a new religion but it also facilitated its perversion by the assimilation of elements foreign to its nature. It was an age of eclecticism, of cultural borrowing. The church was confronted, among other things, with the task of determining how much of the Old Testament and Judaism should be retained and how much should be ignored. The first historical attempt to face this issue was the Jerusalem Conference (Acts 15). They were also required to decide how much of paganism was harmless and how much was dangerous and had to be rejected. This conflict is reflected in Paul's advice to the churches under his care (Rom. 15:1 Cor. 5). It is reflected also in the decision of Justin Martyr to pose as a Christian philosopher and of Clement of Alexander to pose as a Christian gnostic. [14] Likewise in each age and place the Christian must constantly decide to what extent and in what respects he can be a citizen of this world and in what respects he cannot. He will be in the world but not of the world. The criteria by which his decisions must be made include the Scriptures, historical precedent, example of others, advice from good people, the Spirit of God, and his own reason.

The contrast here is between **grace** and **meats**, between the inner spiritual reality and external ritual. This corresponds to the contrast Paul made between the circumcision of the flesh and that of the heart (Rom. 2:25-29). It is the perennial contrast between obedience and sacrifice, between the moral and the liturgical (1 Sam. 15:22; Hos. 6:6; Matt. 9:13; 12:7).

---

13. The Easter letter of Bishop Athanasius (c. 367 A.D.) was the first to present a list of New Testament books identical to ours.

14. Justin wore his philosopher's robe and Clement described the ideal "gnostic" in "Stromata," Book VII (*Ante-Nicene* Fathers; New York: Chas. Scribner's Sons, 1903), II, 523ff.

d. *The two altars (vv. 10-16)*

(1) *The Old Testament system (vv. 10, 11)*

Within this section (10:19-13:25), most of which is devoted to exhortation, there occur additional bits of instruction. This paragraph is one of the most difficult in the entire letter. What does he mean by the **altar?** Is it a Jewish altar or a Christian altar? If it is a Christian altar, does he have in mind the cross (J. Wesley), the mercy-seat (Peake), the Eucharist in the upper room (W. Manson), the cleansed heart (Creed), or Christ himself (Calvin)? [15]   The author is contrasting the atoning work of Christ with the Day of Atonement when the high priest entered the holiest place once annually. On this occasion the blood of the bullock and goat was brought into the holiest place while their bodies were burned outside (Lev. 16:27). Four victims were offered: a ram for a burnt offering, and a bullock and two male goats for sin offerings (Lev. 16:3, 5). The blood of the victims was brought within the veil to hallow the mercy seat, the incense altar and the tabernacle itself. The fat of the sin offering was burned upon the great altar in the court yard (Lev. 16:25). Presumably the ram for the burnt offering was also consumed by fire on this altar. Afterwards the carcasses of the two animals (exclusive of the scapegoat) were not used for food but were burned outside the encampment (Lev. 16:27). Therefore for the Christian, that altar is the place of sacrifice, i.e., the cross. Since the worshippers did not eat the victims on the Day of Atonement, there is nothing in this ceremony to suggest the Christian eucharistic meal.

The main point seems to be that the Christian gospel calls for a separation from Judaism with its cultic practices. Such is the repeated emphasis of Paul, although Paul and the other leaders continued to pray in the temple. To press the analogy further, the Christian has access to the innermost sanctuary by the blood of Christ, as the high priest had on the Day of Atonement.

(2) *Sanctification provided outside the camp (vv. 12-14)*

After following Christ into the holiest place for entire sanctifi-

---

15. For a fuller explanation see T. Hewitt, *op. cit.*, pp. 209-215.

cation we need to follow Him in His exclusion and isolation from "the world," as witnesses of His triumphant resurrection. The movement of the epistle is twofold. There is the necessity of pressing on unto perfection, of following Jesus within the veil (4:16; 6:1, 20; 9:24; 10:19-22). There is also the necessity of going forth into the new community of the redeemed, sharing Jesus' reproach. Thus the author seeks to emphasize the importance of withdrawal from the "city of destruction," from the world that crucified Jesus, from Judaism, into the new but despised Christian community and **an abiding city** which is to come. "It is not [only] the irreligious but the religious world from which we must go out—that, is from everything that is not in harmony with His cross and its spirit of self-sacrifice." [16]

After Henry Lyte experienced an evangelical conversion, he was thrust out from his parish. As he left he prayed:

Jesus, I my cross have taken, all to leave and follow thee.
Naked, poor, despised, forsaken; Thou henceforth my all shall be.
Perish every fond ambition, all I've sought or hoped, or known;
Yet how rich is my condition; God and heav'n are still my own.

What is the connection between sanctification and Jesus' suffering without the gate? Wherein lies the parallel? In the old covenent the victim's blood sanctified the sanctuary and the body was incinerated outside the encampment. What is the significance of going outside the gate to Jesus in order to be sanctified? He is not referring here to eating of the flesh of Christ in a sacramental sense. [17] This is indicated by his failure to allude to the Eucharist at any time in his epistle when he might conveniently have done so. It is rather a spiritual concept in which the emphasis is upon "grace" and not upon food. [18] The point is that the beasts for the sin offering, after serving as the atonement for the priest and the nation, were not eaten in the sanctuary

---

16. A. Murray, *op. cit.*, p. 531.

17. As for example in John 6:53—"unless you eat the flesh of the Son of man and drink his blood you have not life in you" (RSV).

18. Cf. Rom. 5:2, 15; 1 Cor. 15:10; Eph. 2:5, 7, 8; 2 Thess. 2:16; Heb. 2:9; 4:16; 10:29.

as were some of the offerings. Instead the sin-bearing carcass was burned outside. This exclusion from the purified camp was also the pattern with reference to the scapegoat (Lev. 16:21, 22), the sin-offering of the red heifer (Num. 19:2-6), and the relocation of the tent of meeting outside the sinful camp (Ex. 33:7). In the latter instance the reverse process is in effect: the community is infected with sin; hence the removal of the entire sanctuary to a separate location. The parallel is not exact in every detail, but the author's clear intent is to emphasize the twofold fact that Jesus' lifeblood makes possible the atonement and that those who have shared in this new life must separate themselves from the old system and follow Jesus only.

Sanctification here means bringing the people to God "as worshippers purified in conscience" (FFB); it involves being "set apart as holy" (MRV). It is identification with the truth which necessitated Jesus' separation from the community that rejected Him. Much in this letter stresses following a leader. Here again the emphasis is upon following Jesus, "bearing the stigma that he bore" (NEB). The justification for this procedure is that we seek a better city than that which now rejects Christ (cf. 11:10, 14, 16). It is better because it is more enduring, although at present it is less obvious.

(3) Acceptable sacrifices (vv. 15, 16)

Although the Christian does not have an external paraphernalia of ritualistic worship, he is not without sacrifices. But the Christian's sacrifices are spiritual in nature. This feature of the new covenant was anticipated in the old: "I will not reprove thee for thy sacrifices: and thy burnt offerings are continually before me. I will take no bullocks out of thy house, nor he-goats out of thy folds . . . for the world is mine, and the fulness thereof. . . . Offer unto God the sacrifice of thanksgiving" (Ps. 50:8-14; cf. Ps. 27:6; 69:30; 107:22; 116:17; Hos. 14:2). Although the sacrifice of Jesus is completed, the praise continues. The nature of this praise is the "confession" (*homologia*) of the Christian faith. The noun and verb of this term occur four other times in Hebrews (3:1; 4:14; 10:23; 11:13), making it one of the distinctive terms of this letter.

V. 16. The other side of Christian confession is to match words with deeds. Hence the charge **to do good and to communicate** (*koinōnias*). The first is praise directed to God; the second is benevolence directed towards man—good religion as described in the Bible, as having this dual polarity. The "vertical" relationship to God is good only if the "horizontal" relationship to others is good. This dual emphasis is the constant theme of a variety of scriptures in a variety of places.[19]   It is an emphasis common to both Old and New Testaments. The rabbis used to say that the world rests upon three pillars: the Torah, the cultus, and charity or benevolence. They considered good works as of equal importance with the Commandments and the temple worship. In rabbinic stories about who should experience the joys of "the world to come," a humble man of inconspicuous piety is pictured as in heaven because he showed mercy to someone in need (cf. Luke 16:25; Matt. 25:31-46). Benevolence—the showing of compassion—characterized the early church from the start, as evidenced in collections for famine relief (Acts 11:29). This concern for others is described by Harnack as one of the reasons for the rapid spread of early Christianity.[20]   Where the Christian Church has kept in touch with her Head, a readiness for this kind of "communication" may be found.

e. Obedience to leaders (v. 17)

The thought here is linked with verse 7 where they were reminded of the example left by their former leaders (v. 7). The language of the exhortation with its deferment to leaders (*hēgoumenoi*)- is similiar to the exhortations of Ignatius of Antioch who constantly urged obedience to the bishop (*episkopos*).[21]   The matter of discipline is a constant problem in the Christian Church. Without discipline, anarchy ensues. Christianity places the main stress upon the worth of the individual, upon the growth of personality. This may lead to tensions among those whose claim to leadership

19. E.g., James 1:27; Isa. 1:11-17; Amos 5:21-24; Hos. 6:6; Matt. 22:36-40; 1 John 4:20.

20. A. Harnack, *Mission and Expansion of Christianity.*

21. E.g., Ignatius, "To the Ephesians," iv (Loeb Library, *The Apostolic Fathers*), I, 177.

is precarious. The church traditionally follows this admonition; it is not an agency for revolt or even insubordination. What happens if the leaders are going in the wrong direction? These leaders were not of that type, but were "tireless in their concern" (NEB). The appeal is similar to that voiced by Paul when writing to the Corinthians (2 Cor. 1:14). The ideal type of government is a *benevolent* and judicious autocracy. But if the leader is not a good one, it can be the worst type of government. But with leaders such as described here the believer's obligation is clear—he must "defer to them" (NEB).

3. Conclusion (13:18-25)

a. Prayer requested (vv. 18, 19)

It was customary for Paul to request prayer for himself and his work. Before making this request the writer searched his heart to see that there were no hindrances to prayer. The self-examination assures him that his conscience is free from guilt from such sins as unworthy motives. The Psalmist recognized that, "If I regard iniquity in my heart, the Lord will not hear me" (Ps. 66:18). Nothing hinders prayer like unconfessed sin (Isa. 59:2). Wrong motives also make prayer ineffective (James 4:3). For this reason the writer's good conscience assures him that prayer will be effective. "If our heart condemn us not, we have boldness toward God" (I John 3:21). This writer believes that "prayer changes things" and that prayer affects God's providences in the lives of His saints. Some think it naive to believe that the petition of an individual or group has any influence on events. But men of faith know otherwise.

b. Benediction (vv. 20, 21)

This benedictory prayer is the greatest in all the Scriptures. It is not only a benediction but gathers up into itself the thrust of the entire letter in one climactic petition. The gist of the prayer is to "perfect" (KJV, ASV, NEB), a better translation than the RSV "equip" because it is more positive and inclusive. The aim of being well pleasing to God is the sum total of Christian perfection.

This emphasis on pleasing God is another characteristic of

this epistle. The language suggests a servant whose chief objective is to cause his master satisfaction with his performance. This is impossible apart from faith (11:6). Enoch pleased God (11:5). The same term in chapter 12:28 affirms that our service can be pleasing to God (cf. Rom. 12:1, 2). The correctly oriented soul is like Jesus (John 8:29) in that its chief concern is to please God as a lover seeks to be pleasing to his beloved.

> I want the witness, Lord, that all I do is right,
> According to thy will and word, well-pleasing in thy sight."
>
> —Charles Wesley

c. Postscript (vv. 22-25)

(1) Final appeal (v. 22)

The author calls his letter a "word of exhortation." This describes the treatise well. Unlike Paul's letters which begin with instruction and end with exhortation, this letter intersperses exhortation throughout, as the following graph indicates.

EXHORTATION		EXPOSITION	
Ref.	No. of verses	Ref.	No. of verses
2:1-4	4	1:1-14	14
3:7—4:16	29	2:5-18	14
6:1-12	12	3:1-6	6
10:19-39	21	5:1-14	14
12:1, 2	2	6:13—10:18	95
12:13-17	5	11:1-40	40
12:25—13:9	14	12:3-11	9
13:13-25	13	12:18-24	7
		13:10-12	3
Total	100	Total	202

Thus exhortations total about one third of the letter. They are spread throughout the letter but are concentrated toward the end. This feature has led some to identify the author as Barnabas, a man surnamed by the apostles "son of exhortation" (Acts 4:36). This letter appears to have a larger proportion of exhortation than any of the other New Testament epistles. The author's attitude is not so much that of one having apostolic authority, nor one claiming deference as an elder, nor one entitled to respect because he was a spiritual father or founder; he speaks rather as a teacher, one whose words and arguments must be considered on the basis of their intrinsic merit rather than being dependent for their authority on the prestige of the writer.

(2) Personal greetings (vv. 23, 24)

Further evidence of authorship is to be sought in the fact that Timothy is referred to as a brother; it implies that Paul was not the author, since Paul usually referred to Timothy as his son in the gospel. This is the only evidence of Timothy's imprisonment. Since Nero died in 68 A.D., since the letter was apparently written prior to 70 A.D., and since the release of prisoners is more likely after the death of a monarch, one is left with a conjectural date of 69 A.D. as the time of this writing.

A feature common to both secular and sacred epistolary literature of the early centuries was the personal felicitations. The **rulers** are probably presbyters, deacons and overseers; the **saints** (*hagioi*) are the members of the Christian community. The term "saint" was the common designation of a Christian. It was applied to the Corinthian church, even though these members are later described as "carnal" or immature (1 Cor. 1:2; 3:1; cf. Rom. 1:7). The word in these contexts does not designate a superior type of piety but rather designates separation: the "saints" are those separated from the world and separated unto Christ; in this sense all Christians are "holy ones."

The inclusion of brethren in Italy in the salutation implies Italy as the place of the epistle's origin. If Italy is the place of origin, Jerusalem or some city in the Near East could well be its destination.

(3) Invocation of grace (v. 25)

This benediction, coming after that of verses 20, 21, is a bit anticlimactic. **Grace** (*charis*) is the most common factor in epistolary salutations, both sacred and secular. "Peace" was and still is the common Hebrew (and Moslem) form of greeting. "Grace" suggests more of the Greek influence. The term connotes graciousness, gratitude, favor and sometimes joy (M-M). Its Old Testament ancestry conveys the meaning of favor, either of master toward servant or of Jehovah toward the worshipper.[22]   Paul usually combined this term with peace. Grace in its Greek setting often denoted physical beauty and gracefulness. In its Semitic setting it means blessing, the bestowal of a benefaction. Its distinctive Christian meaning is that of a bestowal of the divine nature on the believer, the impartation of righteousness (Eph. 2:8; Rom. 5:15, 17).

The King James version has a subscription that reads, "Written to the Hebrews from Italy by Timothy.[23]   But this is not in the original letter.

Thus the author closes his "word of exhortation," a treatise which is priceless, presenting as it does Jesus Christ as the high priest who offered himself, and challenging readers now as well as then to follow this leader into the throne-room of the Most High.

---

22. Cf. Ruth 2:2, 10, 13; Gen. 39:21; Ex. 11:3; Num. 11:15.

23. As Stuart observes, "It is demonstrably erroneous here; for how could Timothy write this epistle, when the author says, at its very close, that Timothy was *then absent?*" (*op. cit.*, p. 538).

Some Basic Concepts
of the Epistle

A. Some "key words"

1. "Better"

This treatise or epistle is largely structured in terms of comparison and contrast. The basic comparison is between the Old Testament and the New, between the leaders of the old dispensation and Jesus Christ and between the Law and the Gospel. Indeed, a "key word" of this letter is "better." Occurring 13 times in this letter is *kreitton*, where it is employed to show that Jesus Christ is better than angels (1:4), serves a better priesthood (7:7), sponsors a better hope (7:19), mediates a better covenant (7:22; 8:6) based upon better promises (8:6), and provides a better sacrifice (9:23). As a result believers count on better treasures (10:34), inherit a better country (11:16), anticipate a better resurrection (11:35), and share in a better inheritance (11:40; 12:24).

Three times the comparison employs the term often translated "more excellent." Thus Christ is worthy of more glory than even Moses (3:3) because the Creator is entitled to more honor than His creation. He notes in addition that Abel is in the "Hall of Fame" because his offering was more excellent (*pleion*) than that of Cain (11:4).

Thus by the use of three synonyms in more than 18 instances, the comparisons show the superiority of the Christ to His predecessors, the superiority of the new covenant and the greater privileges it bestows upon its participants. In addition to these impressive statistics there is a constant emphasis on the superiority of the new covenant to the old. Three points are stressed as evidence of this superiority: (1) the superiority of Christ to prophets, angels, and Moses; (2) the superiority of Christ's priesthood (4:14-14-7:28); and (3) the superiority of Christ's sacrifice (8:1-10:39) (B. Metzger, *Oxford Annotated Bible*, 1962, p. 1453).

Dominating the whole is the unique superiority of Jesus, the Son of God and Son of man. Jesus is seen to be superior in His *person*, viz., superior to prophets (1:1, 2), to angels (1:5-2:5), to Adam (2:6-18), to Moses (3:2-6), to Joshua (4:8), to Aaron (5:1-10), and even to Abraham (7:1-10). Jesus is also superior, not only for what He is but also for what He does—because of His *work*. He provides the believer with a superior priesthood (7:11-28), a more effective covenant (8:1-13), a heavenly sanctuary (9:1-22), a superior sacrifice (9:23-10:18); consequently the believer faces the prospect of a better country (11:16), a better city (11:10, 16; 12:22), and a better resurrection (11:35; 13:21).

The following diagram makes the comparison stand out more conspicuously.

JESUS

HIS PERSON	HIS WORK
He is superior to	*He provides a better*
Prophets (1:1, 2)	Resurrection (11:35; 13:21)
Angels (1:4-2:4)	City (11:16-12:28)
Adam (2:5-18)	Country (10:19-11:16)
Moses (3:1-18)	Sacrifice (9:23-10:18)
Joshua (4:1-14)	Sanctuary (9:1-22)
Aaron (4:15-6:20)	Covenant (8:1-13)
Abraham (7:1-10)	Priesthood (7:11-28)

The basis for the claim of superiority for the new order is varied. Sometimes the author argues that the new is better because the old has been tested and found wanting, as in the case of Adam (2:8), Joshua (4:8), the priesthood (5:3), the law (7:18, 19), and animal sacrifices (9:9; 10:2-8). At other times he argues that since the new is given, the old is thereby rendered obsolete (8:7-13). Often the superiority of the gospel is considered axiomatic and self-evident since it is heavenly rather than earthly (4:14; 9:23-28; 11:16), permanent rather than changeable (6:16-19; 13:8), final rather than provisional or repetitive (10:10-18), spiritual rather than physical (9:1-6, 11), human rather than beastly (10:13, 14), eternal rather than temporal (7:23, 24; 12:27), attractive rather than repulsive 12:18-28). While Peter speaks of believers as pilgrims (or aliens—I Pet. 1:17; 2:11), en route to a better homeland, and Paul speaks of the Christian life as a race, Hebrews places even greater stress on "pilgrim's progress" toward the heavenly homeland of the soul. This author is concerned with movement; the Christian life is viewed as a journey toward a better land comparable to Israel's pilgrimage from Egypt to Canaan. Leading the pilgrims is Jesus himself in whose victory lies the assurance that the believer will also be victorious if he "runs with patience" like Jesus (12:1, 2).

The emphasis on living in two worlds with a dual citizenship is like that of John's Gospel but with a difference in idiom. John speaks of spiritual life as having begun now, as having already bypassed judgment and entered into real life (John 3:18-21; 5:24; 6:58; 8:51, 52). In Hebrews the believer experiences life only by faith and anticipation (4:14; 10:19-24), the stress being not so much upon the immediate subjective effects (as in Paul) but upon the conditions and consequences of salvation.

Scott has pointed out that the eschatology of this epistle is "more advanced than that of the St. Paul" and less "advanced" than that of St. John. He states also that in this letter is an inconsistent mixture of Hebrew apocalypticism and of the Greek idea of the heavenly world as the spiritual counterpart of the present world (EFS, p. 120). But Scott overstates his case. This author repeatedly reflects his acceptance of "primitive" Christian expectations of the *parousia* and at the same time employs the imagery of the tabernacle to stress the superiority of the spiritual and eternal over the material and temporal. Belief in the present intercession of the high priest does not preclude an expectation of his reappearance in glory "at the end of days."

2. "Consider"

"Consider" occurs (ASV) five times in the epistle.[1] The reader is exhorted to "consider" (*katanōesate*) Jesus as apostle and high priest (3:1). This calls for a careful, thoughtful, contemplative scrutiny of the Saviour (cf. Matt. 7:3; Luke 6:41; Acts 7:31; Rom. 4:19). The same term connotes careful concern for one's brethren (10:24)—"let us consider how to stir up one another to love and good works" (RSV).

The reader is asked to "consider (*theoreite*) how great this man was, a reference to Melchizedek (7:4). The verb calls for a careful survey (as in a theater). It is another challenge to meditation and further study, a summons to see and to reflect.

We are asked again to "consider" (*analogisasthe*) Jesus as exemplifying victory in spite of adversity (12:3). Here the verb connotes a "reckoning" or an "accounting" as Jesus did when facing the cross (M-M, p. 36).

The readers are again summoned to "consider" (*anatheōrountes*) their leaders appreciatively and to follow their example. The verb means to "survey up and down" and is found only once elsewhere in the New Testament (Acts 17:23).

Three different synonyms are employed in challenging the readers of this letter to investigate, to reflect and then to act. Thrice attention is focused on Jesus. From these and similar passages (e.g., 2:9; 4:14; 5:5; 8:1; 10:19; 12:24; 13:13) we recognize in Jesus Christ the courageous leader and exemplar (3:1; 12:3), the faithful high priest, and the victorious Saviour of mankind (1:3; 12:2). A challenge to love and loyalty was never presented more winsomely and persuasively.

3. "Partakers"

"Partakers" is another "key word" which has been treated in some detail where it occurs in the text of the commentary proper. The term appears a total of seven times in this letter.[2] It means sharing, participating, identification, involvement. The kinship of

---

1. 3:1; 7:4; 10:24; 12:3; 13:7.
2. *Metochos, metochō*: 1:9; 2:14; 3:1, 14; 6:4; 7:13; 12:8.

the Son of God with the human race is indicated several times: "beyond thy comrades" (1:9, RSV), sharing in human nature (2:14; cf. 5:7). Believers also share in Christ's salvation in a manner similar to the Pauline phrase "in Christ" (3:14; 6:4). The kinship among believers is also indicated by this term: "brethren, who share in a heavenly call" (3:1, RSV), sons are partakers of chastening (12:8); cf. Melchizedek "belonged to another tribe" (7:13, RSV).

The idea of believers partaking of God's holiness is expressed by *metalambanō*; it is the result of chastening (12:10; cf., 6:8). The third term (*koinōreō*) is used to designate the sharing in flesh and blood which Jesus and God's children experience in common (2:14; cf., 13:16).

The most significant feature of this characteristic in style is the emphasis on participation by Jesus in human nature and the believer in the divine nature. No New Testament author makes it more emphatic and none does so in just this manner. Like Paul, the author often equates the Holy Spirit with the Spirit of Christ (3:14; 6:4). The intimacy and vitality of the relationship of believer to his Lord and of believers to each other receives special emphasis here because the author is eager that his readers distinguish between what is only the correct and time-honored ritual and what is the reality of Christ. He knows that if this is lost or even lightly esteemed, their faith and Christianity itself is jeopardized.

B. Christology

Although in basic harmony with the other portions of the New Testament, the Epistle to the Hebrews presents some distinctive emphases which should be noted. In common with Paul, this author stresses the vicarious atonement of Christ. Although not using the terms atonement, expiation, reconciliation, justification or propitiation, this author speaks of a substitutionary atonement under similar but different idioms. Instead of the language of jurisprudence such as "justification," he uses the language of the sanctuary such as "purification" (1:3; 10:22). He speaks less of God's righteousness than Paul in Romans but more of God's holiness. It is a difference of language and emphasis only, not of basic theology.

1. The Person of Christ is divine and yet human. He seldom uses Paul's favorite term—the term "Christ"—but prefers instead cognomens as "Son," "Jesus," "High Priest," "Author," "Pioneer," and "Perfecter." In speaking of His divine nature this writer prefers the term "Son" (12 times) rather than "Christ" (9 times). Paul uses "Christ" ten times to "Son" once. This is a "high Christology" like that of Paul and John, yet is somewhat more precise than either. In describing the nature of the Son as the "effulgence of God's splendor and the stamp of God's very being" (1:3, NEB), he goes as far as language permits in making the Son like the Father in nature and yet distinct in person. It is even more precise than Paul's "nature (*morphē*) of God" (Phil. 2:6) or John's "My Father and I are one" (John. 10:30, NEB); it defines the intimate relationship more explicitly.

In spite of the author's high Christology, he stresses Jesus' humanity to an equal degree. It is here that he is most original and bold among the early Christian writers. The author's purpose is to present Christ as a sympathetic and approachable mediator. Consequently he presses home the fact that Jesus shares human nature to the fullest (2:5-18), even to the extent of suffering the common trials of humanity, including death itself (5:7-10; 12:3; 13:12). In addition He suffered uniquely, like the Hebrew scapegoat, a vicarious death for others (2:9; 10:13; 13:21). The boldness and originality of this author appears also when he calls Jesus "the apostle," the "high priest," the initiator and completer of faith (3:1; 12:2), terms found nowhere else in the New Testament.

The chief contribution to Christology made here is in depicting Jesus both as a high priest and the sacrificial victim. E. F. Scott notwithstanding, there is little "Alexandrian speculation" in this sphere of his thinking (EFS, p. 146). In most of the epistle, he dwells on the tabernacle in the wilderness and its provision for dealing with sin. He labors to show that as high priest Christ had all of Aaron's merits of sympathy and accessibility but none of his defects of personal sin and mortality. His incarnation and earthly life was only an interlude in His continuing life as Son of God, "an episode in a higher existence, which had suffered no real interruption" (EFS, p. 152). Had the Church been able to keep the truth of Christ's real humanity in perspective, the veneration of martyrs, saints, "the mother of God" and icons would never have usurped the adoration merited by Christ alone.

2. The work of Christ is stressed here even more than His person. The first seven chapters are concerned primarily with Christ's person—who He is, and chapters eight and the following chapters primarily with His work—what He does.

Like other early writers this author is concerned only incidentally with Jesus' earthly ministry to the needy of Palestine. His emphasis is upon Jesus' incarnation and death. He believes in the resurrection but places less stress upon it than Paul. The work of Christ as emphasized in this treatise had two uses: the vicarious death in the past as victim, and the present ministry of intercession as high priest.

Missing in this epistle is the Pauline emphasis on reconciliation (*katallagē*).[3] Missing also is the Johannine language of "Lamb of God" and "Good Shepherd," but the same truth appears as "sacrifice" and "offering" and "blood." Here the emphasis shifts from the lamb of the Passover, stressed in John and Paul, to the scapegoat and the Day of Atonement. The main emphasis here is expressed in sacerdotal language, cleansing, sanctifying, perfecting.

Here, paradoxically, Christ the high priest enters the inner sanctuary carrying His own lifeblood. The offering and the offerer are the same. Also, paradoxically, His work is finished and yet continues. As the sacrificial victim His work is finished once and for all time. Consequently He is *seated* on the throne as evidence that the work is complete (1:3; 7:27; 9:25-28; 10:12). Although His work as offering is complete His work as intercessor continues and His second advent is anticipated (2:18; 4:16; 6:20; 9:28). Always this author's concern is more practical than theoretical. He is eager that his readers experience the benefit of Christ's atonement and persevere in this faith and hope.

---

3. G. B. Stevens, *The Theology of the New Testament* (New York: Scribner's, 1899), p. 513.

C. Covenant or testament?

The idea of covenant (*diathēkē*) is related to the mediatorial work of Christ and is therefore a basic theme of the entire epistle.[4] The term occurs seventeen times in this letter, of which six are quotations from the Old Testament. In six of these instances the term refers to the Sinaitic covenant and nine occurrences designate the new covenant.[5] Twice the term is found in a context which defines it not as a mutual agreement but as a will, a testament or a bequest (9:16, 17).

The old covenant in the evangelical sense began with Abraham. The rainbow covenant with Noah was universal in its application, unilateral and unconditional. This was not true of the Abrahamic covenant which was initiated, tested and reiterated repeatedly in Genesis and later.[6] It was restated by Yahweh at Sinai, at Shechem, at Gilgal (1 Sam. 12), at Jerusalem (1 Kings 8), and in each case it was confirmed or ratified by the people. The sequel shows that the people repeatedly broke the covenant, as Stephen so eloquently declared (Acts 7).

There are many points of similarity between the Hebrew covenant and the contemporary Hittite covenants, as seen in the recently discovered Ugaritic literature. These old Canaanite covenants of two millennia before Christ usually contained specific stipulations, many of which can be paralleled in the Hebrew covenants.

Hittite suzerainty covenants of c. 1500 B.C. contained the following features: (1) a preamble stating the parties to the agreement and its occasion (cf. Ex. 19:3-5); (2) historical prologue reviewing past relationships of the contracting parties up to the present time (cf. Judg. 11:14-23); (3) stipulation of the conditions to which the contracting parties bind themselves,

---

4. Wm. Leonard, *Authorship of the Epistle to the Hebrews* (Vatican: Polyglot Press, 1939), p. 76.

5. *loc. cit.*

6. Gen. 12; 15; 17; 22; it included a promise of land, posterity, protection and blessedness.

the conditions under which the covenant will operate (cf. Deut. 28); (4) provision for public reading (Deut. 27); (5) witnesses to the agreement (Josh. 22:26-29); (6) blessings for keeping and curses for breaking the covenant (Deut. 28; 1 Kings 9:1-9); and (7) provisions for perpetuating and keeping the covenant in force (cf. Deut. 11:13-32). [7]

The usual Hebrew term for covenant, *berith*, occurs some 286 times in the Old Testament. It designates a pact, compact, contract, alliance, treaty, covenant, agreement, league (BDB, p. 136). In Old Testament usage three main thrusts of the term are clearly discernible: (1) It was a contract between man and man, as Laban with Jacob (Gen. 31:43-55) and David with Jonathan (1 Sam. 18:3; 20:8). (2) It was an alliance between God and man as with Noah (Gen. 9:9-17), with Abraham (Gen. 17:2-21), with Israel (Ex. 19:5), and with David (2 Sam. 7). (3) In anticipation of the Christian era the new covenant was announced by the prophets of the exile. It differed radically from the Mosaic covenant in that it was "written not on stone tablets but in the heart" (Jer. 31:31-37; Ezek. 11:19; 36:25-27). The older expression which appears in Jeremiah 31:31 was "to cut a covenant," implying the offering of a sacrifice or the effusion of blood to seal the agreement (Gen. 15:9-20; Jer. 34:18, 19; cf. Mark 14:23-25).

With these prophets of the exile the restoration of the Jewish community in Judea meant a transition from the tribal inclusiveness of the kingdom period to individual responsiblity, since only who chose to return did so. Therefore the members of the Jewish colony in Jerusalem were there by personal choice and the covenant became thereby more personal and meaningful. The same is true of the covenant in Christianity; it has a personal involvement which the Old Testament tribal covenants lacked. No longer could one be a covenanter simply because of his ancestry since God could make children of Abraham "out of stones" (Matt. 3:9), the most common of materials. The basic contrast between the old Mosaic covenant and the new covenant was that the latter called for an "infused righteousness," and impartation of the di-

---

7. Geo. Mendenhall, "Covenant," *Interpreter's Bible Dictionary* (Abingdon, 1962), I, 714.

vine nature, an inward transformation of character to make it effective. It stressed grace rather than duty, love as well as obedience.

This term was usually translated in the LXX by *diathēkē*, which in Greek literature normally means a will or a testament, a bequest. In the LXX the term loses the sense of will or testament since death is not necessary to make the covenant effective. It retains, however, the meaning of a decision by which a benefit passes from giver to receiver (A-G, p. 182).

The difference of meaning between *berith* (agreement) and *diathēkē* (testament) led to certain ambiguities in the New Testament usage. This is particularly apparent in the Epistle to the Hebrews. In chapter nine the "first covenant" is mentioned four times (9:1, 15, 18, 20) as providing only partial and temporary relief from the sin problem. In contrast to it is the "new covenant" (9:15) predicted by the prophets and now identified with the sacrificial work of Christ. The same term in Greek is given a different emphasis in 9:16, 17 where it is compared to a bequest which only becomes operative in the event of the testator's death. Since Jesus the testator died, the believer receives the full benefit of the "will" (RSV). By showing that the first covenant was ratified in the shedding of blood, the author makes the more convincing his thesis that the new replaces the old by showing that Jesus' blood ratifies or authenticates the new.

As always the author's interest is practical. This new covenant, he emphasizes, is even more sacrosanct and demanding than the first covenant. It is not to be trifled with. The great privileges bestowed by that "will" (*thelēmati*, 10:10) by way of sanctification is matched by the awesome responsibilities it entails (10:29). This bequest or will is the body and blood of Christ which alone makes possible the removal of sin and restoration to God's favor (9:28; 10:10-22).

D. Faith

Faith as defined and illustrated in this epistle is different from that found elsewhere in the New Testament. Although Paul appealed to Abraham and to Habakkuk for his conception of faith, this writer is closer to these Old Testament sources in his thinking than was Paul. When Abraham "believed God" he rested in the confidence that somehow in due time God would fulfill His promise of an heir (Gen. 15:6). Paul, noting the words "it was counted unto him for righteousness," used the passage as evidence that even in the Old Testament forgiveness of sin was experienced on the basis of faith alone. Habakkuk was not troubled by a sense of personal guilt but by the moral and theological problem of a divine justice that seemed indifferent to the injustice of the Chaldean invasion. His confidence in God's justice was such that he did not yield to the temptation to cynicism but resolved to wait upon God. He was rewarded by the assurance that by this faith, this confidence in the ultimate triumph of righteousness enables the righteous to live victoriously (Hab. 2:4). Paul, impressed by the word "just," used the passage as a proof text for justification by faith alone (Rom. 1:17; Gal. 3:11). In the mind of the prophet, the just person is made just when he trusts God for this gift of grace.

Faith, as used by the writer to the Hebrews, is closer to the thought of Habakkuk than to that of Paul. It was faith or confidence in God's faithfulness that enabled the two spies to present an optimistic report. It was a lack of this confidence that led the majority of the Israelites to a skepticism that resulted in their death en route to Canaan (Heb. 3:14-19). It is this kind of faith that enables the believer to "hold fast" his confession or commitment to Christ and "to press on to perfection" (Heb. 3:14; 6:1). In the same manner the heroes of chapter 11 were sustained by the conviction that God's cause was going to triumph. Hence Rahab cast her lot with the Israelites rather than with her own kinfolk (11:31); and Moses, taking the long-range view, chose hardship with his people rather than luxury at the Egyptian court (11:25). The emphasis in these instances is not so much on a trust for one's personal salvation as on the endurance of a present hardship and hazard in view of a reward visible only to the "eye of faith."

The change of emphasis between this writer and Paul appears not due to a shift in emphasis from Christ as the object of faith (Paul's view) to Christ as an example, as Scott insists (EFS, p. 172). The difference is adequately accounted for by the different circumstances of their respective readers. Paul wrote to make clear that Christ, rather than the law, is the basis for righteousness, and that this righteousness comes from God by Christ in response to trust alone. The Hebrews already had been partakers of Christ by trust; they now needed new assurance that they had chosen wisely and needed only to persevere in this confidence.

There are affinities between this concept of faith with that of Philo. Like Aquinas, Luther and other saints, Philo insisted that faith involves both a disbelief in the physical world and a compensatory faith "in the only true and faithful God." [8] Such a faith calls for both a *contemptu mundi*, a distrust of the "certainties" of time and sense, and a conviction of the supreme worth of unseen spiritual verities. "It is an intuitive conviction of a world of truth which lies beyond the senses, and from this conviction we can advance, by way of a given discipline, to an ever-growing knowledge" (EFS, p. 176).

Unlike Philo, however, this writer regards faith not so much as a pathway to knowledge but as a God-given conviction of spiritual values. Also this writer is concerned with the future to a greater extent than Philo. The conviction of a final vindication of their faith at the conclusion of their "race" sustained and invigorated the Old Testament saints named in the epistle. In Hebrews faith appears to be more conspicuous than the love which lies at the apex of Christian graces in Paul, Peter and John. This, however, may not be due to a difference in theology so much as a difference in the circumstances of the readers. This epistle is not a general presentation of Christian doctrines but a "word of exhortation" to a certain group of believers. The value of this presentation is that it shows the continuity of the Christian faith with that of the Old Testament, while at the same time it stresses the distinctives in the new faith. Paul did this occasionally as in Romans 4 and Galatians 3, 4, but usually stressed the contrast between the Christian faith and the law.

According to this writer, faith is Christ-centered. For him

8. Philo, *Quis heres.* 18.

Christ is the example who commands fortitude and perseverance. Christ is also the leader who opens up the way of access to God's presence. He is also the consummator or perfecter of faith as well as its initiator or author. More than any other New Testament writer this one stresses the timeless insights of Habakkuk—"the just shall live by faith." If faith sustained the saints of the old covenant, "how much more" should the present ministry of Jesus Christ give assurance to heirs of the new covenant. Such a faith comes from the Word of God (cf. Rom. 10:17), is possible to "all sorts and conditions of men," is consistent with varying degrees of knowledge, and overcomes all things. [9]

E. Perfection

One of the more perplexing problems in the interpretation of Hebrews is its concept of perfection. The careful student of this letter is likely to agree with Spicq, Montefiore, Westcott and others that perfection is the key-note of its message. Specifically, the epistle seeks to prove the perfection of the new alliance, the perfection of the high priest of this new covenant, and the perfectibility of its adherents. The term itself occurs in an English translation (ASV) fifteen times. [10]   As will be noted later the perfection concept is linked with the covenant four times, with Jesus five times and with man eight times. What does the author mean by these terms? Does perfection mean maturity in the Christian life (5:14; 6:1); does it mean adequacy in dealing with the sin problem (10:1, 14); does it mean the culmination in time of God's plan of salvation (7:11, 19); does it mean purity of heart (9:9; 10:1); does it mean resurrection victory (12:23; cf. Luke 13:32); or does it mean wholeness, integrity (13:21; cf. Eph. 4:12)? Interpreters do not agree as to the specific meaning(s) the author has in mind. There is general agreement, however, that the concept of perfection is a central feature of this treatise. [11]   With varying degrees of affirmation Ahern, Flew,

---

9. F. B. Meyer, *The Way into the Holiest* (New York: Revell, 1893), p. 202.

10. Viz, Heb. 2:10; 5:9, 14; 6:1; 7:11, 19, 28; 9:9, 11; 10:1, 14; 11:40; 12:2, 23; 13:21; cf. 8:7 (*amemptos*—"faultless"); 9:14 (*amomos*—"without blemish").

11. Allen Wikgren, "Patterns of Perfection in the Epistle to the Hebrews," *New Testament Studies*, Jan., 1960, p. 159; BFW (p. 63); Spicq (II, 214).

Montefiore, Murray, Wikgren, Wesley and Wiley agree that it has reference to Christian purity and maturity. [12] Others see in the author's usage only the objective aspect of the term, i.e., that perfection refers to the adequacy and finality of Christ's atoning work rather than to its effects upon the believer, that perfection corresponds to the Pauline term "justification" rather than to the Johannine term "perfect love." A. B. Bruce believed that the words "sanctified" and "perfected" have a different connotation here than in the Pauline letters. In the letters of Paul, he argues, "Sanctification is ethical, and means making the Christian holy in heart and life . . . in Hebrews this ethical sense continues . . . occasionally . . . but more commonly the term is used in a theocratic sense, to express the idea of being put in right covenant relation with God" (cf. 10:14). [13]

1. Synonyms

Four terms contribute to the general New Testament meaning of perfection. *Teleios* and its cognates occur 18 times and mean "maturity" or fulfillment; *amemptos* and its cognate form convey the meaning of "blamelessness" (Gen. 17:1; Luke 1:6; Phil. 2:15; Heb. 8:7; 9:14); and *katarismos* with its corresponding verb form means "wholeness" (Heb. 13:21; cf. 10:5; 11:3). Another related term (*hagiazomenoi*, 2:11; 10:10, 14) conveys the meaning of "purity." The three main concepts that emerge are maturity, wholeness and purity.

a. Maturity

Teleios and *teleioō*, the main forms for "perfect" and "to perfect" respectively, come from the root *telos* which means end or goal. This meaning lies behind virtually all usages of the terms in this family. In the LXX it is the usual translation of *tamim* which means "unblemished" and *shalom* which normally

---

12. Cf. H. Montefiore, "His call to Christian maturity and perfection, grounded in the perfection of Christ, is the major positive ethical theme of the Epistle."—*The Epistle to the Hebrews: Harper's New Testament Commentaries* (New York, 1964), p. 104.

13. A. B. Bruce, "Epistle to the Hebrews," Hastings, *Dictionary of the Bible* (1903), II, 334.

means "sincere."[14] In classical usage it means "full-grown, mature, adult, fully developed" (A-G, 817). The "mature" are often equated with teachers.[15] In koine Greek also it designates "maturity, completion, fulfillment" (M-M, 629). Sometimes it was applied to those who have completed initiation in the mystery religions (cf. Col. 1:28; 1 Cor. 2:6).

In the Qumran literature perfectionism is prominent. Perfection was particularily mandatory for the three priests and twelve laymen (IQS, vii, 1). Yet all of the initiates were henceforth expected to live blameless lives (IQS, vii, 20; Hymns v, 6; xviii, 29). Theirs was an ascetic perfection, however, rather than perfection of love.

That the New Testament usage often means more than maturity is clear in such passages as Matthew 5:48 where it is Godlikeness, or in Matthew 19:21 where it involves full consecration, going "the whole way" (NEB). It also means Christlikeness (Col. 1:22, 28), fullness of love (1 John 4:16-21), purity of heart, singleness of motive, freedom from sin and defilement. This comes from its association with righteousness, justice, wholeness and sanctity.[16]

b. Wholeness

The concept of wholeness is conveyed by two terms. Blamelessness (*amemptos*) was sometimes linked with conformity to the letter and spirit of the Old Testament as exemplified in Zacharias and Elizabeth (Luke 1:6). Sometimes it included also conformity to rabbinic traditions, as exemplified by Saul of Tarsus (Phil. 3:6). It also connoted freedom from moral blemish, as in the case of the sacrifices of the Old Testament which had to be without physical blemish (Ex. 12:5; Mal. 1:13; Eph. 5:27; Heb. 9:14; cf. Phil. 2:15).

The other term (*katartismos*) connotes integrity, a corporate

---

14. Ex. 12:5; see G. A. Turner, *The Vision Which Transforms* (Kansas City, 1964), pp. 42-45.

15. Plato, Rep. V, 466a; *Laws* II, 929c; Philo. De Spec. Leg IV 140 (Spicq, *op. cit.*), p. 218.

16. Cf. Gen. 6:9; Deut. 18:13; Job. 1:8; Ecclus. 44:17; IQS v, 7-20; Did. 6:2; Luke 6:40; A. Wikgren, *op. cit.*, p. 162.

perfection or wholeness as in Galatians 6:1; Ephesians 4:12; Hebrews 13:21.

c. *Purity*

The kinship between perfection and purity of heart is clear in several passages in the New Testament.[17] The relationship, however, is not limited to certain texts in which both terms appear. Rather it centers primarily in the kinship, effected by divine grace, between the God who is free from sin, a Saviour who is likewise sinless, and the believer who is united to Christ as a branch to the vine—or, to use another biblical analogy, as the body to the head. Since every disciple shall be "as his master" (Luke 6:40), it follows that disciples of a sinless Christ Jesus should share His concern for purity of heart and motive.

These are the general meanings in the New Testament and contemporary literature. The particular matter in which these ideas are set forth in the Epistle to the Hebrews can best be presented topically. The relation of the perfection concept to the new covenant in general, to Christ and to the believer, will be our next focus of attention.

2. The perfection of the new covenant

a. *Its intrinsic superiority*

Although intimately related, the author makes a distinction between the imperfect Levitical *system itself* and its perfect successor, on the one hand, and the relative *effectiveness* of each system to the other. Three passages speak of the relative perfection or adequacy of the new covenant: there was no "perfection (*teleiōsis*) through the Levitical priesthood" (7:11); "the law made nothing perfect" (*eteleiōsen*) (7:19); and Jesus serves in a "more perfect (*teleiōteras*) tabernacle" (9:11). The comparison evokes the detailed contrast made by this author between shadow and substance, between the temporal and eternal, between the blood of bulls and that of Jesus, between the external and internal.

---

17. Heb. 10:14; 2 Cor. 7:1; Acts 15:9; I John 3:3; Col. 1:22.

He shows that the inadequacy of the old necessitates and hence justifies the new which is adequate or perfect (9:9; 10:4). Conversely, the announcement of the better implies the imperfection of the system which it replaces (8:7).

b. Its effectiveness

As seen in many contexts, sacred and secular, "perfect" has reference to the adequacy or effectiveness in achieving a purpose, task or goal. Judged by this standard, the old dispensation was imperfect because it did not effect the necessary change in the worshipper. The new covenant, by contrast, does just that and hence is perfect (cf. 9:9; 10:1, 14; 11:40). The perfection of the new covenant consists in its deliverance from the guilt and power of sin and in assuring the believer of God's favor.

Christ succeeded in bringing the conscience into a right relationship to God and hence "perfect" (*teleion*) with respect to "eternal redemption" (9:9-12). Because his conscience is now cleansed, the believer is free to "serve the living God" (9:14). The inadequacy of the Levitical system lies in its inability to take away a "consciousness of sins" which Christ is well able to do (10:1-4), thus rendering the recipient of his grace "perfect" or "sanctified." The end result of Christ's work is to render the sanctified one "perfect forever." This does not mean that his is a perfect love which necessarily lasts forever. It means rather that those "sanctified," i.e., those who are Christians, are by this atonement rendered pleasing to God with no need of further sacrifices or offerings. The divine resources released by Christ's death are fully adequate for both present and future needs. Here also the author is chiefly concerned about showing the adequacy of the objective grounds of one's perfection rather than with its subjective effects. This is equivalent to justification in the Pauline usage, or to regeneration in the Johannine nomenclature, or "partakers of the divine nature" (2 Pet. 1:4). This the heroes and heroines of the Old Testament lacked, according to 7:11; 11:40, unless it was by anticipation of the perfect sacrifice to come. The new covenant is "perfect" because it effects full victory over sin.

3. The perfection of Christ

The perfection of Jesus is one of the unique features of this presentation. If Jesus became perfect (2:11), was there a time when He was imperfect? In what sense could the Son of God *become* perfect (5:9)? If Jesus Christ is "the same yesterday, today and forever," how could He "learn obedience" since learning necessitates change? Does the perfection that Jesus accomplished (10:14) consist in a right relation with God which the old covenant failed to provide, or is it, more specifically, cleansing from inner defilement and perfection in love in the Johannine sense?

Noteworthy in the epistle's treatment of Christ's perfection is the fact that Jesus' humanity is more emphatically stressed here than in any New Testament writing other than the four Gospels.

Three distinct applications of the concept to Jesus' person and work may be detected: (1) Jesus himself experienced or acquired "perfection" as a result of the incarnation (2:11; 5:9; 7:28). (2) Jesus' "perfection through suffering" qualifies Him as a sympathetic and hence effective high priest and intercessor (2:17, 18; 4:15; 12:2). (3) Jesus is thereby able to bring believers into a similar state of "perfection" through fellowship with himself (10:14; 11:40; 12:23; cf. 2:11; 13:12, 21).[18]

The perfection of Christ himself is twofold: (1) as Son of God He is sinless and holy, with a "perfect heart" in the tradition of Noah, Abraham and Job (Gen. 6:8, 9; 17:1; 22:12; II Kings 20:3; Job 1:8); (2) as high priest and intercessor He is to share human nature, endure temptations and experience death as an authentic representative of humanity.[19]

Of greatest interest is Jesus' own growth unto "perfection." In the Gospel of Luke note is made of the fact that "Jesus increased in wisdom and stature and in favor with God and men" (Luke 2:52; cf. 1 Sam. 2:26). This mental and physical growth and increasing favor with God implies progress toward "perfection" or maturity. Growth implies change. It underscores

---

18. B. F. Westcott, *op. cit.*, p. 65.

19. C. Spicq, *L'Epitre Aux Hebreux*, (Paris: Galalda, 1952), II, 219.

the reality of His humanity—there is no doceticism here.[20] As a truly human being Jesus experienced and overcame temptation without experiencing sin. He could have sinned but did not (cf. Heb. 2:18). Jesus' growth "moved forward from the imperfections or innocence which belongs to the early stages of a moral career to the completeness which can only be achieved by the processes of testing and struggle." Thus Jesus although truly human was still sinless; His growth consisted "not in the gradual elimination of the evil, but a constantly increasing realization of the good, until He achieved a positive perfection of life.[21] He often agonized in prayer, not as a petitioner for personal purity but in intercession for others (Heb. 5:7). The fitness of this method of preparing Jesus for His work as high priest lay in emphasizing His oneness and hence sympathy with mankind (Heb. 2:14-18). For the same reason Jesus was made judge of all mankind "because he is the Son of man" (John 5:27) and hence able to establish rapport with the condemned.

Perfection or maturity through suffering is indicated in Hebrews 12:2-14 and in Romans 5:2-5. His status as Son did not relieve Jesus from the necessity of suffering like those to whom He ministers (Heb. 5:8). This does not necessitate a previous imperfection. "Rather the meaning is that sufferings introduce a new perfection, a perfection of testedness."[22] Jesus' consistent obedience was not without struggle (John 12:27; Luke 22:42). But because He always did the things that pleased His Father (John 8:29) He qualified as "the source of eternal salvation to all who obey him" (Heb. 5:9, RSV). In most spheres of life it is recognized that the leader who can give commands is the kind of person who himself can take commands. Because Jesus could say, "I have kept my Father's commandments," He can also say to His disciples and to all others, "Keep my commandments" (John 15:10). By means of victory over temptation and constant obedi-

---

20. Doceticism (from *dokeo*) is the heresy that Jesus' human nature was only an appearance. His human nature was real (cf. John 1:14; I John 4:2; II John 7).

21. G. B. Stevens, *The Theology of the New Testament* (New York: Scribners, 1899), p. 500.

22. Leon Morris, *The Cross in the New Testament* (Eerdmans, 1965), p. 281.

ence, "in the days of his flesh," He "became perfect" in that He was further qualified for His role as mediator. Thus our author, with greater boldness than any other New Testament author, asserts the intimate relationship between sanctifier and the sanctified (Heb. 2:11).

The third passage (7:28) speaks "of the abiding work of the Son for men as their eternal High Priest," as Westcott puts it. But may this not apply to the resurrection, to the consummation, as the same term does in 12:23? Here the context seems to indicate an inherent perfection in Jesus, enhanced by the experiences of 2:10; 5:7-9, and consummated in His death, resurrection and ascension. This includes His essential goodness as Son of God, His acquired "obedience" as Son of man, His total adequacy as high priest and the eschatological consummation of these factors in perpetuity. Henceforth He is "the same yesterday, and today and forever" (13:8). In contrast to other priests this high priest is without infirmity (cf. 2:10; 5:9) because of the perfecting process now consummated. As Son of God He is sinless and holy, serving God with a perfect heart (7:26-28; cf. 1 Kings 8:61).

4. The perfection of believers

a. Purity—sanctification

The most difficult and important phase of the subject is perfection among human beings. There is an intimate relationship between sanctification and the perfection to which it leads. But the concept of sanctification also presents difficulties of interpretation. To what extent, if any, does sanctification in this letter differ from the usage elsewhere in the New Testament? The main term for sanctification in its several cognate forms occurs more than 25 times in this epistle. Two of these are translated "holiness," meaning to share in God's nature.[23] One form is the noun (*hagion*) and usually means "sanctuary," and another is the adjective (*hagios*) and means "holy," usually linked with "Spirit" or Christian "brethren." The significant term here is

---

23. *Hagiasmos* (Heb. 12:14) and *Hagiotes* (Heb. 12:10), the latter occurring only here in the New Testament.

hagiazo ("sanctify") which occurs six times in the epistle.[24] This term is used of the Old Testament sacrifices which "sanctifieth unto the purifying of the flesh" (9:13), i.e., "an external state of purity" (FD, II, 94). It is set in contrast to the efficacy of Christ's atonement which cleanses the conscience. The meaning of the term in the context of the new covenant is illustrated in 10:10, "We have been sanctified through the offering of the body of Jesus Christ." Here "sanctified" apparently means "set apart" or to consecrate in the sense of 1 Corinthians 1:2—"sanctified in Christ Jesus." Henceforth they may be classified as "they that are sanctified" (2:11).[25] His emphasis here is more upon the objective basis of the atonement than upon the subjective effects in man. His interest in the subjective effectiveness was a derivative from his interest in the adequacy of Christ's work. Three emphases are noticeable in 10:14; the emphasis is upon the one *final* and adequate *offering* of Christ, its *availability* to those sanctified and its *sufficiency* for their perfection. These are the ones who have been sanctified by the new covenant—set apart, accepted and made righteous—presumably those who gave heed to the gospel (2:1-4) and experienced the peace or "rest" that comes from a cleansed conscience (4:4; 9:14).

In Hebrews 13:12 as in these other passages, the essential meaning of "sanctify" is to put people in a right relation with God. In each case moral renewal, ethical righteousness and cleansing from sin is implicit. Although more implicit than explicit, "the sense of spiritual maturity is also clear" in these passages.[26] The possibility and obligation of spiritual maturity is constantly urged upon those who are "enlightened" and partake of the Holy Spirit but are immature. The saints of the new covenant are those

---

24. 2:11; 9:13; 10:10; 10:14, 29; 13:12.

25. Sanctification in the New Testament has five distinct meanings: (1) It means a recognition of God as uniquely holy (Matt. 6:9; Luke 11:2; 1 Pet. 3:15); (2) separation, dedication or consecration to divine service (John 10:36; 17:19; Rom. 15:16); (3) status imputed by *relationship* to the divine (Matt. 23:17, 19; 1 Cor. 1:2; 7:14; 1 Tim. 4:5); (4) nature imparted by progressive moral *renewal* (1 Cor. 6:11; Eph. 5:26; 1 Thess. 4:3, 4, 7; 1 Pet. 1:2); (5) *complete purity* of heart (Rom. 6:6, 14, 19; 2 Cor. 7:1; 1 Thess. 3:13; 5:23; Col. 1:22).

26. A. Wikgren, *op. cit.*, p. 160.

who have God's law in their hearts and are free from a "root of bitterness" (8:10; 12:14-15). This must include moral purification." [27]

Bultmann observes (correctly) that in Paul's thought the indicatives indicate the believer's standing in Christ while the imperatives challenge him to "walk in the Spirit" and thus make actual the deliverance from sin which is otherwise only potential. [28] But he also states (incorrectly) that in Hebrews no attempt is made to harmonize the declarative aspect of sanctification or perfection (9:14; 10:1, 10, 14, 29; 13:12) and its imperatives—"follow after sanctification" (12:14; cf. 6:1; 12:10). [29]

Here, as in Paul's letters, the work of Christ in effecting salvation provides the necessity and possibility of its implementation. It is therefore as important to "give heed" (2:1), to "hold fast" (3:14), to "press on" (6:1), to "run with patience" (12:1), and to "go forth " (13:13), as it is to experience salvation (6:4).

b. Maturity

The basic meaning of *teleios* is maturity. This is clear in Hebrews (5:1-6:1; cf. 1 Cor. 2:6; 3:1-3; 13:10; 14:20). The "Hebrews," accused of being "dull of hearing" and too immature to accept adult food, are urged to "press on unto perfection" or maturity (6:1). *Teleios* is always a cognate term with *telos* which means "end" or "destination." What is the "end" to the process of maturation? It is nothing less than Godlikeness or Christlikeness. This is seen in Matthew 5:45-48 where "perfect" means treating one's enemies as God does—better than they deserve. In Luke 6:40 it means Christlikeness—like the Master. In Philippians 2:15 it means complete identification with the passion and purpose of Christ (cf. Gal. 2:20). The personal "perfection" or maturity called for in Hebrews 5:11-6:4 is spiritual and intellectual discernment. It has here an intellectual aspect in comparison to the ethical emphasis of 1 Corinthians 3:1ff.

---

27. R. N. Flew, *op. cit.*, p. 87.

28. R. Bultmann, *Theology of the New Testament*, tr. by K. Grobel (Scribner's, 1955), I, 332.

29. *Ibid.*, II, 167, 168.

But here maturity does not exhaust the meaning. Even in the exhortation, "Let us advance towards maturity" (6:1, NEB), more than maturity is expressed. Here is a distinct challenge to go beyond conversion or justification. It is a summons issued to believers to advance toward completeness, to perfection, to holiness of heart and life. The entire epistle is so permeated with this concern that this verse may be said to sound one of its keynotes. A verse such as this is necessary to correct a view which might be obtained from other verses (e.g., 7:11, 19; 10:1, 14) that "perfection" in this epistle is equivalent to justification or regeneration. Hebrews 6:1-3 makes it clear that justification is just the beginning of the Christian life, not its completion or perfection. Ultimately, "perfection" is nothing less than "the possession of the moral image of God." [30]

c. Integrity, wholeness

While *teleios* and its cognate terms means individual perfection or maturity, another synonym connotes corporate perfection. The term *katartisai* or *katartismos* means to repair (Matt. 4:21; Mark 1:19), restore (Gal. 6:1), fabricate (Heb. 11:3), prepare or furnish (Heb. 10:5); also to perfect, to make whole, in an ethical sense, as in 2 Corinthians 13:10, [31] "We desire your perfection" (*katartisim*—Luther, *Vollkommenheit*). Similarly, in 1 Corinthians 1:10, one must "be perfectly joined together in one mind"; and in Ephesians 4:12 Paul prays "for the perfecting (*katartismon*) of the saints." Both passages call for togetherness or spiritual wholeness for unity, for spiritual adulthood (*andra teleion*, Eph. 4:12), for Christlikeness. This is the connotation of the benedictory prayers of 2 Corinthians 13:11 (*katartizesthe*—"be perfect," or "mend your ways"), and Hebrews 13:21 (*katartisai*—"perfect" or "equip"). He prays in the latter passage for the spiritual wholeness and maturity of the Christian community which will enable it to function effectively in the service of the Kingdom. Such passages indicate that "the moral integrity of the individual is merged with the spiritual unity of the Christian commu-

---

30. H. O. Wiley, *op. cit.*, p. 206; cf. Matt. 5:8; I John 3:3; Col. 1:23.

31. Its pre-Christian meaning is "prepare," "equip" or "perfect" something for its full destination or usage—Moulton & Milligan, *op. cit.*, p. 332.

ity.[32] Another fact of this concept is that Christians are to expect from God the grace which enables them even in this life to be Christlike and to serve effectively.

d. *Christian perfection as the design or goal of discipline*

The connection between suffering and Christian perfection is here stressed more vigorously than anywhere else in the New Testament, with the possible exception of 1 Peter. Jesus emphasized that suffering persecution for their faith would place the disciples in the authentic succession of the prophets (Matt. 5:10-12). He also made it clear that disciples should follow their master in the path of unjust suffering and persecution (Matt. 16:21-25; Luke 6:40; John 16:1-3; cf. Phil. 3:10; 2 Tim. 3:12).

The same theme is developed in the General Epistles. James sees that patience under trial produces Christians that are "perfect and entire, lacking in nothing" (1:4). Peter likewise emphasizes that overcoming severe trials culminates in "the end (*telos*) of your faith, the salvation of your souls" (1 Pet. 1:9; 3:18; 4:1-19; 5:10). The same theme, that discipline is essential to Christian perfection, is also prominent in the writings of Paul (Rom. 5:3-5; 8:17, 35-39; 2 Cor. 11:23-12:10; 2 Thess. 1:3-12). In Hebrews the relationship of suffering to Jesus' own perfection is seen in 2:9-18 and again in 5:7-9. The same conviction is applied to followers of Jesus in 12:2-14. Looking first to the example of Jesus triumphing over suffering, and then quoting from Proverbs (3:11), the author, in the most vigorous language to be found in the Scriptures, asserts that chastening or discipline (*paideias*) is not only essential to spiritual maturity but is the condition of sonship. If our natural fathers chastened us to satisfy themselves, how much more appropriate that our heavenly Father chastens us for our profit! The end result of such discipline is partaking of God's nature (v. 10). Suffering will not in itself assure holiness, but the attaining of holiness is impossible without this means.

e. *The "rest of faith"*

Akin to the concept of maturity, and peculiar to this letter, is the emphasis on the sabbath rest for the people of God (4:9).

---

32. G. A. Turner, *op. cit.*, p. 135; cf. 1 Pet. 4:8; Eph. 4:16; Phil. 2:2; 14, 15.

This motif is dominant from 3:2 through 4:16. It is closely related in thought to 5:11-6:12 where spiritual immaturity is denounced, and the readers are exhorted with great earnestness to "press on unto perfection." Likewise in this segment of the letter the danger of arrested progress is emphasized by the historic precedent of the Israelites en route from Egypt to Canaan. Their tragic example is constantly kept before the readers as a challenge and warning: (1) the people were God's people; (2) they were in bondage; (3) they experienced a miraculous deliverance; (4) in spite of all this they disbelieved and failed to press on to their destination; (5) as a result they perished without obtaining the goal which they set out for in the beginning; (6) what happened to them can happen to us, unless we follow our leader in faith and obedience; and (7) this "rest of faith" is both imperative and available to God's people.

The relevance of this long passage to perfection lies in the definition of "rest" and whether it is to be understood as a spiritual condition presently available or as the future abode of the soul in heaven. It certainly includes the latter meaning, but does it also include the former? The present tense at 4:3 here is significant. It is clear "neither that they are certain to enter, nor that they will enter, but that they are already in process of entering." [33]   The chief concern of the writer in this section is to show (1) that this rest is available by faith, (2) that it will be missed unless there is faith, and (3) that it is *presently* available by faith, not just at some future time after death. The emphasis is on "today." The contrast is between those who left Egypt but remained in the wilderness and those who left the wilderness and entered the sabbath rest. Since it is available by faith and therefore available now, it is a stage in the Christian life in which self-effort gives way to God working in one "both to will and do of his good pleasure" (Phil. 2:13). The paradox is expressed by Jesus, "Take my yoke . . . and ye shall find rest" (Matt. 11:29), and by Paul, "I labour, striving according to his working, which worketh in me mightily" (Col. 1:29). Says Murray:

> There are the two stages in the Christian life. The one in which, after conversion, a believer seeks to work what God would have

---

33. Hugh Montefiore, *op. cit.*, p. 83.

him do. The second, in which, after many a painful failure, he ceases from his works, and enters the rest of God, there to find the power for work in allowing God to work in him. [34]

The concept of this rest of faith is the unique contribution which this epistle makes to the New Testament doctrine of Christian perfection. That it is a present option for believers is clearly stressed in 4:3 ("We who have believed do enter that rest") and 4:10 ("He that is entered into his rest hath himself also rested from his works"). Because it is a present possibility it is therefore a present obligation.

f. Glorification

In several texts *teleion* has the meaning of glorification or final salvation. In Hebrews 12:23 reference is made to "just men made perfect" ("just," i.e., *dikaion*, not "good" as in NEB and JBP), in a context which indicates that these are believers who died in the faith and are now in heaven, i.e., "the church triumphant." Theirs is a final as well as full salvation. In such a context the term connotes resurrection as in Jesus' statement that "the third day I am perfected" (Luke 13:33). Paul expected a similar "perfection" following his "resurrection from the dead" (Phil. 3:12). Eleazar is said to have been perfected after his heroic martyrdom. [35] Paul also says, in this context, that his readers are or should be "perfect" (*teleioi*) with respect to this aspiration and goal (3:15). Paradoxically, they are to be perfect in motive and attitude while seeking that perfection which comes only after the resurrection. It also appears on at least one Christian gravestone as *eteleōthē* (M-M, p. 629). The completion or fulfillment conveyed in the term "perfect" is in these texts experienced after the resurrection of the just; this is "final salvation."

The most distinctive feature of the motif of perfection, which is so prominent in Hebrews, is its application to Jesus "in the days of his flesh." The perfection acquired through suffering provided the experience of sharing in the trials of humanity which qualified Him as high priest and as judge.

---

34. A. Murray, *op. cit.*, p. 152.

35. IV Macc. 7:15. This usage appears also in an early Christian martyrology (JM, p. 32). Cf. I Macc. 6:18-31.

In addition, the application of "perfection" to the new covenant in contrast to the old is uniquely characteristic of this epistle. The new is "perfect" and the old imperfect because only the new deals adequately with the sin problem. The new is "perfect" because it alone provides for the worshipper the clear conscience resulting from the removal of guilt and consciousness of cleansing from sin's pollution.

Thirdly, perfection, subjectively considered, is that which is available to the believer who "presses on to spiritual maturity." Thus they become partakers of God's holiness, i.e., God's moral character (12:10). Believers share with Jesus ethical moral progress towards the goal of perfection. Because of Christ's work the believer is "proleptically *teleioi* through initiation and participation in that community of faith which also constitutes this ideal goal" (cf. 11:40).[36] Christian perfection is seen immediately in the Son, mediately in man (CS, p. 224).

To claim "perfection" for the new covenant, for its high priest, and for its adherents was a bold affirmation, but this author dares to affirm it "with a full assurance of faith." Dare one deny its applicability to Christ and His work?

---

36. Wikgren, *op. cit.*, p. 162.

Appendices

A. The time and place of writing

Among the most baffling problems in New Testament studies are the time, place, readers and author of the Epistle to the Hebrews. At best one can only limit the possibilities and make conjectures.

1. Time of writing

Several factors provide clues to the approximate date of composition.

The epistle appears to have been written after the freshness of the Christian mission had worn off. Like the recipients of the Epistle of James the readers were imperiled by discouragement and complacency. They, like the Ephesians, were in danger of leaving their first love (cf. Rev. 2:4). Like those of Laodicea they had endured afflictions only to become somewhat lukewarm (Rev. 3:16; cf. Heb. 2:1). Like those of Malachi's congregation they had reached a stage where they were ready to wonder if the discipline was worthwhile and to relax or even reconsider their commitment (Mal. 3:14; cf. Heb. 5:11-6:8). While situations differ widely from place to place, the implication is that the gospel was generally known from "eyewitnesses" in the area for at least two decades prior to the reception of this letter (cf. Heb. 2:3).

The author's preoccupation with the tabernacle, the sacrificial system and the priesthood makes it extremely unlikely that this was composed after the destruction of the temple in 70 A.D. and the termination of the Levitical priesthood. Note the present tense of Hebrews 13:9-16, especially the words, "They have no right to eat that serve the tabernacle" (v. 10). To have written thus after Jews practiced only synagogue worship would have seemed strangely anachonistic and irrelevant. Although the author had in mind the tabernacle in the wilderness rather than Herod's temple in Jerusalem, the analogy between the sacrificial system and the offering of the Christ would have seemed rather empty and academic unless written either before or long after the cessation of sacrifices in Jerusalem. Even if the sacrifices continued after the temple's destruction, as some have argued, most of the force of the epistle's central emphasis would have been dissipated. If the temple had been destroyed, this fact would have been reflected in the author's phraseology as it would have strengthened his argument. It is conceivable, of course, that the writer, pondering the significance of the destruction of the holy city, at some time removed from the event, could have elaborated his argument as a rationale of the fall, much as Augustine compiled *The City of God* after the sack of Rome in 410 A.D. But this hypothesis seems improbable.

Timothy was alive after his recent release from prison (Heb. 13:23). These factors point to a date not far from 69 A.D.

2. Place of writing

Where were the recipients of this treatise? Where was the letter written? Neither question can be answered with confidence.

One clue is the clause, "They of Italy salute you" (13:24). This has been interpreted to mean, "Those here with me in Italy send greetings." It could also mean, "Those from Italy who are here with me, send greetings." Another possibility is that a group, known to writer and reader as Italians, took this opportunity to send greetings to another congregation as Aquila and Prisca (who were "from Italy") sent greetings to those at Corinth (1 Cor. 16:19). Or it could mean, "Those from Italy send greetings to friends there in Italy." Ephesus also has some claim to be the place of origin (cf. Acts 18:24-28: I Cor. 16:19).

B. The purpose of the author

The author's purpose appears from internal evidence to be twofold. He wants to instruct them in Christology and he wants them to "go on unto perfection," to become established in the faith (Heb. 5:11; 6:1). Christology is the means to this end. The readers have already endured persecution and more of the same appears imminent. They are being stimulated and encouraged to "press on" and are warned against the disaster of standing still or turning back. He is as aware of the danger of apostasy as was Paul when he wrote to the Galatians, and writes with equal earnestness but more dispassionately than did the apostle to the Gentiles.

Indoctrination was a major concern as is seen in the long expositions concerning the superiority of Christ to prophets, Adam, angels, Moses, Joshua and Aaron, as well as in explaining the superiority of the new covenant to the old.

The care with which the author pursues his course implies that he has in mind, in addition to one particular congregation (Heb. 6:9; 10:32-39), a larger Christian community as well. Thus his immediate objective appears to be the strengthening of a certain group while his larger objective is to set forth his own contribution to Christian theology, especially that dealing with Christ as high priest. It would be applicable, therefore, to Christians with a Jewish background who now felt excluded from the synagogue and yet not fully accepted by Gentile believers.

C. The recipients

Who were these readers whom the church fathers labelled "the Hebrews"?

The title, "To the Hebrews" (*PROS EBRAIOUS*) was apparently inserted by an early copyist, for it appears in all of the most ancient manuscripts. Later manuscripts enlarged it to "the Epistle of Paul to the Hebrews" (BFW, p. xxvii).

The argument that the readers were Gentiles because non-Jews also recognized the authority of the Septuagint, and because the title was a mere guess (JM, p. XVI), is not convincing. Scott's conclusion that the readers were mature Gentile teachers, responsible for the future of the congregation, has some things to commend it (EFS, pp. 30ff.). But the recipients are said to be still immature (*nepios*—5:13) and are urged to respect their leaders (13:7, 17). The fact that gross sins are not rebuked may be not so much evidence of their spiritual maturity as it is of their Jewish backgound. Every allusion and argument is directed to those familiar with the Old Testament and Jewish ordinances. Perhaps these believers feared being excluded from temple services and from the messianic kingdom and therefore had become vulnerable to temptations to apostasy.

Many scholars identify "the Hebrews" with "the Hellenists" mentioned in the New Testament—those who were represented in Jerusalem (Acts 6:1), in Samaria (Acts 8:12-25) and in Antioch (Acts 11:20-24). That they were Hellenists—Greek-speaking Christians of Hebrew ancestry seems clearly inferred in the epistle. But the letter seems to appear addressed to a group in a particular place (Heb. 10:32, 33) rather than a general class in widely distributed areas. They were known personally to the author as having been accepted by Christ and having undergone persecution for their faith, yet were now wavering in their allegiance.

The theory that these were Alexandrian believers is weakened by the fact that the Jewish temple at Elephantine never had been under the influence of the temple in Jerusalem and it had no status outside of the Egyptian communities.

In a lengthy and plausible treatment of the subject Montefiore argues that the recipients of this letter were members of the Church at Corinth *before* Paul wrote I Corinthians.[1] But this hypothesis required a date considerably earlier (c. 53 A.D.) than the date usually assigned and implies an audience of Gentiles as well as Jews, "a mixed church, predominantly Jewish in origin."[2] It seems unlikely also that a letter addressed to Corinthians would be so preoccupied with Old Testament institutions.

W. Manson argues persuasively for an unknown author, Alexandrian in training, writing to Christians who were the result of the world mission of Stephen and his disciples. This group he identi-

---

1. H. Montefiore, *op. cit.*, pp. 11-30.

2. *Ibid.*, pp. 12, 16; Heb. 12:16; 13:4 perhaps imply a pagan background.

fies as a minority party of Jewish conservatives in the Church at Rome.[3] Manson assumes that the scrupulous minority (which Paul calls "the weaker brethren") consisted of conservative and legalistic Jewish Christians.[4] But there is equal or greater force to the argument that "the weak" were Christians with a pagan background, hence were more squeamish about food with idolatrous associations than confirmed monotheists would be (Rom. 14:1, 2; 15:1; 1 Cor. 8:7, 9; 9:22). Also the word for "readers" in Hebrews 13:7, 17, 24 (*hēgoumenoi*) is similar to 1 Clement 1:3 (*proēgoumenoi*). Westcott maintains:

> It is quite conceivable that a society of Hebrews in Rome may have been led to develop the sacrificial theory of Judaism and to insist upon it and so to call out 'the word of exhortation.' . . . That which is of real import is the spiritual character of the Epistle. This can be grasped no matter where developed. It is likely—most likely, to have been developed in Palestine (BFW, xli).

Efforts have been made to ascertain the relationship between the recipients of this letter and the community at Qumran. Yadin and other suggest that "the Hebrews" of this letter were Christian believers who at one time had been members of this Dead Sea sect. Because these "Essenes" looked for another prophet, this epistle declares that Jesus is the last and final revelation of God. Because Qumran emphasized the role of angels, this letter devotes considerable space to Jesus' superiority to angels. Because these convenanters went to the "wilderness" to prepare the way of the Lord (Isa. 40:1-3), Yadin continues, this epistle lays stress on the wilderness sojourn of the Israelites and their tabernacle.[5] Their preoccupation with the doctrine of the two messiahs is countered in this epistle by the presentation of Jesus as the only valid successor to the Aaronic priesthood.[6] Against this view

---

3. William Manson, *The Epistle to the Hebrews* (London, 1951), *passim*.

4. *Ibid.*, p. 182.

5. Isa. 40:1-3; IQS, viii, 15.

6. IQS, lx, 11; cf. Heb. 7:26-28; Y. Yadin, "The Dead Sea Scrolls and the Epistle to the Hebrews," *Scripta Hierosolymitana* IV (1958), pp. 36-55; P. E. Hughes, "Current Religious Thought," *Christianity Today*, Dec. 15, 1958, p. 40; See J. Coppens, *Les affinites qumraninnes de l'Epitre aux Hebreux* (Bruges-Paris and Louvain, 1962).

is the fact that the Qumran sect had little apparent interest in the high priesthood since they seldom mentioned the high priest. Rather they were disillusioned with the hierarchical system as they knew it.[7] This fact led some scholars to conclude that the Essenes were hostile to the entire hierarchy at Jerusalem, which would argue against linking Qumran with "the Hebrews" of this letter. The emphasis on the priesthood is, however, common to both.[8]

The emphasis on the priesthood in this epistle has led to the conjecture that it was addressed primarily to Jewish priests converted to Christianity. We learn that "a great company of the priests were obedient to the faith" (Acts 6:7) while at the same time the "Hebrews" were those who should have been "teachers" of other believers (Heb. 5:12).[9] Spicq has elaborated on this theme and believes that these converts had come under the influences of the Essenes of the Qumran community.[10]

The argument that the recipients were "Hebrews" of the Jerusalem community also merits consideration. There are factors that support the position that the scribe who added *PROS EBRAIOS* to the manuscript envisioned a group of Christian Jews in Jerusalem. The Clementine Homilies refer to the "Church of the Hebrews in Jerusalem" (BFW, p. xli). Also the "Epistle of Clement to James" by the same author addresses James as the "bishop of bishops, who rules Jerusalem, the holy church of the Hebrews."[11] This lends plausibility to the theory that when the title was added to our Hebrews, it reflected the scribe's belief that a congregation in or near Jerusalem was the destination of the letter.

---

7. T. H. Gaster, *The Dead Sea Scriptures* (Doubleday, 1956), p. 332.

8. F. M. Braun, "L'arriere-fond, Judaique de quatrieme Evangile et la Communaute de l'Alliance," RB (1955), p. 35.

9. K. Bornhauser, *Empfanger und Verfasser des Briefes an die Hebraer* (Gutersloh), and C. Snadegren, "The Addresses of the Epistle to the Hebrews," *Evangelical Quarterly* xxvii (1955), pp. 221ff.

10. C. Spicq, *L'Epitre aux Hebreux* (Paris, 1952), pp. 226ff.; *Revue de Qumran* (1958-59), p. 390.

11. "Epistle of Clement to James," *Ante-Nicene Fathers*, VIII, p. 218 (Scribners, 1903).

The main objections to acceptance of this theory are that (1) a letter addressed to such a group would have been written in Aramaic, whereas it seems clear that it is not translation Greek; and that (2) the Palestinian group was too large a body to account for the personal matters which seem to be fitting for a local congregation. To the first objection Maclear counters by pointing out that Jews in Palestine were generally familiar with Greek and used the Septuagint no less than did Jews of the Diaspora.[12] The book of Acts witnesses to the presence of more than one synagogue in Jerusalem, divided according to national background and language (Acts 2:5-11; 4:36; 6:1, 9; 9:29). It seems certain that similar differences would be reflected in Christian groups later and that some Christian congregations in or near the Holy City would be characterized as "Hebrews."

But Jerusalem theory seems to many to be improbable because of no explicit references to the temple such as Stephen made (Acts 7:45-50), and because believers in Jerusalem prior to 70 A.D. would probably have heard Jesus firsthand rather than secondhand (Heb. 2:3). It is hard also to think of Jerusalem believers as ministering to the saints (Heb. 6:10) rather than being recipients of such aid (Acts 11:29; FFB, p. xxxii).

The interesting suggestion that these were Hebrew Christians near Sychar where Jesus and Philip preached is made by J. W. Bowman.[13] This might account for the lack of any references to the Jerusalem temple as such and the extensive use of the Pentateuch.

Antioch also had much on which to base such a claim, as Spicq has impressively demonstrated (CS, I, 250-252). It was an important city with a large Jewish community. The Christians there were in close touch with believers in Judea to whom the Old Testament meant much. It had a cosmopolitan atmosphere such as is required by the recipients of this letter. Moreover, they were generous (Acts 11:27-30; cf. Heb. 6:10) as were these people. It had a sizable colony of Romans since it was the capital of the Syrian province and hence could account for the expression,

---

12. G. F. Maclear, *op. cit.*, p. 109.
13. J. W. Bowman, *Hebrews, James,* I & II Peter(London, 1962), pp. 13-16.

"They of Italy salute you" (Heb. 13:24). The New Testament does not refer to persecutions here, however, unless the allusion in 1 Thessalonians 2:14 includes believers in Syria. But it is almost certain that persecution was the common lot of Christians at this time as is reflected in the letters of Paul, Peter and James, as well as in the Gospels, the Acts and the Apocalypse. The advantage of this location is that it was less provincial than Jerusalem, more exposed to "Alexandrian" influences, more sophisticated and yet more oriental than either Corinth, Rome, or even Ephesus. To such a sophisticated group, urbane and cultured, yet predominantly Hebrew and oriental in background, the line of arguments in this epistle would have greater appeal than either to the practical Europeans or the legalistic and conservative Palestinians. Here one would expect to find a mixture of Jewish and Alexandrian concepts to which a letter of this kind would make its maximum impact. Antioch seems to have been the most influential church of the first century and could well have been the recipient of such a letter as this. Fortunately the value of the letter is not dependent upon our certainty with reference to the identity of either author or readers. It claims attention entirely upon its intrinsic merit.

D. The identity of the author

1. External evidence

The first known witness to the authorship of the Hebrew Epistle is Pantaenus (185 A.D.) who attributed the letter to Paul without reservation and accounted for its anonymity by Paul's modesty as the apostle to the Gentiles. With keener insight Clement (fl. 200) of Alexandria said Paul wrote in Hebrew and that Luke translated it into Greek, thus distinguishing between thought and its literary vehicle. [14]

Origen, greatest of the Alexandrian scholars (fl. 225 A.D.), impressed by the linguistic differences from the Pauline letters, concluded that "the thoughts are those of the apostle, but the diction and phraseology are those of someone . . . who wrote down

---

14. Eusebius, *Hist. Eccl.* vi, 14, 3.

at his leisure what had been said by his teacher."[15] After this Dionysius (fl. 260 A.D.) of Alexandria attributed it to Paul with equivocation. Eusebius (c. 325 A.D.) of Caesarea, however, listed it as disputed.

In the west Clement of Rome at the close of the first century quoted from it extensively as inspired Scripture but did not identify its author. It is strange that he did not when writing to the Corinthians if he believed it to be the work of Paul, their founding father. Tertullian (fl. 200 A.D.) credits Barnabas with the authorship but this was not confirmed by others. Jerome (fl. 400 A.D.) decided in its favor because the Eastern church considered it apostolic and because of its acceptance in the churches, i.e., for pragmatic reasons. From Jerome until the Reformation Pauline authorship was taken for granted. In short the external evidence settles nothing and the matter must be settled, if at all, on the basis of internal evidence alone.

2. Internal evidence

Differences of style have impressed readers since the time of Origen. In Paul's writings application follows explanation; here exposition and exhortation alternate.[16] St. Paul "constantly mingles two constructions; breaks off into personal allusions; . . . and leaves sentences unfinished," substituting the syllogism of passion for the syllogism of logic. This writer "is never ungrammatical, never irregular, never personal; he never struggles for expression; he never loses himself in a parenthesis; he is never hurried into an unfinished clause." His style is the style of a man who thinks as well as writes in Greek (FWF, p. 31).

While the main doctrines are in harmony with Paul and other New Testament writers there are differences in emphasis from Paul that preclude his authorship of this letter. These emerge from the contrasts between Paul and the author of Hebrews.

With Paul the law stands in a temporal relationship to the

---

15. *Loc. cit.*

16. In Ephesians, for example, chapters 1-3 deal with God's work, chapters 4-6 with our walk; Romans 1-12 deal with exposition, 12-16 with exhortation. In Hebrews exhortation occurs at 2:1-4; 3:7-4:13; 5:11-6:8; 10:19-39; 12:1-13:17.

gospel, while in Hebrews the relationship is spatial; in other words, Paul thinks of the law as preceding the new covenant in point of time," "The law was our custodian until Christ came" (Gal. 3:24, RSV). This author thinks of the old as existing simultaneously with the new in the relation of shadow and substance (Heb. 10:1). It is true that in Hebrews the new invalidates the old (8:13), but the relationship emphasized is more of the superior and inferior than of the contemporary and the obsolete (Heb. 9:23, 24). The influence or Platonism may account for this emphasis in addition to an appeal to Moses and the Law.[17]

To Paul salvation or reconciliation is described in idiom congruous with the Roman law; in Hebrews, with the Jewish sacrificial system. To Paul the law's moral demands are set over against man's inability to meet the demands because of indwelling sin; in Hebrews the law by means of the sacrifices points the way to the perfect sacrifice for sin. In Paul Christ and His salvation are "apart from law" (although witnessed by it—Rom. 3:21); in Hebrews the salvation of Christ is the natural culmination of the law. In Paul the law is a pedagogue to lead to Christ; in Hebrews the analogy of antitype is different but the meaning is similar. Paul emphasizes discontinuity with Mosaic law; Hebrews stresses the continuity.

Paul emphasized Christ's divinity and glory (Col. 1:13-18); Hebrews, His humanity and intercession (Heb. 2:9-18). With Paul Jesus is now present in the Spirit (Rom. 8:9); with Hebrews Jesus is now high priest at the Father's right hand (Heb. 4:14).

Paul stressed the work of Christ in effecting man's justification in the sight of God (Rom. 3:21-28). In Hebrews the stress is upon both the person (ch. 1-7) and the work of Christ (ch. 8-13). In Paul's letters primary emphasis is upon the resurrection; here, on the incarnation. Paul stressed Christ the risen Lord; Hebrews stresses Jesus the living high priest. In the Pauline correspondence stress is placed upon salvation which reconciles rebellious man with a merciful God (Rom. 5:1-11); in Hebrews stress oc-

17. R. N. Flew, *The Idea of Perfection in Christian Theology* (Oxford, 1934), p. 75

curs on salvation, which leads men with a cleansed conscience
into the very presence of God (Heb. 10:1-23).

The Christology is different in emphasis from that of Paul.
Paul's favorite expression is "in Christ" with stress upon the
subjective effects of the atonement. In Hebrews the emphasis
is on "with Christ" or after Christ, "looking unto Jesus" as
the initiator and finisher of our faith as well as its high priest.
This author stresses the full humanity of the Lord; Paul, His deity.
Like the Synoptics, he is aware that the incarnation includes not
only Jesus' birth but also His healing ministry and even His death.
But while the Gospels depict the facts of Jesus' life with very
little interpretation, this author is eager to point out its *significance*
for the Christian faith. Here is to be found, even more than in
the writings of Paul, Peter and John, the rationale of Jesus' incarnation. One can catch his ardor in such phrases as "consider
him" and "we see Jesus," followed by the respects in which Jesus
Christ excels and climaxes all of His predecessors.

Paul is a mystic who thinks of his relation to Christ as pneu-
matic, as involving death and resurrection with Christ (Rom.
6:1-6). This writer is a teacher whose greatest concern is to point
to Christ (Heb. 3:1; 8:1; 12:1). He points to Jesus Christ as the
One who leads disciples into the throne room of God (Heb. 4:14-16;
10:19-22). His approach is somewhat more objective and deliberate
than that of Paul. He is tender in his portrait of Christ, stressing
His humanity and sympathy, but is more severe even than Paul
in warning of the consequences of rebellion.

For Paul, the believer's body is the temple of the Holy Spirit;
in Hebrews the temple of God is in heaven (and yet presently
accessible). Paul places the emphasis on being converted and
living a holy life; this writer emphasizes insight, loyalty and
perseverance. Paul's emphasis was upon God's immanence and
fatherhood; here the emphasis is upon God's transcendence and
kingship.

For Paul faith is *trust* in God's mercy that brings reconciliation (Rom. 5:1); for this writer faith is *confidence* in the final
triumph of righteousness as it was with Habakkuk and Abraham
(Heb. 11:1, 6). Like 1 Peter the Christian is viewed as a migrant,

a pilgrim en route to the Holy City in the tradition of heroes and heroines of the Old Testament and inter-testamental periods. Paul thought of Christians as colonies awaiting their translation to heaven (Phil. 2:15), rather than struggling to follow the leader and holding tenaciously to their initial commitment (Heb. 3:12-4:16). Paul found time to urge his readers to grow in grace and to translate their new life in Christ into every sphere of life (Col. 3:1-12). This reader is more "other worldly" if possible, placing the stress on the goal. Paul stressed the difference Christ makes in how you live now; here the emphasis, as in both Petrine letters, is upon completion of a successful pilgrimage.

In short, the areas in which he differs from Paul in emphasis most conspicuously are his attitudes toward the old covenant, in his presentation of Christ as high priest, in presenting the Christian way as a pilgrimage and in his emphasis on faith.

One needs to be cautious, however, about pressing such comparisons, for one can draw upon thirteen letters of the Apostle and his messages quoted in the Acts, while we are dependent upon only one letter as a clue to the theology of this author. Each suited his message to his audience. Paul addressed the citizens of Athens in a manner quite distinct from his approach to Jewish audiences. Hebrews likewise is not presented as the author's systematic theology but rather as a "word of exhortation" to fit a particular situation. Still the situations back of the letter to the Galatians and the one to the Hebrews are sufficiently similar to rule out the possibility that the same person would have faced similar situations in manners so dissimilar.

The differences lie not in the grand central truths of the gospel. In such matters as the vicarious atonement of Christ they draw upon a common heritage. The differences are in emphasis and method only and are not surprising considering the different temperaments of the authors and the differences in the congregations addressed. The surprising thing is to find a writer whose knowledge of Jesus was secondhand and who had no "vision" like that of Saul of Tarsus, yet whose insight, balance and independence were not less than that of even Paul and John. For this reason the church rightly considers this anonymous letter indispensable.

3. Other Possibilities

If it is well established that the epistle is neither directly nor indirectly the work of Paul, can the author be discovered with any degree of probability? A number of solutions to this problem have been offered. Barnabas, Luke, Clement of Rome, Silvanus (Silas) and Apollos have been suggested as possible authors.

(1) Evidently the first suggested alternative to Pauline authorship, Barnabas, was made by Tertullian about 200 A.D.[18] Riggenbach and Starthmann supported this view.[19] The primary basis for proposing Barnabas as the author is that according to Acts 4:36 he was a Levite and thus had an interest in priesthood and sacrifice. In addition he belonged to the circle of Paul's friends and companions and was acquainted with Timothy. He also came from Cyprus where pure Greek was spoken, but was also familiar with the Jerusalem circle of Hebrew believers. In addition Barnabas was known as a "son of exhortation" (Acts 4:36), while Hebrews is described as the "word of exhortation" (13:22).

However, the Epistle of Barnabas could not have been written by the same author as the Epistle to the Hebrews. If Barnabas wrote the former he did not write the latter. In any event the evidence for Barnabas' authorship is conjectural and inconclusive, the early advocacy of which was based upon a kind of crude (and unscientific) literary criticism."[20]

(2) There are similarities of style and vocabulary between Luke, Acts, and Hebrews. There appear also to be some correspondences with Luke's Gospel or with the sources he used. He has an interest in the temple and the two covenants. But there is a noticeable lack of awareness of Alexandrian thought in Luke. Although Calvin suggested Luke or Clement of Rome

---

18. *On Modesty*, XX, *The Ante-Nicene Fathers*, eds. Alexander Roberts and James Donaldson, 9 vols.; (Buffalo: The Christian Literature Publishing Association, 1887), IV, 97.

19. E. Riggenbach, *Der Brief an die Hebräer* (Vol. XIV of *Kommentar zum Neuen Testament*, ed. Theodore Zahnizer; Leipzig, 1913), pp. xl-xlii; H. Strathmann, *Das Neuen Testament* (Vol. IX; 5th ed.; Gottingen: 1949), p. 67, cited by Floyd V. Filson, "The Epistle to the Hebrews," *The Journal of Bible and Religion*, XXII (January, 1954), p. 21.

20. Hugh Montefoire, *op. cit.*, p. 2.

as the author,[21] there seems to be little to support this view today.

(3) Silas (Silvanus) has been mentioned as a possible author. H. E. Mueller gives the following considerations in favor of Silas. Like Barnabas, he came into the church on the Pentecostal occasion or subsequently and thus was not one of those who had seen the Lord in person. His name is either of Greek origin or is a Grecianized form implying a Greek background. Silas was sent by the church in Jerusalem with Paul, Barnabas and Judas Barsabbas to carry the decision of the council to the sister church in Antioch (acts 15:22). When Paul set out on his second missionary journey, he chose Silas to accompany him. He must have been a man of ability and demonstrated reliability to be selected first by the church and then by a man like Paul. We find him much in Paul's company thereafter. He and Judas were prophets (Acts 15:32). Since prophecy was for the purpose of exhortation, Silas would fit in there as well as Barnabas. He spent the night with Paul in prison at Philippi, and from his incident we learn that he was a Roman citizen like Paul (Acts 16:21). He is mentioned with Paul and Timothy in 2 Corinthians 1:19 as having preached the gospel among the Corinthians. The writer to the Hebrews placed himself on an equality with Timothy, as Silas would do. As to the closing word of the epistle, these men who were with Paul so much of the time and were in fact his theological students would adopt some of his phraseology, as students today follow their teachers. That Paul universally uses this manner of closing a letter argues nothing. Others, especially those who were so much with the apostle, could use the identical expression. If the words "Grace be with you all. Amen" are evidence that Paul wrote the epistle, then by the same logic he must have written the Apocalypse (Rev. 22:21).[22]

(4) Apollos continues as one of the most popular alternatives to Pauline authorship. Luther suggested Apollos in 1537 but gave no supporting evidence. Lenski, Manson, Ketter, Spicq, W. F.

---

21. J. Calvin, *op. cit.*, p. 359 (on Heb. 13:23).

22. The case for Silas is effectively presented in T. Hewitt, *Epistle to the Hebrews-Tyndale Series* (Eerdman, 1960), pp. 26-31.

Howard, and Hugh Montefiore are among contemporary advocates of this conjecture.[23]

Montifiore, in particular, has marshalled the usual arguments for Apollos. Apollos was of the Jewish race, a native of Alexandria, an eloquent man, powerful in the Scriptures, an accurate teacher of "the things concerning Jesus," instructed in the way of the Lord, "full of spiritual fervor," a bold speaker in the synagogues, indefatigable in confuting the Jews, and adept at public demonstration from the Scriptures that Jesus was the Messiah (Acts 18:24ff.). His influence in the early church is reflected not only in the book of Acts but also in Paul's letters (cf. 1 Cor. 1:12; 3:4, 5, 6, 22; Tit. 3:13). In addition to these considerations which admittedly "fall short of proof," Montefiore seeks to analyze the factors which shed light upon the circumstances, date, composition and destination of the epistle, concluding that "Hebrews was written at Ephesus by Apollos to the church at Corinth, and especially to the Jewish Christian members of it, in A.D. 52-54." [24]

The chief weakness to this theory is that if it were written by so prominent a person as Apollos, it is strange that his link with the writing should have been unknown or forgotten. The fact that he was not an apostle could not have been a deterrent since Mark and Luke were not apostles, yet their work was accepted as canonical. But someone of great competence had to write this letter. Of the candidates proposed none seems to fit the qualifications quite as well as the person described in the New Testament as Apollos. In short, if Apollos did not write this treatise, someone like Apollos did.

---

23. R. C. H. Lenski, *The Interpretation of the Epistle to the Hebrews and the Epistle of James* (Columbus, Ohio: The Wartburg Press, 1946), pp. 21-24; T. W. Manson, "The Problem of the Epistle to the Hebrews," *Bulletin of the John Rylands Library,* XXXII (1949), 1-17; P. Ketter, in *Die heilige Schrift Für das Leben erklart* (Vol. XVI, 1, Freiburg: 1950); C. Spicq, "L'Épitre aux Hebreux: Apollos, Jean-Baptiste, les Hellenistes et Qumran," *Revue de Qumran,* I (1958-59), 365-390; W. F. Howard, "Epistle to the Hebrews," *Interpretation,* V (June, 1951), 8-91; Montefiore, *op. cit.,* 9-32.

24. Montefiore, *op. cit.,* p. 28.

Fortunately the value of this treatise is not dependent upon its human author. The Christian Church from the beginning followed an authentic spiritual insight when it recognized in this anonymous letter a message so important and so consistent with writings of apostolic origin that it was accepted with little hesitation. But the acceptance was not without discrimination. Other contemporary writings of merit were not accepted. The science of literary criticism began in the second century, not in the nineteenth. Time has merely confirmed the judgment of the early church as to the enduring worth of this "word of exhortation."

Bibliography

Archer, Gleason L. Jr., *The Epistle to the Hebrews*. Grand Rapids: Baker, 1957.

Barclay, William, *The Letter to the Hebrews*. Philadelphia: Westminster, 1957.

Barclay, William, *Epistle to the Hebrews*. London: Lutterworth Press; New York: Abington Press, 1965.

Bovel, G. G., *The Epistle to the Hebrews*. Grand Rapids: Eerdmans, n.d.

Bristol, Lyle O., *Hebrews: A Commentary*. Valley Forge, Pa.: Judson Press, 1967.

Brown, John, *An Exposition of Hebrews*. London: Banner of Truth & Trust, 1961.

Bruce, Alexander B., *The Epistle to the Hebrews: The First Apology for Christianity*. Edinburgh: T. &T. Clark, 1908.

Buchanan, George Wesley, *To the Hebrews*. Garden City, N. Y.: Doubleday, 1972.

Calvin, Jean, *Commentaries on the Epistle of Paul the Apostle to the Hebrews* (tr. by J. Owen). Grand Rapids: Eerdmans, 1948.

Carter, Charles Webb, *The Epistle to the Hebrews*. Grand Rapids, Eerdmans, 1966.

Davies, John Howard, *A Letter to Hebrews*. London: Cambridge U. P., 1967.

Delitzsch, Franz, *Commentary on the Epistle to the Hebrews* (tr. by T. L. Kingsbury). Two volumes. Edinburgh: T. &T. Clark, 1868, rev. 1882.

Dods, Marcus, *The Epistle to the Hebrews* (EGT). Grand Rapids: Eerdmans, n.d.

Erdman, Charles Rosenbury, *The Epistle to the Hebrews*. Philadelphia: The Westminster Press, 1934.

Goodspeed, E. J., *The Epistle to the Hebrews*. Macmillan, 1905.

Hall, Asa Zadel, *A Cloud of Witnesses*. Zondervan, 1961).

Héring, Jean, *The Epistle to the Hebrews* (tr. by A. W. Heathcote &P. J. Allock). London: Epworth Press, 1970.

Hewitt, Thomas, *The Epistle to the Hebrews* (TNTC). Grand Rapids: Eerdmans, 1960.

Hoppin, Ruth, *Pricilla, author of the Epistle to the Hebrews and other essays*. New York: Exposition Press, 1969.

Hoskier, Herman Charles, *A Commentary on the Various Readings in the text of the Epistle to the Hebrews in the Chester-Beatty Papyrus P.* (circa 200 A. D.). London: B. Quaritch, Ltd, 1938.

Kent, Homer Austin, *The Epistle to the Hebrews*. Grand Rapids; Baker Book House, 1972 (1937, rpt.).

Lenski, Richard Charles Henry, *The Interpretation of the Epistle to the Hebrews and of the Epistle of James*. (1937, cpt. Columbus, Oh.: Wartburg Press, 1946).

Leonard, William, *Authorship of the Epistle to the Hebrews*. Vatican: Polyglot Press, 1939.

MacDonald, William, *The Epistle to the Hebrews, From Ritual to Reality*. Neptune, N. J.; Loizeaux Bros. 1971.

MacNeill, Harris Lachlan, *The Christology of the Epistle to the Hebrews*. Chicago: The University of Chicago Press, 1914.

McFadyen, Joseph F., *Through Eternal Spirit*. New York: George H. Doran, n. d.

McGaughey, Don Hugh, "The Hermeneutic Method of the Epistle to the Hebrews." (micro-film) Thesis-Boston University, 1963.

Meyer, F. B., *The Way Into the Holiest*. Grand Rapids: Baker, 1951.

Michel, O., *Der Brief and die Hebräer*. (MK) Göttingen: 1949.

Mickelsen, Anton Berkeley, *Methods of Interpretation in the Epistle to the Hebrews*. Thesis (Ph.D.), University of Chicago, 1950.

Milligan, George, *The Theology of the Epistle to the Hebrews*. Edinburgh: T. &T. Clark, 1899.

Moffatt, James, *Commentary on the Epistle to the Hebrews*. Edinburgh: Clark, 1948.

Moll, Karl Bernnard, *The Epistle to the Hebrews*. New York: C. Scribner, 1868.

Montefiore, Hugh, *The Epistle to the Hebrews*. New York: Harper & Row, 1964.

Moule, H. C. G., *Messages from the Epistle to the Hebrews.* New York, 1909

Mueller, H. E., *The Letter to the Hebrews: A Translation.* Minneapolis: The England Press, 1940.

Murray, Andrew, *The Holiest of All, an Exposition of the Epistle to the Hebrews,* New York: Revell, 1960, 1962.

Nairne, Alexander, *The Epistle of Priesthood; Studies in the Epistle to the Hebrews,* Edinburgh: T. & T. Clark, 1913.

Nairne, Alexander, *The Epistle to the Hebrews.* Cambridge: The University Press, 1921.

Narborough, J. D. M., *The Epistle to the Hebrews.* Oxford: The Clarendon Press, 1930.

Peake, Arther S., ed., *The New Century Bible.* Oxford University Press, n.d.

Pink, A. W., *An Exposition of Hebrews, third edition.* Grand Rapids: Baker, 1968.

Purdy, A. C. & J. H. Cotton, *The Epistle to the Hebrews* (IB). Nashville: Abingdon, 1955.

Robinson, T. H., *The Epistle to the Hebrews.* New York & London: Harpers, 1933.

Robinson, William, *The Eschatology of the Epistle to the Hebrews.* Birmingham, England: Overdale College, 1950.

Roddy, Clarence S., *The Epistle to the Hebrews.* Grand Rapids: Baker, 1962.

Rose, Delbert R., *Hebrews.* Winona Lake: Light and Life Press, 1961.

Saphir, Adolph, *The Epistle to the Hebrews,* (Fifth Amer. ed.). New York: Gospel Publishing House, 1946.

Schierse, Franz Joseph, *The Epistle to the Hebrews.* New York: Herder, 1969.

Scott, E. F., *The Epistle to the Hebrews: Its Doctrine and Significance.* Edinburgh: T. & T. Clark, 1922.

Seiss, Joseph A., *Lectures on Hebrews.* Grand Rapids: Baker, 1954.

Snell, Antony, *New and Living Way.* London: Faith Press, 1959.

Spicq, C., *L'Epitre aux Hebreux.* Two volumes. Paris: Gabalda, 1953.

Stuart, Moses, *Commentary on the Epistle to the Hebrews.* 2nd edition. Andover, Mass.: Flagg, Gould and Newman, 1933.

Synge, F. C., *Hebrews and the Scriptures.* London: S.P.C.K., 1959

Tasker, Randolph Vincent Greenwood, *The Gospel in the Epistle to the Hebrews.* London; The Tyndale Press, 1950.

Thomas, William Henry Griffith, *Let Us Go On.* Grand Rapids; Zondervan, 1944.

Vincent, Marvin R., *Word Studies on the New Testament* (Vol. IV). New York: Charles Scribner's Sons, 1906.

Vine, William Edwyn, *The Epistle to the Hebrews: Christ All Excelling.* London: Oliphants Limited, 1957.

Vos, Gerhardus, *The Teaching of the Epistle to the Hebrews,* Johannes G. Vos, Editor. Grand Rapids: Eerdmans, 1956.

Westcott, Brooke Foss, *The Epistle to the Hebrews: The Greek Text with Notes and Essays.* London: Macmillan and Co., 1889.

Wickam, E. C., *The Epistle to the Hebrews* (WC). Second Ed., London: Methuen, 1922.

Wiley, H. Orton, *The Epistle to the Hebrews.* Kansas City, Mo.: Beacon Hill, 1959.

Wuest, Kenneth S., *Hebrews in the Greek New Testament.* Grand Rapids: Eerdmans, 1948.

Other Volumes Relevant to the Epistle to the Hebrews

Flew, R. Newton, *The Idea of Perfection in Christian Theology.* London: Oxford, 1934.

Gaster, Theodore, H., *The Dead Sea Scriptures in English Translation.* Garden City, N. T.: Doubleday, 1956.

Stauffer, Ethelbert, *New Testament Theology* (tr. by J. March). London: SCM Press, 1955.

Stevens, George B., *The Theology of the New Testament.* New York: Scribners, 1899.

Shank, Robert, *Life in the Son.* Springfield, Mo.; Westcott Publishers, 1961.